VEGANS

– VS. THE –

VERSES

A Bible Handbook For The Vegan Activist

STEVEN LEE AUGUST

VEGANS VS. THE VERSES

Vegans Versus the Verses: A Bible Handbook For The Vegan Activist
Published by August Entertainment Inc.

AUGUST, STEVEN LEE, Author
VEGANS VERSUS THE VERSES: A BIBLE HANDBOOK FOR THE VEGAN ACTIVIST

ISBN: 979-8-9865470-0-8

RELIGION / Biblical Studies / General
SOCIAL SCIENCE / Activism & Social Justice

TABLE OF CONTENTS

PART ONE:

LET'S TALK ABOUT ME

CHAPTER 1:
I AM AN ENTERTAINER

W ho am I?

My opening is a whole lotta me talking about myself, hoping to impress you enough to consider what I have to say. I think if you hear my history, you'll understand how I can help you reach Christians with the message of compassion we call veganism.

Or-

You realize I'm an absolute idiot, and if you still have your receipt, you might get your money back on this book. But really, you could save yourself 20 minutes and skip my first four chapters and go straight to part 2.

Physically:

The first thing people notice is my long hair. OK, lots of guys have long hair, but mine is freakishly long, down to my knees kind of long. I'm pretty fit for an older guy (born 1961). I am thin, currently at 9% body fat (thanks veggies), not tall, but not short. One arm is a full sleeve of classic horror tattoos such as Dracula, Frankenstein, and The Wolfman. My average attire is painfully tight jeans, a button-down dress shirt, and a blazer. My T-shirt-wearing friends say that's dressing up, but eh, I don't see it that way. I'm just an old man stuck in the 70s. I'm often told I look like I'd manage a rock band. Now, on to my work.

Professionally:

I'm a Las Vegas variety entertainer that can juggle bowling balls and does close-up magic with classic toys from the 40s thru the 60s. Occasionally, I eat fire or hammer nails up my nose. On average, I perform about 150 times a year in the corporate market of Las Vegas. Many people are unaware of the corporate entertainment market. Imagine working for a soda company, car rental company, or whatever. They have their yearly convention in a Las Vegas casino ballroom. Sometimes it's a small business, and only a couple hundred people show up, or perhaps it's a big company, and 5000 people attend. They hire entertainment for their banquet or trade show booth. That is the corporate market where I work.

A juggling historian told me I was the only guy in history to juggle 3 Blow-dryers, cords attached, plugged in, and running. That was super hard to figure out, but boring for an audience to watch. Most of my notoriety came from an easy stunt (eh, easy for me at least) where I balanced a flaming Bar-B-Que grill on my face and made a 9-foot python appear from the fire. I could juggle seven items by the time I stopped juggling as my primary profession.

As of today, I'm pretty much a "Has-Been." You might have seen me on television juggling dangerous stuff in the late 90s and early 2000s. Just writing that makes me feel proud. OK, proud and old. Back to my entertainment career, I never made it to celebrity status. I got to touch it a bit; eventually, I failed. No shame here. I tried, gave it my best shot, and loved every minute of the struggle. There is something genuinely gratifying in the struggle. As an artist, your reward is more in creating the art than success. But oh, when I had it, success was fun!

Personality:

I am one of those annoying people with loads of willpower. When I decide to do something, I go for it. Self-discipline started for me as a teen with Tae Kwon Do lessons. It was the early 1970s, and Bruce Lee was all the rage. New Kung Fu movies were at theaters every week. Daily begging and pleading eventually got my loving mother to sign me up at Tiger Tae Kwon Do Academy for lessons. It wasn't one of those studios that gave you a Black Belt to keep the money coming in from the mommies. The instructor was an uncompromising teacher. If you didn't do well, they expected you to train harder. They gave no advancement in belts unless you did the work and earned the promotion. I trained five days a week, 2 hours a night, for over three years. I got my butt kicked, literally, over and over until I earned my black belt and then my 2nd-degree black belt. Then, one sad day, a fire destroyed the studio. The new studio was too far away to continue my training, leaving me 2 hours a night of free time. Then I discovered:

Juggling

One lazy afternoon in 1973, I sat on my living room sofa watching reruns of 1966 Batman. That's something I still do. My love for animals was never as strong as it was for our family dog, Charlie. That afternoon, Charlie came to me with a ball in his mouth, wanting to play fetch. There were no VCRs back in the dim-dark ages of the 1970s, so as much as I loved that dog, he had to wait for Batman to go to the commercial before I threw that ball. Finally, Charlie's patience gave out, and he dropped the ball. Coincidently, it rolled to a stop near two other balls on the floor, I got my lazy butt off the couch and went to grab a ball to play a bit of fetch, but something magical happened that day. I don't know what came over me. I don't know if it was God's intervention or what, but I got an idea that I should try to juggle those three balls. I mean, come on now, who thinks like that? Well, I picked up the balls, and much to Charlie's disappointment, rather than play fetch, I tried to juggle.

I could not juggle at all. But thanks to years of Tae Kwon Do training, I knew I had to keep trying, and eventually, I would. So I picked the balls up and tried again, again and again. I could write "again" a thousand more times before pulling off a single solid rotation of juggling... but I did it. And when I did, it was orgasmic. I then committed to learning to juggle.

So there I was, a teenager in the pot-smoking, glue-sniffing 1970s, and many of my friends were doing drugs. I had no interest in mind-altering stimulates. Probably my religious faith had me thinking it was a sin, but saying no was easy. Drugs and alcohol had the appeal of being offered a plate of dog crap. Oh ya, I don't drink booze either. I am what you call "Straight Edge" except for coffee, so I guess I do one stimulant, caffeine. But, I stayed true to my commitment of juggling and I'm so happy I did. I didn't know the benefits juggling would bring. But here I am over 45 years later, and WOW, what a ride it has been. Juggling has had me travel the world, get laid like a rock star, be on TV, make crazy amounts of money, and have fun, fun, and more fun. Thank you, Charlie.

Magic

I enjoyed magic too. I did well with it and even created magic for some celebrity magicians you see on TV, but it was not my artistic passion. To me, magic seemed to be a store-bought talent. Oh, not the manipulation kind of magic, but big illusions like cutting a girl in half. Honestly, you could buy a magic prop on Friday and perform it on Saturday. Not so with juggling. It could take years to perfect a 30-second juggling routine. I loved the physical challenge.

Las Vegas isn't what it used to be. Work as a juggler slowed, and 90% of my income is now from magic. Probably for the best, juggling is a continuous beating on the hands. Because of juggling, I can't write my name without pain in my fingers and knuckles. I gave the art my best, and jugging did me well, so time to quit and move on.

My next decision was to use those 4-5 hours a day once spent in juggling practice to take control of my health; yep, you guessed it, I now lift weights and do cardio 5 to 6 days a week with yoga on my rest days. So I am in the gym seven days a week, twice a day if time and the wife allow.

As I age, I find I am in excellent health. Most guys half my age can't keep up with my 90-minute cardio workouts. Ah, there's that arrogance of mine again. But it isn't bragging if you can do it. Thank you, vegan superpowers.

So here I am, a semi-retired entertainer on a fresh path of vegan activism.

A lil' bit about the Mrs.

My wife Maria is an amazing woman. She is also vegan, and, lucky for me; Maria is a perfect 10. I'm not saying that cause all guys think their wives are beautiful. By today's standards, she is all that, 115 pounds, 5 foot 9, exotic almond-shaped eyes, long dark hair. Maria is so attractive she gets paid to be pretty. She had stopped most of her modeling work when she turned 55, but Maria has been a showgirl, fashion model, magic assistant, and oh ya, she did porn. The sales from her online porn site pay for our animal rescue efforts. You will read more on that craziness later in the vegan section if you haven't written me off yet. Not really a vegan thing, but heck, full disclosure, ya know.

Maria has many talents. It wouldn't be unusual to see her performing for children at schools, churches, or hospitals in the daytime. At night, she performs at bachelor parties naked, often while eating fire. The sexy stuff gets her the most attention (and hate), but if I had to give it a guess, the naughty stuff is less than 20% of her work. The majority is "G" rated corporate shows that require true performance skills, which she has. But, people can't pick on her for that, so it gets ignored.

Am I becoming an author?

My skills as a juggler, magician, and fire-eater require a lot of physical talents, but you will soon see my writing skills are not so impressive. I write as I speak, like an idiot. My activist friends proof-read selections before publishing, and boy, I got my butt reamed. There were lots of compliments but many complaints. If you meet me, I'm not a serious person, more of a goofy guy, but that might not come across in my writing. Christian activists told me I sounded mean. Ouch! But I re-read what they called to my attention, and yep, they were right. When talking face to face, there are tones of voice, facial expressions, and physical mannerisms that make a negative comment sound friendly and acceptable. It's like working at a comedy club when I comedically insult a person in the audience. They see the delivery and know it's all for laughs, making it acceptable. A skilled writer can do that too. Unfortunately for my readers, I'm not a skilled writer. I really needed to hire an editor, but nope, I didn't. No editor, no qualified proofreader, and I'm sure it shows. Wanna know why? Did you know a book editor gets $6,000.00 to $10,000.00? I am an animal activist! That 10 grand could save a lot of animals, so screw that! You are getting me unedited. Please, I ask for your patience because I'm a really,

really good fire-juggler but a terrible, terrible author.

CHAPTER 2:
I AM A CHRISTIAN

Ultra-hyper dispensational, deconstructed, reconstructed, liberated, progressive, Bible-thumping Jesus freak.

I am a Christian. Have been since 1967. That's a long time to be reading the Bible and I still haven't got it right.

Like most kids, you are the religion of your parents. That's the same as "Carnism" (people that choose to eat meat), as you eat what your parents raised you to eat. For me, religion was fun. Mommy is Jewish. She was not really a practicing Jew kind of Jew, but if asked, for the first half of her life, Judaism was her faith. Then came the Jesus Movement of the late 1960s & early 70s. It was the time of the Hippie, and God got in the mix with pop culture. Broadway plays such as Jesus Christ, Super-Star, and Godspell were huge. Music on the radio had many Christian hits, too.

So we flipped from Judaism to Christianity. I guess you could say we read part two of the Bible. To please my *born-again* Mom, I did what any kid would do. I "asked Jesus into my heart" and magically became a Christian. My religious conversion meant as much as it could to a child at that age, but it was my start.

Score: Mommy - 1 / School Principal - 0

Christianity got real for me around the 5th grade. It was the early 1970s, and evolution was being taught as a fact in my school. This began lots of fun confrontations with my science teacher. I was the only kid willing to stand up for creationism, but to my embarrassment, I didn't know enough about it to defend it. That made it very easy for my science teacher to make a fool of me in front of my entire class. Public humiliation from a teacher in front of your classmates can destroy a 10-year-old boy...unless you've got a Super-Mom as I do.

Mom comes to school and speaks to the principal. She presents pieces of evidence that support (not prove but support) creation. This was fun because the principal was as uneducated on creationism as I was on evolution. I watched the principal cringe while Mom put him in his place. The result, they excused me from any tests or studies that involved evolution.

I had another round of the creation vs. evolution debate when I got to high school. Mom up'd her game when comically dealing with my new principal. This is how it went down. A parent-teacher conference was called because I was vocal in my religious views. Mom wore a "Groucho Nose" and glasses for the meeting. Need I say more? I'm sure my younger readers are Googling "Who is Groucho."

I can't tell you how powerful a young man can feel when his mother has his back as my Mom did for me. Her doing these actions is showing me that faith in God requires action. Mom didn't know it, but she planted the seeds for me to grow up to be the activist I am.

Thanks Mommy. Miss you!

Rabbi Chicken

I was 12 or 13 years old when I got my first job. It's as if God was setting me up for this book because the job was working for a Rabbi delivering kosher chicken. I kid you not. I don't think the Rabbi was prepared for a long-haired Jesus freak.

During the day, the Rabbi slaughtered the chickens, wrapped them in white butcher paper, and stacked them in the back seat of his 4-door Chevy Impala. Then, he'd pick me up to help with deliveries three nights a week.

The Rabbi looked just as you'd imagine, the long gray beard, black hat, wise and old. So old, he could not be running up and down the stairs to deliver kosher chickens. So he hired a young kid (me) to do the footwork while he waited in the car and counting the money. We got along fine and had wonderful conversations. I got 10-15 hours a week of one-on-one time with a Rabbi, which led to endless Bible conversations. What a blessing and education it turned out to be. You are going to see that reflected in my defenses of veganism.

Church book stores

It's 1977 and I'm a teen with a car, which means freedom to go where I want to go. So, where did I go? *Nerd-Alert* I went to the comic book store first, but it wouldn't be unusual to see me driving to church. Some churches I attended to were mega-churches. They had things I never saw in the small churches; they had bookstores! I never knew there were books written to help people defend their faith. I grabbed as many books as I could afford, and that old enemy of mine, Darwinian Evolution, appeared again, but now I had information from books to squash it. The feeling of

power that knowledge brings is addictive.
     And then, trouble starts.

Book stores and baptisms

Church taught me water baptism is not something I should do because I feel obligated. Instead, wait until I understand the commitment that baptism is. How I phrased that will let my Christian readers know I had been a standard fundamentalist evangelical Christian up to this time. That means I believed Hell is eternal torment, Jesus had to die on the cross to pay God off for my sins, sex is evil unless you're married, speaking in tongues is real, and tithing is still mandatory. But oh my, a study on water baptism changed everything for me.
     I had mentioned that I attended several churches. While trying to decide which to get baptized in, I spoke to one pastor who said full submersion in water is necessary. Another pastor said they only need to sprinkle water on your head. Yet another pastor said they must do baptism in the name of the father, son, and holy spirit, and you have to be dunked backward, not forward. OK, now this trips me out. These very educated men had different points of view. They each could defend their opposing views from the same Bible. Logically, they could all be wrong, but they cannot all be right.
     To deal with the confusion, I went to those bookstores for books on baptism. I can't tell you how long I studied the sacrament before I made a final decision. I concluded that water baptism is not a part of Christianity any longer. Water baptism was a Jewish purification ritual meant for the Jews at a specific time for a specific purpose and is no longer relevant today. I can hear many of you thinking, "heretic."

I'm an ultra-hyper what?

Moving on to the mid-1980s and I am working as a blow dryer repairman. Ya, they have those. For eight hours a day, five days a week, I sat in the repair room with my headphones on, listening to my Bible study tapes or Christian radio. There was a guy with a call-in radio talk show. He considered himself an answer man for Bible problems (Yes, that was a hint). One day, a caller asked, "is water baptism being necessary in our *current dispensation of God's Grace?*" I just about pooped my pants. Until this time, I thought I was the only one who questioned it. Then this Bible answer person said Christians who do not practice water baptism are called "ultra-hyper dispensationalist." I thought to myself: is that me? Am I one of these ultra-hyper people? How dare he call me a name like that? Wait, there's a name for Christians like me; that means there are other Christians thinking as I do. How exciting! So I needed to look up this "dispensationalism" stuff. Suddenly, I'm a dispensationalist Christian.
     This pattern of discovery has followed me throughout my entire religious life. My views on eternal torment/Hell, sex, open theism,

speaking in tongues, and so many more issues have changed, and I love the journey. I can't wait to see where God brings me in the next decade.

I hope you can see from this that I'm a committed Christian (or maybe you just think I'm a Christian that needs to be committed, haha). If my views differ from yours, don't stress it. <u>You do not have to agree with me to use what's in this book</u> for your activism. I will approach much of this from the average fundamentalist Christian viewpoint. I am familiar with mainline Christianity, and we will kick some Christian butt together.

In the next chapter, you're going to see how I went from a guy thanking God for a prime rib dinner to a radical vegan activist.

CHAPTER 3:
I AM A VEGAN

"I don't think I can eat meat anymore."
—Steven Lee August

It was the mid-1970s. As I walk down Michigan Avenue in downtown Chicago, I get handed a pamphlet attacking vivisection. Vivisection is experimentation on living animals for scientific research. The pamphlet's cover photo is of a monkey strapped on a cold steel table with a nasty-looking metal band restraining his head. I recall streams of blood and disgusting ooze on the screaming monkey's face—nightmare stuff. I close my eyes today and remember the look of terror on that poor baby.

The next day, I started searching for information on vivisection. My school was no help. Teachers are in a position of authority for kids. My teachers said to "ignore that, we need vivisection to save human lives". With so little access to data, I believed my authority figures and let the matter drift away.

Snakes slither into my life

Decades later, I do a juggling stunt of balancing a Flaming Bar-B-Que grill on my face. Yes, that's my job. That alone is an impressive stunt, but with the help of a magician friend, we altered a typical backyard BBQ with a magical twist. The magic twist was doves appearing from the fire pit. I didn't like that idea at all. Imagine watching a juggler on stage with hair to his knees and a fire-filled BBQ grill on his face. I felt it would be a let-down if such a wild stunt ended with a little white dove production. I always liked snakes. One thing led to another, and the magical ending became the appearance of an 8-foot boa constrictor. It's a safe trick for the animal, but not so safe for me.

Having a giant snake in my act got me booked more often. I had no problem working myself to exhaustion, but I didn't want to force my extreme work schedule on the snake. Gee, how thoughtful of me! Ugh. It wasn't just the repetitive work that concerned me, but snakes have times they shouldn't be messed with. Snakes shed the entire outer layer of their skin on average every 5 or 6 weeks. Not a comfortable process for them, so they got those days off. Also, snakes are obligate carnivores that eat the whole prey, be it rats or rabbits. It takes several days to digest. Moving a snake with a 2-pound rabbit in its tummy can cause injury. Undigested bunny toenails and rat teeth can cut into stomach linings if moved abruptly, like in a magical BBQ appearance.

In my mind, to be "humane," I needed another snake to alternate between, so they didn't work during those difficult times. How considerate of me. I shouldn't have used snakes in the first place, but I didn't grasp the exploitation involved. As I look back, I was making the vegan connection. The next two snakes I got were rescues. In my defense, no snake had ever been physically harmed. But isn't that the defense of every animal exploiter? My disconnect was strong, but it was weakening.

Enter, The SnakeBabe

Its the 90s now and I am married. Maria (my mega-hottie wife) started modeling with the snakes. Bikini pics and such. A giant snake on a pretty girl is a brilliant combination to make money.

Maria is not just T&A. She's got exceptional computer skills. She created a webpage (from scratch, HTML programing) for her modeling photos. Time moves on, and Maria develops a large fanbase from her website. I dreamed up a snazzy name calling her "The SnakeBabe."

We both wanted to help animals, so we started Las Vegas' Reptile Rescue. The problem with rescue work is there is always another pet in need which puts shelters in perpetual debt. Maria comes up with a system to limit our rescue expenses. We made a comfortable living as entertainers, so that will be "our money". Maria used the funds from website sales to pay for the rescue efforts. For example, if she sold $1,000 worth of memberships (to her now adult website), we only spent $1,000 rescuing snakes. If she sold $5,000, then we spend $5,000. We are not and never were a non-profit rescue, as many mistakenly assumed. To be above reproach, we never took donations. We funded the rescue ourselves. I got that idea from the apostle Paul. More on this later.

Maria's website had tons of quality info dedicated to reptile care. Emails came from around the world with stories of how her website helped save an iguana suffering with metabolic bone disease, how to treat mouth rot or creating humidity, and so on. Many reptile owners were *too cool for school* and wouldn't go to a proper reptile care site. But, have a naked girl with a giant snake, and they come (yes, that was a sex pun). As for the education, she snuck that in.

Saving animals around the world and still not vegan.

Too sexy

Maria's adult website upsets people. Sex can do that. Heck, I'm sure it's upsetting many readers now. The Peta campaigns, such as "I'd rather go naked than wear fur," brought similar arguments from those in the animal rights movement. Just as Peta did, I too battled animal rights groups on how being naked can help snakes and reptiles. AR groups did not accuse me of hurting animals, but challenged me on the wrongness of using sex to help animals. I argued, if they hung you upside down about to get your skin pulled off, you wouldn't care if it was a porn star or a priest, just help. Every fight I had with animal rights people was only over Maria's sexual activities. No animal rights person ever tried to get us to go vegan. How sad is that?

Not so sexy

We also had a family-friendly website, www.reptilerescue.com, that often got us phone calls when reptiles needed rescue. Most requests came from people who didn't want to care for their pets anymore. We take them on and try to find homes. Police departments, schools and veterinary hospitals end up with unwanted snakes and call us for help. Apartment complex managers call when people move out and leave their snakes. I remember a time I hung by a belt off the side of a building to rescue an escaped iguana. Later that night, I rewarded myself with a steak dinner. So many reptile lives saved, but I still hadn't made the connection—still not vegan.

If you saw what I saw!

There were benefits to being a "B" list—no, make that less than "C" list celebrity. When performing, I got backstage access at rodeos, circuses, and various shows that exploit animals. This allowed us to witness things the audience doesn't. At rodeos, I could pet, cuddle and hand-feed the docile bulls that violently bucked cowboys the night before. At circuses, I observed elephants shackled in parking lots, unable to escape the sun's heat. Lions housed in the back of U-Haul vans. Adult tigers, caged, pacing in circles for days on end.

Maria and her sexiness got us special access at reptile expos. At the time, Maria was "one of them," so we got into the private areas. Early mornings, before the expos opened, we saw salespeople flush dead snakes and lizards down toilets. The deaths were from exposure to cold while left overnight in the expo showrooms or stress from constant handling during sales. Witnessing all this suffering was wearing thin, yet I still didn't make the connection. But my wall of disconnect was crumbling. Oh, how I wish one big mouth aggressive vegan had ripped into me back in those days.

We were brought up to believe humans must eat animals to survive, and Maria got the idea that range-free food was the way to go. We ate only free-range meat for a couple of months, thinking we were doing the animals a favor. I mean, if *we had to eat animals*, let's make it a happy, free-range life. Unfortunately, range-free food is not always available on tour. Also, finding out that 'free range' is a myth, our efforts soon fell by the wayside.

I was arguing with myself

I trust you're seeing a pattern develop in these stories. I can't say precisely what pushed me over the carnist wall into *vegan-land*, but best as I can remember, I was having burgers with a Christian friend who hunts. Not for food, but trophies. My argument started with a question. How can a Christian justify killing innocent animals as amusement? This guy was rich enough to do anything he wanted; why kill was my thought. My second attack was animals only have one thing, their lives, and you take that from them. It cut him deeply as it made him aware of his greed and selfishness. Something happened during that argument. Maybe it was God's intervention. My thoughts were so out of nowhere that they couldn't have been born of my intelligence. Remember my introduction to juggling? Ya, like that again.

The Christian hunter and I battled back and forth with scriptures about how God gave us animals to eat. I agreed, but I argued for being compassionate and not killing animals unless we have to eat, not for pleasure like skins or trophies. Then I got a 1-2 punch. I noticed my hypocrisy right there on my foot. It was my leather boots. I was wearing an animal's skin. Somehow, my mind told me I could have worn canvas shoes. My feet did not need leather. While that was spinning in my head, punch number 2 hit me when this hunter said, "you sure take pleasure in that cheeseburger." I remember that line. It echoed in my head a million times in that one moment. It got to me. I just didn't know it.

I squelched it with standard replies such as we have to eat animals to survive, blah blah blah. Ultimately, I won that argument, not because I was right, but because I knew the Bible better than that hunter. Also, as a performer, I was a much better speaker.

For the next few days, I continued to rerun that conversation in my mind. You know what I discovered? My argument wasn't with the hunter. I realized I was arguing with myself. I was wearing and eating animals for pleasure. But it is not the 1970s, and I'm not a school kid anymore. I did my research and learned there is absolutely no biological need for humans to eat animals.

So now I have to deal with my morals. I was able to defend meat-eating from the Bible but the question that kept nagging me was, does God want me to kill his creation if I don't have a need? Obviously, the answer is no. God made animals with the intention of them being able to experience and enjoy their unique instincts and behaviors or He would not have given them those desires. Instead, because of my "pleasure," I denied animals all that God wanted for them.

Bunny, I don't think I can eat meat anymore.

Maria (I call her Bunny) and I are having dinner with another couple. As we sat at the restaurant, my internal vegan spark was burning me badly. It began quietly, in my soul, privately building to a huge flame. I didn't plan what I was about to say or even know how I came to speak it. But out of nowhere, just nowhere, it happened. I looked up over the top of my menu and said to my wife, "*Bunny, I don't think I can eat meat anymore.*" And it was over.

The decision came from a hidden place deep inside me. Maria had no idea what brought it on. Minimal discussion followed, and we ordered. I got a pasta meal; it was vegetarian. I didn't know the difference between vegan to vegetarian. Now when I think about it, what exactly is a vegetarian anyway but a pig-lover, ya know? They kill cows for dairy; they kill chickens for eggs, so really, all vegetarians do is save pig lives, they are pig lovers only. Eh, but I made my decision to go vegan. Remember what I said about my personality? I decide, and I do it. Be it learning to juggle, earning a black belt, or working out daily. I decided, and Maria knew there was no turning back.

Maria is much smarter than I am, but so are most 10-year-olds. She looked online for recipes and learned they killed animals in making dairy products. I stopped all dairy at that moment. Had I known, I would've stopped dairy that meatless night at the restaurant. When asked, I say I went vegan instantly because I rarely have the time to explain that vegetarian week, but it's all good. Maria followed me to veganism. She adjusted the websites to reflect our new, cruelty-free lifestyles.

So now I'm a vegan. The simple explanation is that I don't think God wants me to eat or wear anything produced from animal abuse. Not as detailed as the actual definition, but when I share that explanation with Christian meat-eaters, it slaps them hard. That style of answer is what my activists' friends have called "The Steve August Back-Slap." The Back-Slap is the sneaky way I ask or answer a question to trigger a person's thoughts, making them feel I slapped them in the face—but nicely. To respond in that manner makes people aware they eat food produced from animal abuse. You'll learn more about this method later.

A Christian vegan has differences from regular vegans. Kind of like saying, I'm a musician. That could mean several things; I could be a singer, a guitar player, or a drummer and still be a musician (Ok, maybe not a drummer). The result is still music. Christian vegans put God first. Compassion for all creation (the heavens, the earth, the water, fellow man, and the animals) reflects the moral baseline every Christian should have. There are differences but the result is still vegan.

Now let's look at my Christian journey in the next chapter.

CHAPTER 4:
I AM A CHRISTIAN
VEGAN ACTIVIST

I s Christian vegan even a thing?
I never completely stopped being an entertainer. Juggling, magic, and comedy are my art; when an artist stops creating, its emotional death. I perform occasionally, but I'd guess 75% of my time is spent on animal activism, including research for this book.

Not an animal lover

For longer than I can recall, I have been arguing to stop animal abuse. Even while I was eating them. Gadzooks - I was an idiot. Glad I straightened that out. But, I don't consider myself an "animal lover" as many activists are. When I am invited to speak at vegan events such as farm sanctuary visits, there are often live animals. I don't enjoy playing with the pigs, cows, or chickens. It was fun to snuggle with a 500-pound cow, sit in the mud with the pigs and feed the chickens. Once, but not something I'd do again.

I'm not a person who likes to get dirty. I love doggies and, of course, reptiles. Bats fascinate me, but I can't bring myself to curl up with a cat. God made loving creatures called dogs, and Satan tried to copy God, and that's how we got cats, evil, heartless cats. OK, I'm teasing; even if the animal isn't on my list of favorites, I am 100% opposed to animal abuse. I'm just saying I am not that kind of vegan. My veganism is an issue of Christian morals first. If we take God out of the equation, I'd say I am vegan for justice.

Becoming "The Religious Guy"

I was holding a sign at a rodeo protest. In between random cowboys stopping to spit on me and call me faggot, one activist invited me to get involved with a group called "Anonymous for the Voiceless". They meet once a week in front of a restaurant that flaunts its unhealthy, meat-based meals. "Eat yourself into a heart attack," is their gimmick. We stand outside in the 115-degree heat that Las Vegas offers while advocating a vegan lifestyle to thousands of world travelers that visit our proudly immoral city.

Downtown casinos offer round-the-clock cocktails, so the tourists visiting are often drunk. In addition, we have 24-hour, open carry, public drinking downtown, making advocacy challenging.

When I started, it became clear to the rest of the activists that I was "The Religious Guy" in a group of predominantly Atheist vegans. How did they know? Funny but true story. While outreaching a Pentecostal family of three, they experienced a heartfelt conviction of their sinful eating of meat. Score one for the animals. The father agreed to go vegan and asked me to pray with them. So, kneeling on the cold concrete of Fremont street, with our hands in the air, we prayed as hundreds of drunks walked by. Afterward, we hugged, and they were on their way. So ya, everyone in the group caught my vibe right away. Oh, I am not a Pentecostal devotee, but that was not the time to argue about our theological differences. My aim was veganism, so I met the family *where they were at* in their lives and religious doctrines. You will learn more about this method later.

From that point on, when a meat-eating Christian offered the typical "God gave us animals to eat" response, the activists tapped me into the conversation. Of course, I welcomed it since I based my veganism on my faith. The next thing you know, I'm the *go-to guy* for the tipsy religious tourists that stumble onto us. This allowed me to work out the methods I share in this book.

The Lord works in mysterious ways.

Book classes and more cheesy God stuff

In 2018, I had the idea of putting my activism into a book. I wanted to empower other vegan activists by giving them the information that worked for me and my outreach to Christians. Unfortunately, I was busy with my magic/juggling shows and such, so I just did the research and writing in my free time. A few hours one week, skip a month, then an hour while I wait for the wife to get done working. So this book was a thing to do at my leisure. I'd say God had other plans for me. If this smells like religious mumbo-jumbo, I agree, but there has been a series of essential "coincidences" for the birth of this book that seems to have lined up perfectly.

Several professional speakers attend my current home church. They invite me to be part of their Bible study that meets at a local coffee shop.

Cool beans. We talk of God, the Bible, and random churchy stuff. Everyone orders breakfast and the conversation goes to veganism when they see what I order. They get defensive. Typical.

One guy runs a school that teaches public speaking, and—are you ready? How to write a book. He invited me to attend both classes for free. I attended because, like I said earlier, I'm Jewish and he said tree.

As much as my theology won't let me accept it, something inside says God (or maybe you think Satan) had this book planned for me. I got the book training, public speaking training, and cash flow coming in, but I just didn't have the free time to finish. *Gee Whiz*, I would need a worldwide pandemic to hit so I could stop working and dedicate myself to this book. Nahhhh, that'll never happen.

Hello Covid

There was a time when I was doing three shows a week. During the year and a half (or more) of this Covid pandemic, I did not do a single show at all. So what's a vegan religious fanatic do? I dived into this full-time. It wouldn't be unusual to see me at my favorite vegan restaurant for 10 hours a day working on this. Not kidding, I'd be typing away on my laptop, drinking coffee, writing this book, drinking more coffee, peeing, studying the Bible, watching sermons and, again, more coffee.

Geez, my pee smells like caffeine.

PART TWO:

PREPARATION

CHAPTER 5:
GOOD MORNING CLASS

ey boys and girls, school's in

Hopefully, my story from part one impressed you enough to read what I have to share. I am guessing it did because you're still reading. Or, you're on the toilet and may as well continue until you say goodbye to last night's vegan burrito.

I feel like I am talking to a classroom full of vegan activists, and I am your instructor. Oh, that's pretty sad to have me as an instructor. I have no qualifications, no PHDs, and no university training. Heck, I've never even lead a youth group. This is going to be a train-wreck. But, with the little I know, I'm confident I can provide the info you need to prove Christians should stop eating products created from animal abuse. That sounds ridiculous, doesn't it? Having to convince Christians that animal abuse is wrong.

The human understanding of right, wrong, or morality can vary, but not so much for Christians. Christians willingly commit to a set of rules, a code of moral conduct not of human invention but determined by their God and shared with humanity via the Bible. Activists can use that to defend veganism.

I submit veganism is a forgotten, or more likely, an ignored component of Christian values. When you finish this book, you'll see that veganism is an essential ingredient of the Christian faith. Let me give you a brief sense of how this works:

Every Christian believes animal abuse is a sin.
Every Christian believes bestiality is a sin.
Every Christian believes gluttony is a sin.
Every Christian believes they must care for the poor.
Every Christian believes their body is a temple of the Holy Spirit

And so on and so on. This book shows veganism is an avoidance of these evils and a fulfillment of their moral obligations. I will provide information to attack Christians on their participation in those issues, leaving them no choice but to consider and accept veganism. Not always because they can't eat animals, but because they shouldn't. My hope is one day, when someone says they are Christian, people will automatically assume that means vegan too.

Row Call

We have two different vegan activists in our class, the Atheist and Christian. Whoa, talk about challenges! The challenge multiplies with the Christian activists and their various denominations as they understand the verses differently. Each Christian denomination thinks they alone hold the truth and if you disagree with them, you just haven't studied the Bible enough. I get that; I am doing it too. But you don't have to be afraid of me should my views differ. If I'm wrong, all that happens is you'll have less cruelty in your diet. God will not have a problem with that.

Let me first address the:

Christian Vegan Activists

I am really excited to be talking to you. I assume your vegan conversion came packaged with many difficulties, as did mine. Maybe your church accuses you of joining a cult, or Christian family members feel judged as you gather for dinner. I am sure you struggled as I did when reading Bible verses of animal cruelty. If these circumstances are familiar to you, I trust this book will bring some peace with new, vegan understandings of many scriptures. But I'm telling you up front, the Bible is not a cruelty-free book for animals or humans. I can not answer all your concerns, but I am sure I'll help you find ease with many.

I'm going to be stepping on religious toes here. I'm sure I'll upset you many times. Hah! And you paid for this abuse! Even though I am a Christian, I may present alternate religious perspectives to your denomination. I hope you won't take it as an attack; trust me, I can relate to your discomfort. It was hard giving up Chicago deep-dish pizza, but I did. I also gave up many cherished religious beliefs (remember what I said regarding water baptism?). Admitting I was wrong made my faith so much stronger.

However, *you do not have to agree with my views or change your beliefs*. If you stay open to what I share, you will find many vegan nuggets while staying within your denomination's limits. Treat me like I'm a bag of "Skittles". If you see a color (a theory of mine) you don't like, throw it away. You can still enjoy the rest of the bag—uh, book.

(Yes, Skittles are vegan)

For my Atheist Vegan Activist

I am a Christian, so we disagree. But I am not here to prove theism or convert you. My goal is to educate any activists on how to reach meat-eating Christians. I fear I might turn some Atheists off when explaining Bible stuff on why we Christians believe the kooky things we believe. Sorry, but I have to. Christian knowledge is essential to this subject, it's unavoidable. You're going to have to be prepared. You don't have to believe anything in the Bible, but the Christian meat eater you're speaking to does. But hey, I'm sure you're ready, or you wouldn't have bought this book. I will try to be respectful of our differences, but if I cross a line into Bible-thumping evangelism, please stick with me. Soon, you'll be able to argue veganism with most Christians you meet.

Ah, I see sneaky people in the back of the classroom that aren't vegan.

Meat-Eating Christians

There are Meat-Eating Christians that took my class just itching to prove me wrong. Ya, I realize you're here, looking for cracks in my theology to pounce on and allow comfort in your bad habits. No need to hide; we rejoice you are here. But I warn you, *I didn't write this to you.* This book is written by an animal activist to fellow animal activists. I will often sound harsh or insensitive as I share my Christian/vegan war stories in a very open and unapologetic nature.

If you are the type to get all *Butt-Hurt* by my crass presentations, all I can say is: oops, leave if you want; I'm not changing. My days of quietly holding signs in hopes Christians will extend God's love and compassion to animals are over.

If you decide to continue reading, here is your first lesson. Frequently, I will call you a "Carnist" or a "Carnist Christian." It has a nice ring to it. What is that? A Carnist (Carnism) is a person who society has conditioned to eat select animals. I learned the term from Dr. Melanie Joy in her book "Why we love dogs, eat pigs and wear cows." Everyone should get her book or at least check out her YouTube presentation. It is an hour-long speech and so worth it for understanding *Cognitive Disconnect*. Cognitive dissonance or cognitive disconnect describes the mental discomfort resulting from holding two conflicting beliefs, values, or attitudes. For us here, that means Christians claiming animal abuse is sinful while paying others to do acts of animal abuse on their behalf. Just reading that might make you feel some cognitive dissonance right now. That's a good thing.

I will be pretty blunt while talking to the vegan activists, pulling no punches. If you are a Christian that eats meat, this book is a kick in the teeth. It may sound as if I make Christians out to be my enemy. That is not my goal. I am criticizing the moral disconnect involving you and your taste buds. I will introduce viewpoints that will challenge the comfort and safety you find in your current beliefs. I will shine a light on your cognitive dissonance. It hurts, I know. I was once where you are now.

I hope what I share drives you to the scriptures to search for truth. Even if your aim is to prove vegans are wrong, please do your research. If you can prove compassion is ungodly, tell me! 'Cuz I'd like to have a meat-lover's pizza again. (yep, that was my "Back-slap")

So I've got three types of readers. I'll be jumping back-and-forth as I speak to each, I hope I don't get you confused.

Just the tip.

Everyone wants a quick one-sentence answer. Unfortunately, God doesn't work like that. I could write an entire book on each animal-related verse, but to keep it brief, I'll give just the tip of the answer, enough to get you through a vegan conversation with the average fundamentalist Christian. We can go deeper with my social media pages if you need.

Since you are all activists, I know you've done your homework on how veganism improves health and is better for the environment. I don't want to add more to this book, so just go watch "Cowspiracy" or read Earthling Ed's book "This is Vegan Propaganda" and save us both the trouble of having to deal with 1000 footnotes. I want to focus on the Christian stuff here.

Because I'm an idiot, I've avoided big words. Because I get bored easily, I've kept each chapter under a 15-minute read. My goal is to provide easy-to-read information, allowing you to formulate your own conclusions. How you bring it together is up to your style of activism.

Am I a liar?

My answers can contradict from chapter to chapter. That is because my replies might not be what I believe scripture teaches, but based on what the average carnist Christian holds true. That may sound messed up, but each denomination sees things differently, and sometimes, one answer does not fit all.

As a result, I will post replies I may not wholly believe. It may appear as if I am confused or lying. My effort is to build off whatever belief the carnist Christian holds true.

I have experimented and used all variations of the answers I give. None will work 100% of the time, but all can be effective. Each chapter will offer several opinions, some you might use, others you might hate. Heck, several of my replies are downright stupid. Use what you like; disregard the rest. The parts you disregard may be just the right answer other activists need. It's all good.

Crossover stuff

Activists told me they wanted to open to a single chapter to get the info they needed when confronted with a specific verse. In part three of this book, I attempt that. As a result, I often repeat myself to put the basics of the answer in each individual chapter.

Example: You'll find repeats in the chapter on "Made in God's Image" and the chapter on "Dominion." More crossovers in chapters on animals having souls and animals having moral agency. They have similar answers but may contain minor twists that support each other. Please, just roll with it. Actually, it will help you memorize stuff.

Factory farms are Hell.

All are welcome to read this book, but I wrote it specifically for the working activists. I assume I don't need to document the hellish abuse animals suffer in our world for food, clothing, and entertainment. I am sure my activist readers have memorized the basics.

But-

If you are a carnist Christian reading this book and you are not familiar with the monstrous horrors animals experience to become food, you won't fully understand why vegans are so passionate about their activism.

The meat you eat does not come from farms like those of Bible times; it comes from modern Factory Farms. There are many ungodly, horrible differences. Today's factory farms are highly developed slave camps of never-ending animal cruelty. Their purpose is to make a profit as fast as possible. There is no concern for the animals suffering if pain relief will cut into the farmer's profit.

Factory farms don't exist for human need but only to satisfy human greed. They ruin our health, destroy our ecological system, they bring in pandemics, antibiotic resistance illnesses, all while perpetuating animal torture. I do not see how any righteous person can innocently feed themselves or their children from such places. It is beyond the boundaries of the Christian faith. Future generations of Christians will look back at us with shame, just as we look back at Christians who supported slavery only a short time ago.

Please, before you go further in this book, go online and watch at least one of these documentaries:

1 - *Earthlings* (Highly graphic video)

2 - *Dominion* (Highly graphic video)

3 - *Land of Hope and Glory* (Highly graphic video)

The USDA estimates over 95% of the food humans eat comes from places seen in these films. You may not be the person doing these horrendous actions, but you are complicit in the suffering these innocent creatures endure.

Veganism is not only for animals; it benefits human well-being too. Try to watch one of these:

1 - *What the Health*

2 - *Eating You Alive*

3 - *The Game Changers*

4 - *Cowspiracy: The Sustainability Secret* (Environment)

I beg you, please don't skip this. If you can, watch them all and pray. I will pray for you too.

CHAPTER 6:
HOW I READ THE BIBLE
(5Ws)

The Bible didn't just plop down out of heaven one day. The Bible is 66 books; has 1,189 chapters containing 31,102 verses. It took at least 40 different authors over 1,500 years to complete. Those writers were kings, slaves, murderers, tax collectors, doctors, tent makers, and prisoners. There are songs, poetry, and letters showing God's ongoing revelation of himself to specific audiences during ancient times of ever-changing historical and political situations with developing beliefs. The Bible is not a textbook, it's art, it's literature.

Many of today's Christians don't grasp that. They seek scientific information in stories that were never meant to give scientific information. They read a 2 thousand-year-old letter that was written to correct problems in a Greek church, then try to apply those same corrections to their American church in the 21st century. Then, they wonder why they are so confused. Oh, and my personal pet peeve is when people view the Bible as a rule book on how to avoid Hell. To them, the Bible is nothing more than some kind of cosmic fire insurance for their soul.

I once believed in those ways too, but I've learned it's OK to be wrong. In my efforts to better understand and correct my mistakes, I got into hermeneutics. No, that's not a cult.

Hermeneutics, or my 5Ws

The Bible has many nasty verses about exploiting animals, speciesism, and animal sacrifice. It's easy to get the impression animals are here for whatever humans want. I thought the same until I learned how to navigate and read the Bible.

I got an epiphany (oh, look at me, I'm using fancy words) from a Superman comic book. Perry White, the editor of the Daily Planet newspaper, told reporter Clark (Superman) Kent to ask the basics of every story, Who, What, Where, When and Why. The **5Ws** of writing a story. As I applied these simple basics to my Bible study, things popped into place in exciting ways with new understandings. It forced me to bypass my preconceived bias and read the scriptures as the writer intended them to be understood. It cleaned up many (not all) concerns on animals.

These **5Ws** were my way of stumbling upon something Christian Apologists call "Hermeneutics."

Hermeneutics: *the branch of knowledge that deals with interpretation, especially of the Bible Literature.* To understand a subject, verse, or word, we first need to consider the context, history, meaning, application, culture, bias, language translations, genre, etc.

How does that 5Ws work?

It's not that difficult, I'll show you. With each troublesome, non-vegan verse, I asked a few of the following:

Who wrote what was being said?

Why did they write it?

Who was the intended recipient, and how would *they* have understood the verse?

What is the history or need for that information?

When was it written?

Where is this going on geographically?

What is the current political and religious culture of the people writing or receiving the information?

Get it? To understand an ancient Bible, we need to stop reading it through 21st-century understandings.

Using my vegan eyes to "Veganize" the Bible

The Bible has many insane stories of rape, slavery, genocide, and more. Today's Christian apologists (a person who argues in defense of something) will apply hermeneutics and present alternative understandings and explanations for these evils. That's good. But somehow, when a "vegan apologist" (me) comes along presenting alternative explanations on verses with animal exploitation, Christians call me a heretic. Or in my case, a "Hair-atic" haha, get it? You will be called names too. Don't let it get you down. You're breaking through their preconceived defenses. But ya, it hurts and it ain't fair.

Inkblots

Studying Scripture is like looking at a Rorschach Ink-Blot test. Those are printed inkblots a psychiatrist shows and asks, "What do you think the inkblot is a picture of"? The inkblot represents nothing in particular, but what you see is what your personality brings into it. You might think a blot looks like a butterfly landing on a flower, or a dragon biting a baby's head off. It varies from person to person.

Apply that to when you read the Bible. Are you an angry person? If so, maybe you see a vengeful, wrathful God. Are you a person who is happy? You'll see the love of God in the Bible. What is in your heart projects into your understanding of the Bible. This is partially why 2 people reading the exact same scripture can get 2 contradictory meanings. If you have a preconceived bias, you will find what you are looking for.

Is bias bad?

If you are a vegan activist, you're going to be accused of having a vegan bias (a prejudice in favor of or against one thing) you read into the scriptures. The accusations will be you are cherry-picking select scriptures to support the point of view you have.

I don't have a problem with that!

I admit, I read the scriptures with a bias of love, mercy, and kindness. The question is, why doesn't every Christian share the same bias? Why do Christians blast my partiality toward eating with mercy and compassion, yet they go to the same scriptures with a bias to approve eating from violence? I guess they see a dragon swallowing a baby in the inkblots. I'm good with the butterfly.

Next thing to learn, you can't read just one:

Chapter or verse.

When the Bible originated, there were no verses. Around the 13th century, church people (monks supposedly) broke the Bible up into chapters and verses. It is easier to navigate an enormous book when the passage you are looking for has a chapter/verse location. But this has also created confusion. Christians will quote a single verse as if it's all they need to know. They never read the entire passage. To fully understand the context of that one, single verse, you may need to read the entire chapter.

Vegan activists will deal with this often when talking to Christian meat-eaters. The carnist knows *one verse* but not the full context, leaving them with bad theology. Often, the true context supports veganism, other times it does not. We will discuss both pro-vegan and anti-vegan views in the chapters to come.

Vegan activists also make this "single verse" mistake. On social media, I often see single verses being taken out of context by well-meaning vegan activists to prove a verse is vegan when it isn't.

Just because I am on *team vegan* doesn't mean I will purposely misrepresent a verse. Oh, if it has any ambiguity, I'll twist it, squeeze it and do what I can to *Veganize* it, but I am a Christian first. If I'm mistaken, then so be it, but I will not lie to justify a vegan theory. The Bible has non-vegan verses, and it sucks. I'll teach you how to handle those as they are. No lies needed.

A fun Bible analogy to help you make sense of it:

A Picture Puzzle

I know Bible study is confusing. Imagine putting together a billion piece jigsaw puzzle without seeing the cover photo on the box. You hold one piece in your hand and think to yourself, "hey, it's a green leaf on a tree." So you confidently put that piece in place. A week later, your confidence is shot to heck when you realize it's not a green leaf but part of a green car. Oh, but wait! A year later, with 10,000 more pieces in place, you discover you were wrong—again. It's an armpit on a green frog...ok, maybe not an armpit, but you get the idea. So reading only one verse, or one story, or one chapter leads to confusion, as with one puzzle piece.

This book will come across similarly, in small pieces. I'm saying you won't understand the *Animal Sacrifice* chapter until you finish the *Dominion* chapter. You won't understand *Dominion* until you figure out what being *made in God's image* means. But you won't understand being *made in God's image* until you get done with *Dominion*. See how it circles around? Maybe I'm just a lousy writer, but eh, what do you expect from a juggler?

Here comes a shocker:

Rightly Dividing

All the Bible is written for us, but *none of the Bible is written* to us.

Uh, so the 10 Commandments are not for us? Well, yes, they are, but no, not really. With that answer, I could be a politician, huh?

It's like this, consider the laws of driving a car. Compare driving in London during the 1920s to people driving in Los Angeles today. Yes, those 1920s laws were 100% true laws, but they don't apply throughout all time and all locations. In America, driving on the left could get you killed. Good law, wrong location. Recognizing what verses belong to **who**, and **where**, and **why** is essential. That's Rightly Dividing, get it?

I didn't grasp this for almost 20 years of Bible study. This was my biggest Christian embarrassment. Sooooo wrong on sooooo many issues. I wasn't "Rightly Dividing" as instructed by the apostle Paul:

2 Timothy Chapter 2:15 Study to shew thyself approved unto God, a workman that needeth not to be ashamed, <u>rightly dividing</u> the word of truth

Rightly dividing is an excellent help to vegan advocacy because you will not have to waste time justifying exploitive animal verses. After all, they may not be for us today. They are what they are, which is done and over.

Words change.

If it was the year 1950 and I wrote these 3 lines:
1- I went to the store to buy a TV
2- The clerk swiped my credit card
3- So I called the police

In the 1950s, the word "swipe" was slang for stealing. Reading that in 1950 sounds as if the clerk had stolen my credit card. By the year 2021, calling the police in verse 3 makes no sense. Why? Thanks to the invention of magnetic strips, credit cards are now "swiped" across a card reader, so we understand that same word very differently.

There will be words and terms in the Bible like that. To figure out the meaning, we must consider the times of the people when they wrote it (hermeneutics). We will have to read the verses as if we are them, sharing their culture, their level of enlightenment. This will be important when we study verses about eating animals. For example, there were no factory farms, and free-range had a different understanding. I'm not saying free-range is OK, but it was a different world then. We will dig more into that in upcoming chapters.

Thees and Thous

The Bible was originally written in Hebrew, Aramaic and Greek. If you are reading the Bible translated into English, then you are reading someone's interpretation. There are three common types of Bible translations used today.

Literal Translations: A word-for-word version that seeks to stay as close to the original language as possible. These are the ones I will quote most often.

ESV- English Standard Version
CSB- Christian Standard Bible
KJV- King James Version
NKJV-New King James Version
NASB- New American Standard Bible
NIV- New International Version.

And just so you know what the others are called:

Dynamic Equivalent: A thought-for-thought translation.

Paraphrased: This version tries to make the Bible easier to read and more understandable.

The King James Version (KJV) of the Bible is perhaps the most anti-vegan translation. I will quote the KJV most to get you prepped for the worst of the worst. The Elizabethan English is hard to read, but it will most likely be the source the carnist Christian will quote and accept.

Some churches think looking at any translation other than the KJV is comparable to looking at porn. Funny thing, the "KJV only" Christians still pray using the words "thee" or "thou:, thinking that's how God speaks. Not realizing the Bible was written in Hebrew, Aramaic, and Greek, not English of any kind. All those hard-to-understand "these" and "thous" didn't get into the Bible until the 1500s. But- we work with Christians where they are intellectually, so there you go. Or should I say, *"There thou goest."*

For my study, I read the other translations and the non-canonical books for contextual understandings, but never put non-conicals on an equal level as the Bible. There is so much we can learn from non-canonicals. It helps me understand the societies, the way they view life, how they view themselves, their philosophies, pretty much, their outlooks on everything. You can't get those insights from the Bible alone.

Last thought on this translation thingy here. Each translation we read today was done by people living in a meat-eating culture. The translators looked at each verse they were translating with the presupposition eating meat is normal and animals hold a low place of importance. We will read many verses proving the opposite. The original authors held contrary views during the times of original writing.

Christian: *The Bible clearly says…*

Me: *If the Bible was clear, we wouldn't have over 1000 denominations* :-)

CHAPTER 7:
MY CLOBBER
QUESTION

Christian Meat-Eater says: You're a F**king heretic ya hear me! You got to stop this God-D**n compassion bulls**t, it's from the pits of Hell, ya hear me?

That quote is from a conversation I had with a born-again Bible-believing Christian during a demonstration on Fremont St. in Las Vegas in 2019. If it wasn't so sad, it would be laughable. You can get a Christian really agitated when pointing out their cognitive dissonance by utilizing their own Bible against them.

How did I get him so mad? I asked my:

"Clobber Question"

If a Christian has a choice of food created from animal abuse or compassion, Shouldn't a Christian always choose compassion?

That question took no theology degree or Bible training. Any activist can use this question. You can use it with any Christian denomination. Ask your pastor, your group leaders, or anyone. Actually, I hope you'll post it on your favorite meat-eating pastor's YouTube Channel and hashtag this book!

I built this question on three premises. Let's review those now.

My Premises:

Premise #1: Animals raised on factory farms are animal abuse.

Premise #2: The distinguishing principles of being a Christian are mercy, kindness, and compassion.

Premise #3: Humans have no biological need for animal products in their diets.

Conclusion (my Clobber Question): When a Christian has a choice of food created from compassion or animal abuse, their choice should always be compassion.

Let's dive into each premise.

Premise #1

Animals raised on factory farms are animal abuse.

You may need to prove this on the spot, so download video footage of factory farms to your cell phone. Then, if they argue it's not abuse, just show the video and ask, "Is this how God wanted us to treat animals we eat"?

Yes, I said, "we eat." In my first steps of vegan advocacy, I often skip past the argument of eating or not eating animals. I feel a better connection with the person when I include myself in my criticisms. I don't appear as preachy, and I did eat animals for the first 45 years of my life. You get the point. I just want them to acknowledge that God disapproves of what is happening in our factory farms, where over 95% of their food comes from.

You can also ask, "does God consider this animal abuse?" By asking this, you make them argue against God, not you. In part 3 of this book, I will present firm evidence of how God wanted animals to be treated.

For both questions, the carnist Christian must stop eating animals to be a consistent moral believer.

Premise #2

Distinguishing principles of being a Christian are mercy, kindness, and compassion.

You can quote **Galatians chapter 5 verse 22**

> *But the fruit of the Spirit is love, joy, peace, long-suffering, gentleness, goodness, faith,*

Or

Colossians chapter 3 verse 12
Therefore, God's chosen ones, holy and loved, put on a heart of compassion, kindness, humility, gentleness, and patience,

Or

Psalm chapter 145 verse 9
The LORD is good to all; he has compassion for all he has made.

Or

Luke chapter 6 verse 36
(Jesus says) *Be ye therefore merciful, as your Father also is merciful.*

Ya, I could list many, many more.

Compassion and mercy are essential elements of Christianity. No believer will argue against these principles. The Bible is packed with similar verses showing compassion for both humans *and animals*. I will list more of these verses as you progress through this book. Premise #2 is an easy win.

Premise #3

Humans have no biological need for animal products in their diets.

This is important! Humans do not need to eat meat—ever. You can quote the Academy of Nutrition and Dietetics (AKA: American Dietetic Association);

"It is the position of the American Dietetic Association that appropriately planned vegetarian diets, including total vegetarian or vegan diets, are healthful, nutritionally adequate, and may provide health benefits in the prevention and treatment of certain diseases. Well-planned vegetarian diets are appropriate for individuals during all stages of the life cycle, including pregnancy, lactation, infancy, childhood, and adolescence, and for athletes."

The Academy of Nutrition and Dietetics (formerly the American Dietetic Association), founded in 1917, is the world's largest food and nutrition professional organization.

The American Dietetic Association is not alone; the British Dietetic Association agrees.

The Mayo Clinic agrees.

Harvard Medical School agrees.

Dietitians of Canada agree.

And neither of these associations is a vegan group.

This is one of those quotes to have saved on your phone. Premise #3 is a scientific and medical fact proven by hundreds and hundreds of doctors, nurses, scientists, and medical professionals worldwide.

My Conclusion

If a Christian has a choice of food created from animal abuse or compassion, a Christian should always choose compassion.

As I continue through this book, you will notice *The Conclusion* being used in many variations. I want you to understand why I underlined the word compassion. By saying it this way, you will bypass arguing their so-called *"God-given right"* to eat any animal and go straight to their

Christian morality. My intended use of the word *compassion* allows them to keep their speciesist stance (just for this moment) while forcing them to go vegan or deny their moral obligations to God. Chances are, they deflect to other subjects. So try to hold them here and stay focused on getting a direct answer to your question.

Reword

You could change it up. I have found that "mercy" and "violence" are also good.

If a Christian has a choice of food created from violence or mercy, shouldn't a Christian choose mercy?

Or make it a statement—

When a Christian has a choice of food created from animal abuse or mercy, a Christian should always choose compassion.

The original is my favorite version, but each works on the same principles: You are challenging the Christian's obligations based on biblical moral guidelines. This technique has been much more effective for me than arguing animal rights or speciesism.

Examples:

Let me show you a couple of examples of how I use *The Conclusion* to hit back at common rebuttals.

1- Christian Meat-Eater: *God gave us dominion*

Vegan Activist: I agree with you on that, but my question is, does God want us to use our dominion to inflict pain on animals or show compassion to animals?

2- Christian Meat-Eater: *God made humans superior to animals*

Vegan Activist: I have read that, but did God give us superiority to hurt animals, or does he want us to use our superior abilities to show compassion to his creation?

3- Christian Meat-Eater: *God said we can eat animals*

Activists: God said we can eat plants too. So, given a choice of food that comes from violence or compassion, which do you think God wants us to choose?

In those 3 examples, did you notice I didn't argue about their "right" to eat animals? Instead, I made the conversation about the Christian's moral obligation to be compassionate about the things they choose to eat. So in my initial confrontations, I try to make compassion, mercy and love the battlefield we fight on and let the Christian discover veganism is the only option they have.

I don't know the Bible well.

That's ok; neither do most Christians. Hahaha, just teasing, but not to worry. You can discuss veganism without having to memorize a bunch of verses. With just some Bible basics, you can crucify their meat-eating habits.

First, go online and grab videos of animals kept on factory farms and load up your phone. You know which videos rip at your heart; I suggest you grab those. Your passion will come through when you show them. Now, ask these questions.

Question #1: *Is animal abuse a sin?*
(Show them footage on your phone)
Follow-up Question: *Is this animal abuse?*
Follow-up Question: *Is this where your food comes from?*
Question #2: *Is beastiality a sin?*
(Show them footage of artificial insemination on your phone)
Follow-up Question: *Is this Beastiality?*
Follow-up Question: *Is this where your food comes from?*

See how that works? Christians agree that animal abuse and beastiality are sins. No scripture quotes are required. All you do is help them connect the dots.

Questions about beastiality are great when dealing with Christians who don't believe mercy and compassion apply to animals. But, ya, there are many Christians like that. Sad, isn't it?

You've read my Clobber questions; now I want to share with you my Clobber Answers. I answer by introducing God into the conversation. I am much more comfortable arguing veganism that way. You will be too when you finish this book. I will list a couple to show the formula and explain why I say it the way I say it.

Carnist: *Why are you vegan?*
Steve: *I don't believe God wants me to eat anything produced from animal abuse.*

Let's dissect that. I brought God into the conversation. If they continue, their argument is with what God calls abuse, not what they personally think is abuse. I did not tell them they were animal abusers, but they will draw that conclusion themselves.

Carnist: *Why don't you eat meat?*
Steve: *Because I'm a Christian.*
Carnist: *What do you mean? I'm a Christian, and I eat meat.*
Steve: *Huh? Can Christians eat food products made from beastiality, abuse, or violence?*

See how that Back-Slap works?

In the following chapters, you will get additional info on bestiality, abuse, and gluttony.

CHAPTER 8:
HUMAN
EXCEPTIONALISM

Humans are exceptional...but so what?
    Carnist Christians act as if humans are the cherry on top of God's creation. They get this idea from incomplete teachings of Genesis chapter 1 verse 26.

And God said, Let us make man in our image, after our likeness: and let them have dominion over the fish of the sea, and over the fowl of the air, and over the cattle, and over all the earth, and over every creeping thing that creepeth upon the earth

The key elements in this verse are "Dominion" and "Being Made in God's Image". Christians combine them into a view called "Human Exceptionalism". I will discuss the concepts of "Dominion" and "God's Image" in part 3 of this book. But here, I want to focus only on the idea that "Human Exceptionalism" does not mean human superiority or speciesism.

Is it Exceptionalism or Speciesism?

These theories are often considered the same, but Human Exceptionalism and Speciesism are two distinct views.
    Speciesism is the belief that all other animal species are inferior.
    Exceptionalism is the condition of differing from the norm.

Looking at its definition, exceptionalism does not make humans superior. It only means humans differ from the animals. What is that difference? Humans are uniquely made to serve God to a farther degree than the rest of creation (animals) can.

Having been created in God's image, humans are given abilities the animals do not have. Does that imply animals are inferior in the ability to serve God? No, not at all. Humans have 100% of the abilities they need to serve God. Likewise, animals have 100% of what they need to serve God. All of creation stands on its own before God. We were not created in competition. Christians must learn to accept that. Humans and animals can be different, but equally precious to God. Part 3 of this book contains more on this.

Hospitals and Symphonies

In efforts to prove humans are superior, meat-eating Christians will say things like "humans can build hospitals and write symphonies, let's see an animal do that!"

They are missing the very point of being exceptional. God never intended the animals to build hospitals or write music, so their inability to do those things does not make them inferior. The exceptional skills humans possess are to do the things God wants us to do. We are made in God's image to do things like helping each other when we are sick (build hospitals). Or creating art (symphonies) for our mutual enjoyment. Animals do not need those skills because God does not require them to build hospitals. To say that humans are superior because they can do things animal can't is ridiculous. That's like saying a hammer is superior to a banana when hammering a nail. It's not superior. Bananas were never intended to hammer a nail. A hammer is made to hammer and nail, while a banana is made to supply nutrition. Ask any carpenter, hammers and bananas are not in competition for a place in his tool belt.

Exceptional to God? How's that work?

Here is *a thought experiment* to help explain how Biblical Exceptionalism plays out with humans and animals.

Imagine yourself driving home from work. The radio is on, and a newscaster breaks in with horrible news. He reports 3 children are shot dead at a local school; it is the same school your child attends. What do you do? Do you pray to God that *your child got shot* so some other child lives? Of course not. Your heart wants your child to be safe. And it's not because your child is superior to the other children, *but your child is unique and exceptional to you.*

Do you see how "Exceptional" works?

Human Exceptionalism means humans are distinct in their relationship to God, just as your child is uniquely connected to you. Now consider the other 2 kids. Are they of less importance or value? Of course not, but how you feel toward those other kids is how God feels toward his animals. That is "Exceptionalism".

Vegans need exceptionalism

Exceptionalism allows all people, vegans and Christians included, to deal with the fact that no person can live without harming other creatures. I recognize exceptionalism as God's "release valve," making it possible to overcome a sense of murderous guilt when I accidentally step on an ant or cause the death of a field mouse in the harvesting process of foods.

Last thoughts

There are Bible verses where animal status is equal to humans. Yay! Other verses imply their status is secondary to humans. This book will show several ways to discuss those without approving speciesism. I'll suggest you only recognize speciesisms' use centuries ago and move on to the moral need for 21st century Christians to go vegan. The moral need is the key. It's not always proving speciesism wrong…at first.

If this sounds confusing, don't sweat it. You'll see this played out further in upcoming chapters. I'll give alternate answers when I can if you are uncomfortable with this tactic.

Dairy Farmers: We care and love our cows like they're our children.

Vegan Activist: Then why are you so upset when we say animals and humans are equal?

CHAPTER 9: GOD'S ACCOMMODATION

God accepts you as you are, even if you're an idiot

Throughout the Bible, God dealt with humans as he finds them; He accepts them at whatever level of enlightenment they have, no matter how crazy and far off they are, because God does not violate free will. God does not force people to be moral, He wants them to choose to do good on their own. So when people do something evil, God's action is to move humanity toward a peaceful goal, not with *his force*, but by *our choice.* This is what's called God's accommodation.

Let me apply this to vegan advocacy. Imagine yourself speaking to the owner of a factory chicken farm. Everything he does is legal. He doesn't have to give animals more space. The law is on his side. Is the factory farmer doing evil? Yes. Does it need to stop? Yes. But we vegans don't have the power (yet) to free the chickens. So we begrudgingly take whatever win we can get without giving up our end goal of total animal liberation. That's accommodation or acquiescing (the reluctant acceptance of something without protest).

Understanding this approach will allow you to *"Veganize"* many troublesome non-vegan verses. When we read of eating animals, sacrifices or other such horrors, we advocates can claim, it is not what God wanted. He is just taking whatever win He can get short of using force. Since the earth is under man's dominion, God is only acquiescing rather than wiping out humanity (again) and taking over.

I'm not making this up.

Christians might argue this concept is ridiculous. God is God and all-powerful. He will always do what He wants, not bow down to human desires.

Uh, not so, and the best way I can prove this concept is by showing patterns of accommodation from the Bible. I will use 2 examples involving the worship of false gods and the sanctity of marriage. When carnist Christians recognize God's accommodation for these two activities, it will be hard for them to argue that God doesn't acquiesce (accept something reluctantly but without protest).

Many gods

My first example is how God accommodated belief in many gods. Yep, He did that.

Deuteronomy chapter 6 verse 4
Hear, O Israel: The LORD our God is one

We know this prayer (verse) as the "Shema." Jews recite it twice a day. Christians use it to support "Monotheism." Monotheists believe only one God ever existed. Christians are monotheists.

In the old days of the Hebrew Bible, AKA: the Old Testament, many of the people of Israel trusted in many gods. They were "Monolatrous." Monolatry is the worship of one high God without denial of alternative gods.

God acquiesced and let them keep their cultural, religious mindset (monolatry) while working to win them over and become the people's "Highest God" amongst the other gods…even though there were none other than He. Kinda confusing.

God could have said, *"Hey, no other gods exist, you're wrong,"* but He didn't. He recognized the people in a monolatrous (many gods) culture were incapable of understanding monotheism (one God). Knowing the people held tightly to the belief their gods were legit, God methodically proved He was the greatest of all gods.

Here is the backup for this view.

Psalms chapter 95 verse 3
For the LORD is a great God and a great King above all gods.

The Psalmist affirms other gods exist. Notice there were no heavenly bolts of lightning sent to scorch his idolatrous butt. Instead, God accommodated his monolatry and let it slide.

You can view a lot more monolatry stuff during:

The Exodus

God's acquiescence is noticeable in the Exodus story.

Do you remember when God sent Moses to rescue the slaves from the evil Pharaoh? Moses used random plagues of frogs, blood in the water, and the sun going dark, to name a few. Well, they weren't that random; God sent those crazy plagues to show the people He was supreme over the "gods" they assumed existed. He could've said He was the only God, but no, He accommodated their beliefs—for a short time.

Check this plague stuff out, and you'll notice what I mean.

Nile River god

The people thought several gods ruled over the Nile river. Their names were Khnum, Anuket, and Hapi. God showed he was more powerful than Khnum, Anuket, and Hapi by turning their river to blood. The people saw this as a direct attack on those gods. See, these plagues weren't so random or crazy, were they?

Frogs

To the Egyptians, frogs were a sign of fertility. Really? Frogs were fertility? I'm sure a sperm/tadpole joke is here somewhere. The frog plague was an attack on Heket, their fertility god. Having children was a big deal; if they upset Heket, they feared they would all be childless. God used this plague of frogs to prove his power over their fertility.

The Sun god

Moving on to Exodus chapter 10, the real God takes on *RA, the sun god*. God turns the sky black, proving He is greater than Ra.

Fear of the fake gods

These people (Israel) had an absolute fear of attack from these imaginary gods. The real God proved He could kick the butts of these fakers and keep Israel safe from their vengeance.

Got it? These people trusted in many gods. The *real God* worked within those beliefs to make his point. He allowed belief in false gods to get the people on his side by proving he was more powerful than their gods. It's a Long Con game done for their own good.

The top ten and accommodation

Move up to Exodus chapter 20. We get into the Ten Commandments and guess what? God still didn't say He was the only God. He is still accommodating their belief in other gods.

Verse 3:
Thou shalt have no other gods before me.

God didn't say there were no other gods but Him. Did you catch that? God let them keep and even reinforced their monolatrous beliefs when He said you cannot have any other gods before Him.

Here in **verse 5**:

Thou shalt not bow down thyself to them, nor serve them: for I the LORD thy God am a jealous God,

This commandment starts with orders not to bow down or serve the other gods. He did not say other gods didn't exist. He did not say He was the only. Nope, He is still working within Israel's monolatry. He even used jealousy. Think about it, if no other gods exist, then what's He got to be jealous over? God is giving the people of Israel reason to continue on with their belief other gods exist.

I trust by now you see God accommodates people's customs, beliefs, or, let's call it, stupidity. It is being done to move them gently with love, not force, toward a time when they can handle the truth of monotheism.

This accommodation to their cultural beliefs and monolatrous religions is so crucial to understanding the violence and craziness in the Old Testament. You will see how this works for your advocacy as we progress.

1st Samuel chapter 8

God preferred a theocracy (a system of government in which priests rule in the name of God). But Israel demanded a human king. So, again, God accommodated the people's decision and let them have King Saul. Hosea says, He wasn't happy about it.

Hosea chapter 13 verse 11
I gave thee a king in mine anger, and took him away in my wrath.

If this is confusing, let me hit you with a my 21st-century view of accommodation that gets me in trouble when speaking to church groups.

God is a meth dealer.

Think of how a medical clinic deals with a heroin addict. If a drug-addicted guy goes into a hospital wanting to get clean, did you know they give him more drugs? It's like this: the addict is in a bad way. His body is physically addicted to heroin. Pulling him off instantly could cause other medical issues and even death. So doctors give him a different drug called methadone. Methadone is a drug that is easier to quit than heroin. It will allow the addict to come down from his addiction in baby steps to avoid the physical damage he may suffer if he were to quit instantly. Then, once his condition is under control, they wean him off the methadone, which is a much easier addiction to kick.

Keep this *"God is a meth dealer"* story in the back of your mind. You will notice this with rules on animals for sacrifice, animals for work, or animals for food. God is weaning them off these non-vegan activities.

New Testament accommodations

I've presented several examples of how God's accommodation works. Despite that, I ran into Christians that fight this concept because my examples are from the Old Testament. They claim the New Testament Jesus never gave in to this so-called "accommodation stuff."

Oh ya? Look at Jesus in

Matthew chapter 19 verses 7 & 8
7- They say unto him, Why did Moses then command to give a writing of divorcement and to put her away

8- He saith unto them, Moses, because of the hardness of your hearts suffered you to put away your wives: but from the beginning, it was not so.

In these two verses, we have Jesus confirming God's accommodation exists. Even though God doesn't want divorce to happen, He will reduce his moral requirements, enabling Him to meet the people where they are at in their cultural development. But God will put restrictions on that harmful activity to curtail it and move it in the direction it should.

Paul and accommodation

We have more New Testament accommodation stuff going on years after Jesus dies with the apostle Paul.

Acts chapter 21 verse 26
Then Paul took the men, and the next day purifying himself with them (Old Testament Law rituals) *entered the temple to signify the accomplishment of the days of purification, until that an offering* (sacrifices) *should be offered for every one of them.*

The death of Jesus is the line Christians draw between salvation by Grace and the end of the sacrificial Law of Moses. However, this was written years after Jesus died. The Apostle Paul *was still* willing to make sacrifices showing his accommodation to the Old Testament Law. By working within their cultural norms, Paul did this to show that he wasn't an enemy of the Jews with his "new" message of Grace. See how it comes together?

Active or Permissive will

Think of all this as the active will of God and the permissive will of God.

God gave humanity the free will to do what they want. He will not force us to do what is right. Instead, God works to guide us within our abilities. As a result, some verses allow for the eating animals. However, when you dive beneath the surface with an understanding of the need for accommodation, you can come out with a vegan-friendly explanation. I think you will enjoy this when we get to those verses in part three.

CHAPTER 10:
ANIMAL SACRIFICE

I s God Bipolar?

The Bible teaches about how to sacrifice animals, but some prophets said God never wanted animal sacrifices. How confusing is that, right? Carnist Christians will often use sacrifice to prove killing animals is acceptable. God wants us to kill animals, animals are made for human needs etc, etc, etc.

Exodus chapter 29
Put your hands on the head of the ram, and you shall kill the ram, and you shall sprinkle the blood all around the altar.

Isaiah chapter 1
I have no pleasure in the blood of lambs and goats.

I could write an entire book on animal sacrifice. Thankfully, we don't have to know much. This chapter will show God never wanted sacrifices, animal sacrifice were of pagan origin and more. All good stuff for your activism, so pick the one that floats your boat. Let's dive in.

5Ws

Today's carnist Christian thinks, *"Hey, if God says we can sacrifice animals, then killing animals is OK."* But, like everything else, you need to know the 5Ws to make sense of it. Looking into the culture these laws originated (the When), considering the people they addressed this to (the Who), and the purpose they wrote it (the Why), I came to the same conclusion the Prophets Jeremiah, Isaiah, Ezekiel did. God never wanted animal sacrifice, humanity did. All God sought was a relationship of love with a sincere heart to serve him. Animal sacrifice was an evil pagan ritual that humans used as a way of releasing their guilt feelings.

Just say no to sacrifice.

The meat-eating Christian will have the viewpoint that God must have blood to forgive sin. I think that's crazy talk. Somehow, you and I can forgive a person, but without bloodshed, God can't. As a kid, I believed God could not look at me if I so much as stole a candy bar unless I sacrificed my pet gerbil.

That is so far from the truth. Today, I am grateful (so is my gerbil) that I see God as a loving, forgiving father who is more concerned about our relationship with him.

Sin matters, but it doesn't matter to God *as much as we think*. God's concern is how sin hurts his children; that's us. Sin is not more powerful than God. God can forgive any way he wants, anytime, and without bloodshed. How foolish of us to think God created a formula of His own device that limits His ability to forgive. Too often, Christians put limitations on God that are of pagan origin.

We will first review the verses (my thoughts inserted) showing God never wanted sacrifice and He can forgive without bloodshed.

Let's begin Sunday School:

Psalms chapter 40 verse 6
Sacrifice and offering you did not desire, but my ears you have opened: burnt offerings and sin offerings you did not desire.

David (Assuming it's David speaking to God) gets it. God did not crave animal sacrifice; the Psalmist says God wanted his people to love him by serving him, not repeatedly killing animals.

Isaiah chapter 1 verse 11
I have no pleasure in the blood of bulls and lambs and goats

Do I need to explain that?

Isaiah chapter 29 verse 13
Their worship (sacrifices) *consists of man-made rules.*

It says here that sacrifice was man's invention.

1 Samuel chapter 15 verse 22
Behold, to obey is better than sacrifice, and to harken (listen) *than the fat of rams.*

The comparison is this; God prefers we obey and listen rather than offer sacrifice. In Hebrew, "Listen" doesn't just mean to hear the words audibly, but to take action on the words you hear.

Jeremiah chapter 7 verses 21–24
21- thus saith the LORD of hosts, the God of Israel; add your burnt offerings unto your sacrifices and eat flesh.

God is saying eat it yourself!

22- For I spoke not unto your fathers or commanded them in the day that I brought them out of the land of Egypt concerning burnt offerings or sacrifices.

During the Exodus, God didn't tell them to sacrifice; it was their idea.

23- But this thing I commanded hem, saying obey my voice and I will be your God, and you will be my people and walk ye in all the ways that I have commanded you

God just wanted obedience, no commands for animal sacrifice here.

24- But they listened not or inclined their ear but walked in the councils and in the imagination of their evil heart and went backward and not forward.

The prophet Jeremiah tells us, when God brought Israel out of Egypt, He did not command the people to make animal sacrifices. They maintained their own evil ideas and went backward to pagan rituals of animal sacrifices when God was trying to move them forward away from animal sacrifice. This is seriously good vegan stuff for you to use.

Hebrews chapter 10 verses 4-6
4- It is impossible for the blood of bulls and goats to take away sins
    5- therefore, when Christ comes into the world, he said: "Sacrifice and offering you did not desire, but a body you have prepared for me,"
    6- with burnt offerings and sin offerings, you were not pleased.

Killing animals was worthless, as they could never remove sin. God did not desire sacrifices, nor did they please him.

Hebrews chapter 10 verse 11
Day after day, every priest stands and performs his religious

*duties; again and again, he offers the same sacrifices, which <u>can</u>
<u>never take away the sins.</u>*

Once again, the Bible says sacrifices were a useless religious ritual.
No matter how many times they performed it, sacrifice couldn't take away
sin.

Amos chapter 5 verses 21-25

In chapter 5, Amos told Israel their legal system was corrupt, and the
people needed to turn back to God. They ignored God's way of love and
continued in their customs (sacrifices) to please God.

*22- Though ye offer me burnt offerings and your meat offerings,
I will not accept them.*

Again, sacrifices are unwanted, but move on to verse 25, and we get
another powerful anti-sacrifice bit of information that we spoke of earlier:

*25- Did you bring the sacrifices and offerings 40 years in the
wilderness, people of Israel?*

Verse 25 is a rhetorical question, and the answer is NO. When Israel
wandered in the wilderness with Moses for 40 years, God did not require
them to perform animal sacrifices!
We repeatedly see that humanity's obsession with animal sacrifices
was something God only tolerated. All God wanted was for Israel to come
back and love Him.
There is thought the Levites (a member of the Hebrew tribe of Levi
that provided assistants to the priests in the Jewish temple.) may have
offered a small number of sacrifices throughout those years but not the rest
of the nation. I doubt anyone but a Rabbi will hit you with that.

Hosea chapter 6 verse 6
*For I desired mercy, and not sacrifice: and the knowledge of God
more than burnt offerings*

OK, we see God can forgive sin without the shedding of blood. Now
let's look at verses that show God's acceptance and forgiveness by doing
the right thing.

Genesis chapter 15 verse 6
And he (Abraham) *believed in the LORD, and he counted it to him
for righteousness.*

All Abe had to do was believe.

Micah chapter 6 verses 6-8
6- Wherewith shall I come before the LORD, and bow myself before the high God? Shall I come before him with burnt offerings, with calves of a year old?

7- Will the LORD be pleased with thousands of rams or with ten thousand of rivers of oil? (This is a rhetorical question.) *Shall I give my firstborn* (Child sacrifice) *for my transgression, the fruit of my body for the sin of my soul?*

8- He hath shewed thee, O man, what is good; and what doth the LORD require of thee, but to do justly, and to love mercy, and to walk humbly with thy God?

People can offer every kind of sacrifice imaginable, but no need. God says all he wants (requires) is for humans to act in justice, love and mercy. Jesus affirms this in

Matthew chapter 9 verse 13
But go ye and learn what that meaneth, I will have mercy, and not sacrifice: for I am not come to call the righteous, but sinners to repentance..

Matthew chapter 12 verse 7
But if ye had known what this meaneth, I will have mercy, and not sacrifice, ye would not have condemned the guiltless.

How did it start?

OK, so we got lots of verses showing God has no interest in animal sacrifice. Now the question is, if God didn't want sacrifices, What, When, Where, and Why did sacrifices start? There are those **5Ws** again.

Many pagan doctrines taught that the "gods" were mad at humans. To appease their anger or try to get favors from these gods, humans felt they must visit holy places, pray a specific way, withhold physical pleasures or do a bloody sacrifice. Israel adopted these rituals of sacrifice from pagan religions of the time. Not good.

But how...

By the time we read of Abraham in the Bible, it was the Bronze Age (around 3000 BCE), and these people had gods for everything imaginable. They had gods for the sun, gods for rain, gods for harvest, and more. For example, people prayed every morning for the sun god to do away with the God of the night. I'm not kidding; they were whacked out.

The Bronze age farmer guy needs to grow food.

I want us to have a good grip on this, so time for a story. It's 3000 years before Jesus is born and there is a farmer guy that wants to grow food. The pagan farmer down the block tells him there is a god of the harvest and if offered a portion of grain, the harvest god will give him bigger crops. So, the Farmer guy is like, OK, how? He gets instructions to burn his crops so the smoke will rise to the heavens, and the harvest god will "smell" it, showing his acceptance of his offering.

In the 21st century, if a farmer told me to burn stuff so a god could smell it, I'd assume he was high on crack. But that was the mindset of that time.

But back to the process.

Farmer guy burned his grain. If luck had it and that day it rained, then the Bronze Age farmer guy now thinks he has the formula to please this god of the harvest. With the notion this sacrifice and the rain were connected, he does it again, and again, and again. But - what if it doesn't rain, huh? What then?

Well, maybe Mr. Farmer needs to increase his offering and sez to himself, "I'll burn extra gain." The problem intensifies because no rain again. "I guess I need to spice up my offering," says Mr. Farmer guy. "Let me see…if grain is not enough to convince the rain gods, then I need something of more value. Hey, I value this old goat. What if I offer that"? So now Mr. Bronze age farmer guy is making animal sacrifices. If by chance it rains, then he has established a system of animal sacrifice. But what happens when it doesn't rain for the next goat he sacrifices? He thinks, "geez, the gods must want more. Maybe I'll present two goats or instead of one old goat? Or offer an extra valuable young perfect goat. Perfect as in no blemishes". That's the way people thought then. Crazy but true.

Here is where it gets insane. Mr. Bronze Age Farmer guy grows greedy and thinks, "To get more from the gods, what if I offered something of higher value than an animal, like a human?" Now the farmer thinks, "I'll just grab a random homeless dude, no one will miss him," and human sacrifice begins.

That continues on till no rain again. So, time to up the offering…again. But what if the next homeless guy is rejected? Farmer guy thinks "What is more valuable than a random human? Oh, I know, a human of more value would be a relative or loved one, like my wife." Say Bye-Bye to the Misses. That works for a bit, but what if it doesn't rain? Farmer guy searches for something he treasures even more, then it hits him. His daughters, or perhaps he offers his youngest son. That works, once. But what of the time it doesn't. These gods always need more. How does it increase from an innocent child? Well, there is a sacrifice which he will only ever have one, his firstborn child.

Do you see how this sacrifice formula can get insane? Sadly, pagan religions operated that way. This system took deep root in Israel's culture. God had to deal with that. Got it?

The Exodus

By this time in history, animal and human sacrifices (including child sacrifices) are happening around these newly freed slaves. Some slaves were Israel, and other slaves were pagan. They had no idea how to worship this unknown Hebrew God of Moses, so they did what they always did: they sacrificed stuff.

The real God gets involved, and rather than cut them off, God accepts people as they are, mentally and culturally. God begins to move them in the direction they need to go. So God is like, *"NO, stop with the child killing. Here, just offer…ummm, this goat, ya, let's just go back to goats, that's better than your child".*

Is it making sense yet?

Now, if you're vegan, you scream Speciesism, and yes, but try to see the big picture. God is ending a horrible system and moving people toward no animal sacrifices at all.

I hope this shines a little light on those contradictory verses commanding animal sacrifice while at the same time, God saying He never wanted sacrifice.

Now let's read examples of:

Offerings without death

Sacrifices or offerings are not always animals. Read these verses.

Exodus chapter 30 verse 11-16: They could pay money for atonement.

Exodus chapter 32 verse 30: Moses felt he could just ask God to forgive.

And then a few places in Leviticus.

Leviticus chapter 5, verses 11-13 claims the poor can bring some flour and burn that.

God did not need blood to forgive sin. But wait, there's more!

Leviticus chapter 14 verse 29 says the priest can pour oil on your head to make atonement. Today, it sounds like deep conditioning for split ends, but back then, these rituals meant a lot.

Numbers chapter 16 verse 41-50: They burned incense.

Numbers chapter 31 verse 48-54: Bracelets, rings, necklaces, and earrings are accepted.

I think those verses show God can forgive in any way He wants *without blood or animal death*. It should be getting real obvious sacrifice was a thing humans wanted.

Only & If

Now let's consider how to argue with a carnist Christian who won't accept God can forgive without blood. The upcoming verses will show none of these rules apply to anyone but the Jews.

Leviticus chapter 1 verse 2

Speak unto the children of Israel, and say unto them, if any man of you bring an offering unto the LORD, ye shall bring your offering of the cattle, even of the herd, and of the flock
   3- if his offering be a burnt sacrifice of the herd, let him offer a male without blemish. He shall offer it of his own voluntary will at the door of the tabernacle of the congregation before the LORD.

Reread verse 2 and ask, at *who* are these rules being directed? Answer: *the children of Israel only.* Not you, not me, not anyone anyplace else in the 21st century. Remember, God had specific rules for specific people at a specific time and for a specific purpose. He never instructed people in other cities to sacrifice animals. Moses received instructions to give these rules ONLY to Israel. Have a peek at the first few verses in Leviticus 4:2, 9:3, 11:2, 12:2, 15:2, 17:2, 18:2, 19:2, 20:2, 24:2, 27:2. These rules are only for Israel during the time of the first and second temples. Just one small pocket of people in the entire world. Those rules applied for a limited time, maybe 1200 years total and done. No one today can use the old Levitical permissions for justification to eat or kill animals today.

The next underline in verse 2 was of the word *IF*.

This was only *IF* any man wanted to sacrifice. God is not demanding sacrifice here. God is guiding them, but *only if* they first choose.

Now let's consider what I underlined in verse 3. It says burnt offerings must be voluntary. That means God does not demand offerings, and the person has a voluntary choice.

If you keep in mind that animal sacrifice is voluntary, then reread the rest of the rules, you'll see those verses from a much different perspective.

If you consider that stretching it, check out **Leviticus chapter 22**

   18- Speak unto Aaron, and to his sons, and unto all the children of Israel. That will offer his oblation for all his vows, and for all his free-will offerings, which they will offer onto the Lord for a burnt offering;
   19- Ye shall offer at your own will a male without blemish.

Again, this is *not required*, but of the person's free will. God is not ordering it, and this was intended only for the children of Israel.

God didn't start it

Moses gave us rules on sacrifice hundreds of years after the sacrificial practices had already started. In history, both human and animal sacrifice was an ongoing part of pagan religious worship. A lot of Christians don't understand that. They read the Torah (the first five books of the Bible) and assume God was the one who ordered it first. Nope, God hijacked the existing pagan practices of that Egyptian culture. Then, transposed their idolatry to worship him only. Once they accepted Him as their highest god, then He changed their rules of sacrifice, making it extremely difficult to do.

The New God In Town

Imagine their situation, out of nowhere; this Moses dude comes in saying:
"Hey everyone, you don't need to do that sacrifice stuff anymore 'cause your gods, well, they don't exist. And your beloved children you killed, ya, they died for nothing. And those gods you have served and trusted your entire lives aren't even real so your just peein' in the wind. So ya'll need to stop eating that yummy sacrificed meat you've been eating for years, oh—and stop praying to your gods and pray only to this new God that I alone talked with"!
Uh, with their Bronze Age mindset, they would have killed Moses on the spot. So God gives Moses the "Welfarist" approach as an easier sell to these uneducated people. It's not what God wanted, but animal sacrifice was the only religious worship these people understood.

Welfarist style

I can hear vegans saying animal sacrifice is cruel or why didn't God just say no? That's a legit question. I had to stop thinking as a Chicago punk growing up in the 20th century and put myself in the Israelites' shoes (or should I say sandals) to understand it. I would have been a slave in Egypt, taught the Babylonian gods must have sacrifices. I would have killed hundreds of animals in my life (and possibly humans) in my efforts to satisfy those gods. The people I trusted would have taught me to eat animals and even drink animal blood to connect to the gods. That is some seriously messed up commitments to non-existent pagan deity. But that's how bad the people were. That depth of devotion isn't likely to go away overnight. Think of the American Civil War when slavery was passionately embedded into American economics and the way of life. When threatened with an immediate stop, many states were wiling to go to war. Hundreds of thousands of people died to keep slavery in their way of life. I think maybe God saw the death and destruction resulting from demanding a cold, hard stop to the sacrificial system. Demanding instant change might shut them off entirely. So, Moses drops a ton of rules (mostly in Leviticus) to choke back sacrifices. People can be fragile and their pride is strong. It is better (not correct, but better) to work with them where they are than to lose them completely. Welfarism is 100% wrong, but in an evil world where "take it or leave it" is a vegans only option, any win is preferred over nothing.
I hope it does not come off that my end-goal is acceptance of welfarism. Abolition is the "home run," I try for every time I step up to bat. But I am living in "their world". If I only get on 3rd base, I'll take that

as a transitory win…for the moment.

Wrap up

We have a new God introduced into a pagan culture. These pagans habitually killed animals any place, at any time, and in any way they wanted. They did it to appease anger or get favors from false/pagan/non-existent gods. After the sacrifices, they selfishly took pleasure from eating these sacrificed animals, which doubled their reasons for continuing sacrifices.

Knowing the mental addiction of sacrifice wouldn't change overnight, God put many burdensome restrictions in place to ween everyone off the ritualistic slaughter. No longer can sacrifice be done anywhere, but only at the temple. It has to be performed by a priest with particular ancestry and training, conducted at sunset, and more and more restrictions. By redirecting the sacrifices to Himself and only Him, God cut out sacrifices to the many other gods, thus cutting the overall number of sacrifice. Now, the people didn't kill ten animals to ten different gods, just one was enough to relieve them from their feelings of guilt. That is why the Bible gives rules on how to do animal sacrifice, but at other times, tells us God never wanted sacrifice.

All God wanted was for his people to turn to him with sincere repentance. More details and lots more repeating of this (sorry) in upcoming chapters.

CHAPTER 11:
JEWISH DIETARY LAWS

T *za'ar ba'alei chayim,*
   To avoid the suffering of living creatures.

Laws improve human relationships when love for one another does not exist. Judaism has statutes that demand compassion in everything, including diet. We are going to consider how the dietary regulations in the Torah can help activists show carnist Christians they need to stop eating animals.

5Ws

The Bible is full of laws specifically made for the Jews. In the Torah (the first 5 books of the Bible), there are over 100 on how to eat animals. That's a lot of crazy rules for a Bar-B-Que, yet so few requirements on eating a banana.

In this chapter I am going to show how to work within these "non-vegan" rules. You will not have to prove the carnist is wrong for eating meat. God's rules will do that for you.

But why did God make rules about eating meat and

Why didn't God tell us we can't eat animals?

Well, he did. In Genesis chapter 1, He said:

> *29- Behold, I have given you every herb bearing seed, which is upon the face of all the earth, and every tree, in the which is the fruit of a tree yielding seed; to you, it shall be for meat* (Oklah = food).

30- And to every beast of the earth, and to every fowl of the air, and to everything that creepeth upon the earth, wherein there is life, I have given every green herb for meat (Oklah = food): *and it was so.*

In the beginning, a vegan earth was God's original blueprint for humans and animals alike. God let people do what they do because he gave humankind "Free Will." Between the time of "original sin" (Genesis 3) and the Flood (Genesis 7), people used their free will and started eating animals. In part 3, you will see God was so upset, He flooded the world, more on that later. I'm just building foundations here in part 2.

Fast forward, past the Garden of Eden, past Abraham, and up to when Moses delivered dietary rules to the Jews. The people were doing horrible things to animals before eating them. Here is an example.. They did not have refrigeration in Bible days. There was no way to kill a large animal and keep its decaying body fresh to eat later. An accepted practice was, if you wanted a leg of lamb, you take it. You cut a leg off a fully conscious lamb, pack the wound with dirt, salt, or preservatives of any kind, and hope the animal lived because later, there remain three more legs to devour at another time (this specific law is known as "ever min ha'chai"). The animal was eaten, one leg at a time/ Yes, it was that bad.

Sounds like veganism

Jewish dietary regulations have a decree: "Tza'ar *ba'alei chayim*" *to prevent the suffering of living creatures.* Sounds a lot like veganism, doesn't it? When permission to eat animals is given, it must be done with minimal suffering. They could've just stopped eating animals, but you know how people are. Humans are just as bad today. We quit using straws to save fish, but we won't quit eating fish to save fish. Humans were often idiots then, and humans can be idiots now.

Side note: I read that 46% of the plastic in oceans is from discarded fishing nets and we think straws are the problem, ugh.

My Rabbi friend (a meat-eater) used to tell me the inconvenience of the multiple rules were to teach people how to refine and control their gluttonous appetites for animal flesh. God did not want his people to give in to the lusting for animal flesh, as in the book of Numbers. You will read more on that in part 3.

If a meat-eating Christian claims they have approval because the Old Testament (Hebrew Bible) says so, then they must accept every biblical law that goes along with that approval.

Laws such as:

Only being allowed to eat animals that are 100% healthy. In America now, over 80% of antibiotics made are injected into, or fed to, factory farm animals. Why? Because factory farm animals are continuously ill from overcrowding, improper diets, lack of exercise, and living much of their lives hoof deep in their own poop. So no, you can't eat any animals from factory farms as they all are unhealthy. That eliminates over 95% of the food Christians eat. Vegan Win!

See what I am doing here? I am using laws that allow animal consumption to stop animal consumption. God gave Moses these laws and activists can use them in the same way.

Here's another law. Ask the carnist Christian, "was the blood of the cow killed for their cheeseburger spread over an altar as required in the book of Leviticus"? Ask them "if the knife that cut the animal's throat was a perfect knife without a single nick in the blade". Oh, and the fat, they can't eat the fat, and they must remove the sciatic nerve. And I mentioned cheeseburgers, my bad, they can't eat meat and milk simultaneously. Obviously, no one is doing everything God required to consume animals, so they can not use those laws for their defense.

Do you see how these laws on how to eat meat impede the eating of meat? Fun, huh?

Shepherds then to factory farms now

This is a tricky method showing Christians must stop buying any animal products based on the horrible treatment of animals on today's farms. But be mindful to establish this for comparison only. It can sound like you are approving of today's free range lies.

Let's consider how Shepherds cared for animals when these "permissions" for eating meat started. There were no factory farms, no genetically modifications of animals, no hormonal treatments, no drugs in their food. The animals were under the care of a shepherd who would leave 99 sheep to save one (Luke 15:4). If "free range" was a thing, it was in action when shepherds like Moses, Abel, or Joseph raised animals.

Animals could graze the natural foods God created them to eat. Foods that were free from pesticides or any growth-enhancing chemicals, so they only grew to a size God intended them to grow. The animals lived in fresh air and sunlight on mountainsides, not in extreme confinement, or alone in dark, filthy cages. The animals could reproduce the way God intended, without humans sexually interfering. Shepherds in Bible times allowed the animals to raise their own young naturally, according to God's plan. The animals could interact with their own species, just as God wanted them. Animals kept indoors were set loose on the Sabbath (Luke 13) to graze. *Absolutely none of these* activities are available today on a factory farm where Christians get most of their food. Let's be real. Can any Christian honestly tell me that God, Jesus, or the apostles would approve meat created on factory farms?

Meat-eaters argue its impossible to supply enough meat for the world under those circumstances. They are correct and that is the position activists can run with. If animals can't be raised with the "Humane" rules set in place by God, then the world needs to lower its meat consumption. Better yet, stop completely, duh!

Shall be your food

In Genesis, God commands every living being to eat only plants. But later on, things changed. In Leviticus 11, we get a list of animals *we may eat*. Don't let that trip you up. It's a list of what *may* be eaten, not what *has* to be eaten. Also, that was a concession for a specific group of people with *no limits* on meat eating. God giving permission to only eat *limited kinds* of animals was a hinderance to discourage their meat-eating lifestyle.

Unnecessary eating and suffering

Starting with Moses thru the time of Jesus, what was *necessary* or *unnecessary* is radically different from what people experience today. For example, we have grocery stores! Yippie! We can hop in our cars and, within minutes, be at a grocery store with access to great-tasting, cruelty-free plant food from around the world. We are not limited to what a small fishing city sold in open markets back in the first century. Fish just might have been the only food option available for their survival. In our current culture, to cause "the least amount of suffering" means we never eat animals because we don't need. They did, we don't. It is that simple.

What if they eat:

Kosher

Many Christians assume kosher food is nothing more than meat blessed by a Rabbi. Wrong! There is an entire process in making something kosher. The system includes the minimal suffering rule: *"Tza'ar ba'alei chayim."* This is not only in the slaughter but also allowing animals to *live* a healthy life. Currently, farmers can cut the horns off cows with no painkillers. They can cut the beaks and toes off chickens with no painkillers. Any farmer, not qualified veterinarians, but any farmer can legally cut the testicles off pigs with no anesthesia. Farmers can keep animals confined in cramped, dark, filthy cages their entire lives. These conditions make animals so sick they need huge amounts of antibiotics to keep them alive, but only long enough to grow to a profitable size for slaughter. All meat and milk from factory farms violate requirements for food to be permissible to eat. So again, NO!

Another thing, meat was permissible only when connected to animal sacrifice (Leviticus 17:3) or it was considered "meat of lust". These people raised their flocks themselves before taking them to a priest for slaughter in what was the most painless way possible. That is not something any Christian does when they visit a fast-food joint. Your drive-thru burger suffered unimaginable pain.

Frequency

I'm babbling on, I know, but I want to add that many of these people were poor. Meat was a luxury item eaten once a week (Sabbath) or less, maybe 6 times a year (usually festivals).

We can eat as Jesus did.

Today's carnist Christian will argue the kosher laws only apply to the Old Testament Jews; Christians are now free to do as Jesus did. Here is a fun rebuttal. These restrictions apply to everything Jesus ate because—are you ready? *Jesus was a practicing Jew.* The Old Testament Law wasn't done away with until *after Jesus died* on the cross. Any approval from Jesus regarding food would still be the Kosher /"Tza'ar *ba'alei chayim"* rules. Actually, everything Jesus did has to take Judaism into consideration as they practiced it during the second temple times. I use this argument often and it's powerful.

Maximize animal suffering

But really, consider what the carnist Christian implies with their comment. Kosher laws aren't vegan, but they require absolute minimal suffering. A carnist Christian's refusal of the kosher rules means they don't want to be held accountable to rules that minimize suffering for animals. Are Christians saying they can thoughtlessly take part in industries that maximize animal suffering? It's crazy talk, it's gluttony, and useable for vegan advocacy.

If they hold to the claim, kosher laws don't apply to New Testament believers, you don't have to argue. I have had outstanding success by asking: *"Why don't the Old Testament laws that minimize animal suffering carry over to New Testament times"* Watch them squirm as they try to defend inflicting maximum misery with "uh, we have dominion".

What beneficial reason?

What benefit was there for God to make these meat laws? None. Was there a benefit to humans for these meat-eating laws? Nope. Did the rules make meat taste better? Nope! Did it make the meat more accessible? Again, nope!

Think about that. Every meat-consumption law God gave is another roadblock to access meat. This makes it so obvious that God begrudgingly gave permissions to a people that were lustful and gluttonous. If the carnist disagrees, ask, "If God wants us to eat meat, why did he block its access by demanding all these insane laws but very few laws for veggies"? I think there was a rule on grapes used for wine, and checking grains and greens for bugs, but that's it. Compare that to over a hundred strict rules on meat.

Also, meat-eaters were required to know all the laws. If they didn't, they might violate a law making the meat "Treif" (un-kosher), thus, inedible. If one wasn't sure of every single, tiny requirement, best to pass on the meat. Geez, you needed a master's degree in kosher law to eat a steak. Actually, the Talmud (Jewish civil and ceremonial law) says that one who didn't study Torah was not permitted to eat meat. Yep, more restrictions on eating meat.

No laws require the eating of meat...kinda:

This is an activist warning. I have seen several videos where Christian vegan activists say "no where in the Bible does it demand Christians to eat meat".

Deuteronomy chapter 27 verse 7
And thou shalt offer peace offerings (often meat)*, and shalt eat there, and rejoice before the LORD thy God.*

Verse 7 sounds like, if you make an animal offering of peace, you have got to eat it on the spot. We can combat this. Point out this was only directed to Jews concerning meat sacrificed at the temple. The temple has been gone for 2000 years. This no longer applies to anyone.

Leviticus chapter 10 verse 12
And Moses spake unto Aaron, and unto Eleazar and unto Ithamar, his sons that were left, Take the meat offering that remaineth of the offerings of the LORD made by fire, and eat it without leaven beside the altar: for it is most holy:

It seems Aaron was ordered to eat the meat offering. When the King James Version translates the word meat, it doesn't always mean animal flesh. Have a look at how other Bible translations see it:
New American Standard Bible (NASB): *Take the grain offering that is left over...*
English Standard Version (ESV): *Take the grain offering that is left of the LORD's food...*
New International version (NIV)
Take the grain offering left over from the food offerings prepared...
Only the KJV says meat. You will read a lot more on this later. Now look at the next verse;

13- And ye shall eat it in the holy place, because it is thy due, and thy sons' due, of the sacrifices of the LORD made by fire: for so I am commanded.

Aaron is told to eat this offering because it is his due. This is not an order to eat meat, but accepting payment for priestly services rendered.

This is how many priests supported themselves. Aaron could refuse or accept this payment.

CHAPTER 12: MURDER? RAPE? HOLOCAUST?

Murder, Rape, Holocaust, and other fun words
Vegan activism has slogans such as "Meat is Murder" or "The dairy industry is the rape industry," or "The Animal Holocaust." I'm right there with you all; these words are 100% accurate. But just because we can, doesn't always mean we should.

1st Corinthians chapter 10 verse 23
"I have the right to do anything"—but not everything is constructive

I am not against using these "trigger" words, just cautious with them. The carnist Christian has a human-centric understanding of what murder, rape, holocaust are. It's frustrating as heck to hear people call animals an *"it"* or consider the slaughter of an animal as something less than murder. I have to bite my tongue and hold my thoughts back, but I do. Why? I've seen the success of agreeing with the Christian just long enough to get the vegan message in first.

Let's kick this around, starting with the word "Murder."

Murder

When I search online for *"What is the definition of murder?"*, The first 3 are:

Murder: the <u>unlawful</u>, premeditated killing of one <u>human</u> being by another.

Murder: the <u>unlawful</u> killing of another <u>human</u> without justification or valid excuse.

Murder: the crime of <u>unlawfully</u> killing a <u>person</u>, especially with malice.

The underlined words shared in these definitions are "human," "unlawful," and "person." In the Christian culture, and in the eyes of the world, it is not <u>unlawful</u> to kill an animal, nor are animals considered as <u>persons.</u> Therefore, *to Christians, murder* does not apply. It is possible for vegan activists to prove *murder* applies, but it creates an enormous battle that disrupts the discussion of veganism. **How?** When I offer biblical foundations for applying the word murder, it preoccupies, or more often angers, the Christian mind sorting out that new information. It impedes the overall vegan message I am trying to bring. I can do it, but I think it's a small win, not worth the effort.

The defense I'll give for applying the word murder is lengthy and way above the education level of most Christians. I find more success when I work with the Christian at their level (you'll hear this a lot). It's your choice to use the word. You are technically correct, but that does not mean you will be effective to uneducated minds (1ˢᵗ Corinthians 6:12). I don't mean that to be insulting, but this is not a subject the carnist Christian had any reason to study unless they meet a vegan Christian, very rare.

Replacement words

I'm guessing many of you have used the word murder and done well. I say bravo, good for you! But for me, I haven't been that successful in using murder with Christians. If I am having a *"decent and civil"* discussion, I focus on veganism and not whether a word like Holocaust can apply to animals. I'd rather they consider veganism first. They will see the connection to the animal holocaust later, on their own. Since I avoid saying murder, the words kill, slaughter, or abuse will navigate the conversation equally well. It builds off the Christian where they are at.

But- if they are absolute total jerks, sometimes the words murder, rape, and holocaust could be a necessary attention getter. When you're in the moment, I'm sure you'll make the right decision.

Yes, you can use the word murder.

Finally, here are the goods. But first, a warning. When I use the words murder or rape, I make sure they realize <u>I am referring to the evil nature of these actions and not the equality of the victims</u>. These are acts of violence against living beings. The victims do not have to be equal for the action to be evil. <u>The act of violence being done is wrong, regardless of who the victim is,</u> human or animal. Get that out upfront. Especially when speaking to a victim of rape or someone who has lost a loved one at the hands of a murderer.

There are verses where the Bible considers killing animals to be murder, but it has complications. Let's start with the book of Leviticus, where Moses gives instructions on animal sacrifice. Believe it or not, the animal you have permission to kill can be the animal that gets you killed.

Leviticus chapter 17 verse 3
What man soever there be of the house of Israel, that killeth (slaughter) *an ox, or lamb, or goat, in the camp, or that killeth it out of the camp,*

4- and bring it not unto the door of the tabernacle of the congregation, to offer an offering onto the LORD before the tabernacle of the LORD, blood (Hebrew: dahm = blood guiltiness) *shall be imputed unto that man; he hath shed blood; and that man shall be cut off from among his people:*

We are dealing with a verse saying animal sacrifice has to be done in a specific way to be lawful. Example: If someone kills an animal at any location, they must bring it to the temple and made into a legit offering. A qualified priest must drain its blood, and that blood must be poured on the temple altar (nasty!). Any other slaughter is unlawful and punishable.

If they did not do this *blood/alter/temple* thing, the person killing the animal is responsible for what is called *dahm* "blood guiltiness" (murder). As it says in my Hebrew translation, *the guilt of bloodshed* (murder) *shall be imputed to the man.* That is saying killing this animal is murder.

This gives us good ground for calling animal death "Murder," but it has complications. If the priest *followed* the proper ritual rules (blood/alter/temple/sacrifice), the killing would have been Okie Dokie.

The killing laws we have today are similar. For example, if you are being attacked, killing them in self-defense is not murder. But taking a person's life for a trivial accident, like stepping on your toe, would be murder. Got it?

According to these verses, if people inappropriately slaughter an animal, that's murder. Got it? Establish that and ask, "are you following 100 or more laws for preparing food"? If not, *you are committing the murder* of an innocent animal. You won't hear that brought up at a church BBQ fundraiser.

More of the 5Ws here.

The *Who* and The *When* may be an objection. Some may claim this "blood guiltiness" is only for the Old Testament times, but **verse 7** says not so.

This shall be a statute forever unto them throughout their generations.

Forever is forever.

There was a change when God expanded their borders, and I will discuss this later, but it doesn't change that improper killing of an animal can be considered murder. So the answer is yes, God gave this law to Israel during the Exodus, but verse 7 says it was to continue throughout all Israel's generations. Most important take-away for vegan activism is God said animal death can be "murder".

Let's consider another place where Scripture uses the term "blood guiltiness" (Hebrew: Dahm) as murder. It isn't about animals, but it will add confirmation the term "blood guiltiness" means actual murder. It additionally helps activist with the stupid "I didn't kill the animal, I just eat them" argument.

Psalm chapter 51 verse 14
Deliver me from bloodguiltiness, oh God, thou God of my salvation, and my tongue shall sing aloud of the righteousness.

This is a confession of King David. He got a woman named Bathsheba pregnant while her husband, Uriah, was away at war. Uriah was a faithful soldier in King David's army. To cover this adulterous mess, King David sent Uriah out to battle and instructed the rest of the military to back off and leave him alone on the front lines to die. What a jerk!

In the Psalm quoted above, we read of David feeling super guilty for having his friend Uriah killed. Please notice the wording. David had a man killed. He doesn't call it an accident; he doesn't backpedal out of it either. Instead, David calls it precisely what it is: murder. He uses *Blood Guiltiness,* the same word God uses when we kill an animal. See the connection?

Others kill 'em, I just eat 'em

Many times in vegan outreach, Christians claim innocence, saying, *"Hey I'm not the person physically killing the farm animals, I only buy the product in the store."* Thanks to King David, this is not a legit excuse for Christians.

King David did not physically kill Uriah, yet he admitted to God *he was guilty* of Uriah's murder. Just because the carnist Christian is not physically killing the animal, they arranged its death with their money at the grocery store. Therefore, buying the products makes the carnist Christian guilty of murder, as David was. This is useful in our vegan advocacy. Interesting fact, Charles Manson killed no one, but he was in jail for first degree murder. Thanks to King David and Manson, we can see how that "guilt" thing works. Manson and King David in the same sentence. Never thought I'd see that one.

The "V" word

As long as I am nit-picking words here, sometimes, just sometimes, I avoid using the word "vegan" when talking to a Christian. The problem is, they have been taught a flawed idea of what a vegan is. Heck, some Christians even think vegans are in a religious cult. This presents roadblocks I don't want to deal with. I sidestep it with something I call my *back-slap*. It's a way I ask (or answer) a question that is a bit of a slap in the face, while leading them in a direction I want to go. Let me give an example:

Christian: *Are you one of those vegans?*

Back-slap: *I just don't think God wants me to eat food produced from animal abuse.*

See what I did there? All I did was answer their question without saying vegan. I didn't tell them they had to go vegan or they couldn't eat meat, but the way I answered, makes them think about their obligations to God with what they eat. Now they have to deal with the knowledge they are eating food produced by animal abuse, and animal abuse is a sin. Arguing about the details of what a vegan is according to their ideas isn't as fruitful.

My Atheist activists can try: I just don't eat or wear anything produced from animal abuse.

Answers like this bypass their flawed perception of what a vegan is, and go straight to the heart of the matter. This kind of reply brings them to the battleground of their ethics and morals based on their Christian duties.

Are Animal Rights wrongs?

Activists know Animal Rights are moral principles based on the idea animals deserve to live as they wish, without being enslaved to the wants of human beings. But, Animal rights is another phrase I avoid when outreaching Christians. It's not the actual meaning, but *the perceived meaning* that gets in the way. Christians hear the term through their understanding of human rights only. For example, the average chucklehead will respond, *"You crazy animal rights people think dogs should be able to vote?"* There is also the Christian that clings to the idea humans are vastly superior to animals; therefore, animals don't deserve any rights.

To make the vegan argument, I bring God to my defense. I say vegans only demand animals get the chance to live the life God created them to experience, without interference from the gluttonous lusts of humans. So, no, we don't want them to vote. Although considering the leaders we've had, the animals might choose better.

In my vegan outreach, I use "animal kindness." Suggesting *kindness to animals* will open a door to further vegan conversations. As we progress through part 3 of this book, I will give several arguments to show that even if animals don't have "rights", God does not want them hurt.

He/She/It

Calling an animal "it" feeds into human superiority and approval for humans to treat animals as property. I understand the need to use "he" or "she" when describing an animal, but again, I have concerns. First off, I admit, I should say human and non-human animals in my talks. But I skip past it for the same reasons stated above with the other words. It becomes a roadblock to making vegan conversation. Christians have a mindset of superiority that is best dealt with *after* I make the point of compassion, being God's plan for our food.

Kind of in the same realm, I use "it" as a generic describer when I do not know the sex of any being, even humans. For example, when friends are having a baby. The day of delivery, I'd call them and ask, "is *it* a boy or a girl?" Calling a newborn baby an "it" is not seen as derogatory.

When I speak to carnist Christians, I might use "it" to avoid confusion in our conversation. Saying "she" for a cow takes the brainwashed meat-eater out of their reality and moves their minds off the subject of veganism at that moment. They will want to discuss if it is proper to call a cow "she" or a rooster "him". It takes us off track by sidestepping the main issue of veganism and I don't want to do that. I keep tight to my principal subject and not deflect on some side issue. To me, pronouns are a secondary issue to deal with later. My utmost target is to get their commitment to veganism. So looking at those words, He/She, I ask, "Why waste myself on a minor battle when I have an entire war to win"?

When I am on stage speaking, the situation allows me to use murder, holocaust, he/she because I have the luxury of time for explanation. I start my vegan outreach using "it" and if I see/feel them agreeing, I may move to He/She, I will also use He/She with my family that already knows my vegan views in advance, but for "hit and run" outreach, I find it best to gain as much ground for veganism I can.

Let me add one more to this list.

The Hebrew Bible

The Hebrew Bible is pretty much the Christian's Old Testament. It might be a good habit to quit calling it the Old Testament when talking to Jewish people. I might be overly nit-picky here, but better not upset somebody when our goal is to share the vegan message. Jewish individuals do not accept the New Testament; therefore, the Old Testament is not an "Old" anything. It is the *only* testament. Are you catching that? If not, don't worry, but it's nice if you can.

My view, just to be clear

I think unnecessarily taking the life of an animal is murder.

Sexual activities with an animal are rape.

Animals are beings; he or she, not an "it"

But I avoid those words because I'm not there to convince the Christian is wrong in these words' applications or meanings; I only need to convince them that the action is sin, no matter what word we use.

When dealing with a fundamentalist Christian, I am more concerned with how they perceive the words. If I use murder, holocaust, or rape, we end up in a tug of war whether those words should be used regarding animals. My goal is to prove God considers these activities are wrong even if done to, in their terminology, "lesser beings".

I am using language that will bring productive dialog to a group of people with preconceived ideas of what these words mean. I prove that regardless of the word we use, be it murder or kill, rape or sexually molest, God did not intend these actions to happen to any of his creation.

CHAPTER 13:
BEASTIALITY

Artificial Insemination is beastiality!

Artificial: made or produced by human beings rather than occurring naturally, especially as a copy of something natural.

Insemination: the introduction of semen into a woman or a female animal by natural or artificial means

To most people, the term Artificial Insemination creates an image of a clean hospital room where doctors and nurses work together to bring hope to barren women. Nothing wrong there if you are a consenting human woman. Artificial Insemination is radically different for unconsenting animals. AI is conducted in filthy barns, where female animals are forcefully restrained, while standing hoof deep in their own crap.

Artificial insemination for humans overcomes medical issues to create life. Artificial insemination of animals is not done for medical need. AI is forced on unwilling beings that will lead to inescapable torment and death. This is not done for animals to experience motherhood, but to create products for a human's temporary experience of sensory (taste) pleasures. They will kill every baby animal created 100% of the time. AI has no benefit to animals at all.

Leviticus chapter 18 verse 23
And you shall not lie with any animal.

Exodus chapter 22 verse 19
Whoever lies with an animal shall be put to death.

Deuteronomy chapter 27 verse 21
Cursed be anyone who lies with any kind of animal.

Ask any Christian, <u>sexual contact</u> between humans and animals is a sin. I have never met a believer who disagreed, so beastiality can become a fantastic lead into vegan conversations. Much of the meat, dairy, and eggs the carnist Christians buy are results of sexual contact between humans and animals. Unfortunately, Christians never think of this. When activists connect the dots for the Christian, they will fight it. But we can fight back.

Stop paying for humans and animals to have sex.

If you are a meat-eating Christian reading this, I'm going to assume you are not aware of the Artificial Insemination processes used to bring your milk, eggs, and meat to your dinner plate. <u>So this chapter is just for you.</u> Remember earlier I warned you I will be blunt? Here it comes.

Let's start with a look at Artificial Insemination in:

The cattle industry

A 12-month-old stud bull will be molested by a human up to three times each week in a process called:

Electro Ejaculation

You need bull sperm to get a cow pregnant, so let's discuss how farmers get the sperm out of a bull. There's such a thing called "Electro Ejaculation." First, they immobilize a bull with a colossal metal frame of equipment. Next, farmers will use what is essentially a big electronic dildo that gets stuffed in the bull's butthole. They send electric current through it, which will stimulate the bull to get an erection. Once fully erect, the farmer takes his hand to grab hold of the bull's penis. This often requires hand movements (jerking the bull off) from the human farmer to assist in ejaculation. Upon orgasm, the farmer directs the sperm towards a receptacle to collect and store for later use.

As the animal gets older, its sperm count lowers. Younger studs will replace the bull. I don't want to tell you what happens to the used-up older bulls. Awww, shucks, I'll tell ya.

After a lifetime of being sexually molested by human beings, people assume they might leave the bull to run free in a field somewhere until it dies. Nope, they get shot in the head, hung upside-down, and have their throats cut so their skin can become the cover of a Christian's leather-bound Bible.

But wait, that's not all! I'm just getting started. Next, I'm going to discuss the female bovine, the cow.

Cows

This is so horrible that I can't imagine any Christian would (knowingly) pay for this to happen. I am not making any of this up. I got this information straight off of farm websites with video tutorials. Google it yourself if you don't believe me.

The sexual molestation begins when the cows are as young as 15 months old. They are only babies considering God made their lifespan to be over 20 years. Cows are restrained in what they call a "Rape Rack." This is not what I call it; this rape rack term is the farm industry name for the metal framework required to restrain a cow and stop its efforts to escape this sexual abuse from humans. If an animal has to be restrained in something known as a rape rack, calling this *Artificial Insemination* is very misleading. I'd call that fisting a cow.

Next, a farmer (not a licensed veterinarian), wearing a rubber glove covering hand to shoulder, will (hopefully) put lube on the glove and begin by sticking their hand up the cow's butt/vagina/rectum. Got that? "Mooooving" on with this description, before they can squirt the previously collected bull sperm into the cow, they got to clean the rectum (poop-shoot). Farmers will use that gloved hand to scoop out whatever crap might be in the way. The next step is to use a catheter (tube) to pump the sperm inside the cow's cervix and she gets pregnant. The average cow can only get pregnant so many times before her youthful body gets worn out and can't produce babies or milk. This typically happens after five years. Then, as with the bull, her 20+ year life is cut short at maybe 5 or 6 years when she gets a knife to the throat and bled to death.

Let's take a moment and consider the never-ending pregnant life of the cow. Constant physical discomfort and being fed unnatural foods laced with antibiotics (which humans end up consuming) are all part of this animal's daily existence. Why? Because cows don't make milk nonstop. A cow must be pregnant or recently had a baby to produce milk. I am shocked meeting adults that didn't know this. Cows only produce milk because they have babies that need to drink that milk.

Speaking of the baby calf, they take her baby away, usually in less than 24 hours. Mother and baby cry for each other, but to no avail. Why the separation? Because humans want that cow's milk for themselves and to allow nursing the baby means less for human consumption, and cuts into profits.

If the baby calf is female, the entire process repeats as she becomes another milk machine like her mother. She will be fed all kinds of chemicals, making her produce more milk than God designed her to make. This causes mastitis. Bovine Mastitis: an inflammation of the mammary gland caused by trauma or an infection. It is very painful for the cow but were Christians dang-it; we have dominion and we want cheese. If it's a male calf, it will become veal. You see, the veal industry is the leftovers of the dairy industry.

Before we finish this milk talk, do Christians ever consider how humans physically get the milk? Ya, from a cow's udders. Udders are the equivalent of breasts in primates. Milk drinkers are paying for humans to grab cow boobs. I remember youth pastors preaching that grabbing the boobs of a female is sinful. I guess that does that not apply when feeling up another species. And ladies, think of how heavy and achy a woman's breasts are doing pregnancy and breastfeeding. Imagine being swollen and sensitive your entire lives…until the day you are slaughtered.

John chapter 10 verse 10
A thief comes only to steal and to kill and to destroy. I have come so that they may have life and have it in abundance.

In John chapter 10, Jesus is the Good Shepherd that gives up his life to save his sheep. Compare that to the bad thief that comes to steal, kill and destroy. That bad thief sounds like what the dairy industry does to cows, yet Christians subsidize such activities with every slice of cheese they purchase.

Pigs

The males are called Stud Boars.

Once again, Mr. farmer manipulates the stud boar's penis to collect the sperm. Essentially, he is jerking off a boar. Heaven forbid letting pigs have sex the way God wanted. That is too costly and inefficient. Farmers can't make enough money with God's system of doing things, so they get involved by molesting the animals to increase reproduction speed or handle their growth.

As the boar ages and his sperm production slows, he will be killed so carnist Christians can have their bacon on Sunday before they go to church.

Breeding Sow

Let's discuss the Artificial Insemination of the lady pig.

The female pig is called a Breeding Sow. These sows get molested at around eight months old. With a 15–20 year lifespan, the poor things are babies during their first pregnancy. Farmers force this on pigs at a young age because they are sent to slaughter at about 2-4 years of age.

Farmers might choose a more hands-on approach to this insemination ordeal. Farmers physically sit on the breeding sows back to fool the sow, giving the illusion a stud boar is mounting her. Can you guess what's next? While pretending to be a boar on the sow's back, they insert a sperm-filled catheter into the sow's vagina.

Are you Christian readers truly comprehending how much physical contact with animal genitalia these non-medical procedures have? None of these activities are done for health benefits to the animal, but to satisfy gluttonous humans. Come on Christians, how can this not be bestiality?

The next step for that tormented pregnant breeding sow is 16 weeks of confinement in gestation crates. Gestation crates are iron cages only inches bigger than the pig itself. Got that? Only inches. Imagine yourself in a coffin so tight on you can't move an inch in either direction. Imagine being stuck like that, while pregnant, on a concrete floor. These iron crates immobilize the pig so she can do nothing more than lie on her side in her own poop or stand up straight. The gestation crate is so tight the pig cannot turn around to scratch her own butt. Sows do not get to enjoy fresh air or interaction with other pigs. After several molestations by humans, the sow can no longer physically produce babies. They are hung upside-down and have their throat slit open so that people can eat pieces of their bodies.

And now it's time to discuss beastiality and chickens. What? You didn't think it happened to them?

Chickens

Artificial Insemination doesn't happen with hens as often as cows and pigs, but it happens. The farmer holds the rooster so he cannot escape being violated. They try to escape as hard as they can, but no match against a heartless human. The farmer will begin by stroking the rooster to stimulate sexual arousal in the animal. They apply finger pressure to squeeze the sperm from the rooster.

Now we get to the hen. The animal is not volunteering for this sexual molestation, so it must be restrained. The farmer will expose the cloaca (a bird's butthole and vagina combined) and take the collected sperm and insert it into the hen.

Turkeys

For farm turkeys, Artificial Insemination is always necessary. They have bred turkeys in a way that makes them grow almost double the size God intended them to grow. As a result, it has become physically impossible for turkeys to have sex as God planned. I guess God got that wrong, huh? (Sarcasm)

Turkeys are locked into restraining devices allowing humans to stimulate them to orgasm to collect their sperm. Later, the female is restrained, allowing humans to forcefully insert the sperm.

Fish

If you're not disgusted enough, let's keep going with fish. Surely, since Jesus and his crew ate fish, there was no bestiality needed.

Back in the first century Palestine, that was true, but today, that's not profitable. So fish don't escape Artificial Insemination either. You could be a shrimp (which gets their eyes cut out to make them breed faster), or even an ity-bity honeybee, and humans will molest these creatures. All these activities are to profit from their babies, secretions, or body parts.

And now, back to my activist.

This topic is gold for vegan outreach. As I said, beastiality is an issue Christian meat-eaters and vegans are in total agreement. The problem is, Christians rarely know the facts. Their minds directly go to the human experience of artificial insemination, which is cleaner, kinder, and, of course, consensual.

Rape

I wrote of this earlier, but I want to remind activists to keep your outreach target of *veganism* in mind. You are speaking to Bible-believing Christians that eat animals. They believe animals are not on the same level as humans. As much as you want to use the word rape, I avoid it. Christians feel rape only applies to humans. Saying rape might pull you away from what could be a valuable vegan conversation.

Look at all I just wrote. I was able to get the horror of rape across using alternate words to make a powerful connection while staying within the Christian mindset.

Sexual contact
Sexual molestation
Genital contact
Masturbate the animals

You can still work the shock value for your outreach with these phrases:

Jerk off the bull

Take a handful of bull sperm and shove it up a cow's butthole

Be creative; you get the idea. This is another one of those times where I don't argue Christians' allowance to eat animals. The sin of Beastiality is enough, and that's the beauty of this argument. Christians will not find a non-beastiality source. Various farm websites report that over 60% of livestock begins with artificial insemination.

What they are doing is not "Sex."

When I have brought up bestiality to Christians, they laugh, saying Artificial Insemination is not sex. I combat this working within their Christian Speciesist view by asking them to think back when Bible shepherds raised animals. Artificial Insemination was not a thought they had. Knowing the laws against beastiality, they wouldn't have done artificial insemination even if they could.

Can you imagine God recommending artificial insemination to (King) David when he was a shepherd boy? Of course not. Do any Christians think Jesus would've walked up to a shepherd and said:

"Hey guys, you can do this reproduction thing better than the way God designed it. Why don't you jerk off a bull and get its sperm? Then, lock-up that cow's head between a couple of trees and shove a fistful of that bull jizz in her vagina-butthole. Consider the money you'll save rather than wait for it to happen God's way."

NOT.

To get Christians past their cognitive disconnect to the sexual activities involved in meat eating, I've tried some pretty twisted comparisons. This is one I'll be hated for:

Masturbation

Some Christians will claim only penis-vagina-intercourse is beastiality; touching animals in the ways mentioned above is not considered sex. Carnist will use any excuse, huh? Working in their mindset, I use some of the sexual contact you just read about and apply it to humans. For example, since grabbing a bull's penis, or sticking a dildo up and animals butt hole is not sex, can I use an electric dildo in my butt while holding my penis until I orgasm? Can a Christian do these activities to themselves? After all, it's not sex, right?

See how that Back-Slap works? You're not disagreeing with them. You are just asking their perimeters for what constitutes sexual activity. This is a perverse method I've used to make carnist see a connection. I say it in a snarky, obnoxious way that telegraphs an attitude of absolute wrongness in both actions. But, chances are, it's a lost cause if you have to go this far. However, if others are listening, it will make the Christian's disconnect painfully obvious to the onlookers and you might make some inroads with them. If you got the personality to pull it off, go for it. If you're one of the "Earthling Ed style" activist, this is probably not for you.

Less offensive questions

OK, that last one was pretty messed up, so I'll leave you with less offensive questions on how to present beastiality in your outreach:

Activists: *Do you believe beastiality is a sin?*

Christian Meat-Eater: *yes*

Activists: *Are you aware people are paid to molest animals in the production of milk, eggs, and meat?*

Activists: *Can Christians claim beastiality is sin yet, pay human farmers to arouse an animal to orgasm?*

CHAPTER 14: GLUTTONY

Philippians chapter 3 verse 19

Whose end (destiny) *is destruction, whose God is their belly, and whose glory* (bragging) *is in their shame, who mind* (focused only on) *earthly things.*

Every Christian knows gluttony is a sin that involves eating too much. But in the Bible, gluttony is much more than just excess calories. The Bible applies gluttony to an unrepentant lifestyle of selfish indulgence, laziness, and more. Gluttons seek immediate pleasures no matter the cost to their health, family, the environment, the sick, the poor, or the animals.

Vegan activists can use gluttony but be careful. Just speaking the word gets me labeled a "Fat-Shamer". I do not shame carnists for their weight, I criticize them for ignoring the harm done to God's creation so they can selfishly satisfy their lust for animal flesh.

Funny thing tho, carnist Christians repeatedly tell me I am too skinny and I need to eat a steak, but that's not considered "skinny shamed". Eh, some I just can't win.

What is Gluttony?

Gluttony's meaning has changed over the years. Let's look at the translations. In the Hebrew Bible (Christianity's Old Testament), the word for gluttony is "zowlel".

Zowlel: *to be worthless, vile, to make light of, to be lavish with. To squander.*

That Hebrew definition has no mention of eating anything. Ya didn't expect that, did ya?

Now compare that to today's dictionary.

Gluttony: An excess of eating or drinking.

The Bible does not limit gluttony to over eating. Gluttony can be an overindulgence with cars, TV shows, stamp collecting, even *church!* Any desire (lust), so strong (addiction) that it hinders your Christian responsibility to serve God, can be gluttonous. I suggest activists get that info out fast, especially when speaking to overweight people.

Let me present a few questions to get this out of the realm of fat shaming.

Let's do a fun Gluttony test.

1- Is it Gluttonous for a Christian eat food manufactured from animals that were sexually molested by humans?

2- Is it Gluttonous for Christians eat chickens knowing 50% of the chickens hatched suffer a painful death in a blender-like machine while fully conscious?

3- Is it Gluttonous for Christians to eat food produced from animals denied the natural behaviors God wanted them to experience?

4- Is it Gluttonous for a Christian to eat food produced from animals fed drugs that made them grow bigger than God wanted them to grow?

5- Is it Gluttonous for a Christian to pay someone to chop the tails off cows and pigs with no pain medications for an unnecessary food item?

6- Is it Gluttonous for a Christian to pay someone to use hand tools like pliers to break out a pig's teeth? Or castrate animals with an ordinary utility knife? And with no anesthesia? Just because they like the way something tastes?

7- Is it Gluttonous for a Christian to buy food products that are destroying the rainforest, polluting the oceans and destroying the land God put in our care?

I have a hundred more "Is it Gluttonous for Christians" type questions, but that's enough to make the point. These questions will help carnist Christians connect they are paying for products made from sinful sources, only to satisfy their gluttonous desires. Also, none of these questions are about being overweight. Gluttons can be skinny.

How serious is Gluttony?

Gluttony has become as acceptable as telling a white lie. But the Bible considers gluttony a serious thing. Sadly, Christians rarely hear gluttony preached in church. I'll tell you why. The Centers for Disease Control says 36% of Americans are obese, and another 32% are overweight. So, with 2/3 of America being pudgy, if a pastor preaches on gluttony, they will aggravate 2/3 of the congregation, and there goes 2/3 of the donations. Also, we can assume 2/3 of the pastors are overweight, so they would look embarrassingly hypocritical. Hmmm, did I just upset 2/3 of my readers? Eh, I'm sure I'll upset the last third somewhere else in this book, so the rest of you, wait your turn.

Preachers may avoid preaching on gluttony, as it's bad for business, but the Bible isn't so politically correct. Check out a few verses.

Deuteronomy chapter 21 verses 20 & 21

20- And they shall say unto the elders of his city, our son is stubborn and rebellious. He will not obey our voice. He is a <u>glutton</u> and a drunkard.

21- And all the men of his city <u>shall stone him</u> with stones, <u>then he die</u>.

In these verses, gluttony is <u>a sin worthy of death</u>. But wait, there's more!

Ezekiel chapter 16 verse 49

Behold, this was the iniquity (immoral behavior) *of thy sister Sodom, pride, <u>fulness of bread</u>* (gluttony)*, and abundance of idleness* (laziness) *was in her and in her daughters, neither did she strengthen the hand of the poor* (Charity)

In the verse above, God destroyed Sodom and Gomorrah because of their serious sins. The prophet Ezekiel tells us one of those sins was gluttony. God saw gluttony (along with not helping the poor) to be evil enough to burn down the entire city. Ouch!

Proverbs chapter 23 verses 1&2

1- When you sit to dine with a ruler, note well what is before you,
2- and put a knife to your throat if you are given to gluttony.

It's bad enough that gluttony can get *you* killed, but the book of Proverbs suggests it's better to *kill yourself* than be manipulated by appetite. OK, context is not saying you should off yourself. It's hyperbole (an over-exaggeration for emphasis), but you can see, food-related gluttony is serious.

But we all like to eat

Don't stress out. In John chapter 2, Jesus turned water into wine for people who were already drunk. But it was a party, not an everyday thing. From that story, we can gather getting drunk at an occasional party and being a daily drunk are different things. Apply that formula to food. Overeating at a party now and then, eh. Not really gluttony, overeating every day is.

OK, so an ongoing overindulgence is gluttony, and gluttony is a bad thing. Let's look at how to use it in vegan outreach.

The hungry, the sick, and the poor

To care for the sick, feed the hungry, help the poor, and maintain the planet are all Christian duties. How does gluttony fit? Because eating meat is unnecessary. It is done only for human pleasure at the cost of innocent animals' lives. Gluttons ignore the destruction of our environment and seek only their immediate gratifications. Eating meat perpetuates hunger in poor countries, eating meat causes bodily harm and so much more. Let me give you some info so you can you see the connection.

Gluttony and World Hunger

A while back, the New York Times printed an article about ending world hunger. Notice, I said *world hunger,* not just hunger in America. The report contained a quote from the United Nations saying it only takes $30 billion to end world hunger each year. OK, so what's my point?

Recently, the American government gave farmers over $30 billion dollars in subsidies and bailouts. Farmers used the money feeding grain to the animals on factory farms.

Do you hear that? $30 billion can end world hunger. American farmers got $30 billion but couldn't end hunger in just America! Why is that? Let me tell you, because farmers use the money to maintain billions of animals in factory farms, so carnists (Christians included) can eat them. $30 Billion is plenty to grow fruits, grains, and veggies to feed the entire world's poor for a year, but no, that $30 billion was spent to satisfy an American lust for meat, and that still wasn't enough. Do you see the gluttony in this? Humans grow enough food to feed over 60 billion farm animals, but can't seem to feed only 9 million people (worldwide) that will die of hunger this year. There is plenty of food! If farmers changed to growing food directly for human consumption, we could end world hunger several times.

Christians answer to a higher calling. To care for the poor outweighs one's personal "right" to eat meat. Sadly, gluttonous desires stop Christians from joining together and giving up meat to end world hunger.

Heal the sick

We have a terrible health care crisis in America, and gluttony is a reason. I've read estimates claiming up to 70% of hospitalizations are results of poor eating and lifestyle habits. Don't believe that? Think about it; no doctor sends a person home saying, "you need to exercise less, cut down on the broccoli, and eat more processed meats."

The chronic diseases from animal consumption puts added stress on our health care system. It's so bad the poor have little access to quality medical care. Putting an end to the health care crises should be the duty of a Christian. By joining together, we could practically empty the hospitals. All it would take is the 200 million American Christians to eat what God told us in Genesis, plants. Vegans have lower mortality rates, lower cancer rates, lower cholesterol, lower rates of heart disease, lower diabetes risk, and lower hypertension. Knowing its negative influence on health care, it is absolute gluttony to continue with a meat-centered diet.

Let's also consider the billions of dollars spent on drug research to cure conditions that would end if people ate a whole-food, plant-based diet. The lives it would save are numerous. The research money could help the needy. But this gluttonous addiction to animal flesh is so strong most can't overcome it for their personal health, much less for poor families or the environment.

Gluttony and the environment

Remember me talking about "Tza'ar ba'alei Chayim"? It means to prevent the suffering of living creatures. There is another Oral Torah Mitzvah (Law) I like known as "Bal Tashchit", which means do not destroy. It is based on verses in Deuteronomy, chapter 20:19 & 20. We are to stop senseless damage to the environment, even if it belongs to our enemies.

Let's peek at how the eating of meat destroys the planet's resources.

Grain waste

It takes at least 3 pounds of grain to make a single quarter pound hamburger. With that much grain, we could give breakfast to a dozen hungry children. Instead, the carnist Christian gets one, just one single meal. Let me give a comparison of calories. On average, a cow eats 9 calories of grains to create 1 calorie of meat on its body. Got that? 9 calories into a cow only converts to one calorie out. Such a gluttonous waste of food when children are starving to death every day. Wake up carnists!

Water waste

Almost half the water America uses goes to livestock needs. It takes at least 600 gallons of water to make a single quarter-pound hamburger. I use about 20 gallons of water for a shower. That's more than most, but I've got a lot of hair to wash. I could take 30 showers with the amount of water used to make a single quarter-pound burger. Activists can also compare that to how many gallons to grow fruits and veggies. It takes less than 50 gallons of water to make a pound of apples, 25 gallons to make a pound of potatoes, and 35 gallons to make a pound of carrots. Using our limited water for meat production is a waste of the earth's resources and violates Bal Tashchit.

Poop

Farm animals produce over 9 times the amount of crap than the entire human population of the United States. Farmers keep that poop in retention pools the size of football fields. Those pools of poo (never in my life did I imagine writing the words *pools of poo*, yet here I am) give off toxic gasses like hydrogen sulfide and ammonia, which contaminates the air. The EPA says 80% of ammonia emissions are from animal waste.

To get rid of this fecal poison, they spray much of this urine and feces in the air over enormous fields. People living near those fields often get sick with respiratory illnesses. They dump a lot of this poop soup into the rivers and oceans, causing destruction. This violates *Bal Tashchit.*

Greenhouse gases

Animal agriculture (I'm talking cow farts) is a huge cause of Greenhouse Gas. A large percentage of Christians whom I have spoken with don't see greenhouse gas as a threat or have yet to decide if greenhouse gas is real. If you choose to introduce the greenhouse effect and it gets denied, I have saved the conversation when I switched to saying our air, land and water are only getting worse because of animal agriculture. I stick with pollution, avoid the Greenhouse gas debate. But, if you're one of those activists that knows your animal agriculture statistics, go for it and have some fun.

Rainforest

The rainforest absorbs carbon dioxide and gives off oxygen. Hunans need that for survival. Corporations level hundreds of rainforest acres every day for animal agriculture. They will run out of land one day. This violates *Bal Tashchit.*

Now let's look at a gluttonous comment activists hear often.

I can't live without cheese

Ever get a Christian say, "I couldn't live without cheese"? As an activist, you can stop them dead by asking, *"Isn't that's gluttony?"* Use these verses.

2nd Timothy chapter 1 verse 7
For God gave us a spirit not of fear but of power and love and self-control.

Proverbs 25:28
He that hath no rule over his own spirit is like a city that is broken down, and without walls.

Gluttony is lack of self-restraint, especially around cheese, it would seem.

Philippians chapter 4 verse 13
I can do all things through Christ which strengthens me.

Yes, Mr. Carnist, as a Christian, you do have the strength (through Christ) to give up cheese. Self-control is a Christian strength and obligation. We can fight their cheese comment with these verses, it's great. If you are an Atheist, you can really, really, really mess with them. Reply, *"Oh, thanks for the compliment of telling me I am superior to your god. I mean, if vegan Atheists can give up cheese but Christians can't, we unbelievers are obviously superior in our moral strengths than your god can provide."*

Your body is a temple.

Your body is the temple of the Holy Spirit. Christianity teaches we shouldn't pollute our temple (body) with sins like lust or drinking booze. That would also include eating toxic foods (like meat) that can cause heart disease, diabetes, several kinds of cancer, high blood pressure, stroke, obesity, erectile dysfunction, acne, Alzheimer's disease, and so much more.

Let's look at this temple stuff for more vegan advocacy:

1 Corinthians chapter 6 verse 19
What? Know ye not that your body is the temple of the Holy Ghost which is in you, which ye have of God, and ye are not your own?

The people of Corinth built incredible temples to worship pagan gods. In these pagan temples, they had "temple approved" prostitutes. Enjoying sex with these temple prostitutes was a way to connect with the pagan gods the prostitutes represented. In verse 19, the apostle Paul is correcting them, saying, Christians shouldn't join themselves to false gods because a Christian's body is already a temple of the real God. Got that? Cool. But today's pastors preach this passage only concerning the sexual immorality. However, to get <u>all of Paul's concerns,</u> we have to step back to verse 12 & 13. Part of this warning includes misuse of food.

12- All things are lawful unto me, but all things are not expedient: all things are lawful for me, but I <u>will not be brought under the power of any</u>.
13- Meats for the belly, and the belly for meats (food)*: but God shall destroy both it and them. Now the body is not for fornication, but for the Lord; and the Lord for the body.*

Verses 12 and 13 are warnings against <u>being brought under the power</u> of both food (gluttony) and sex. This prepares us to better understand verses 19 and 20. Activists can make use of the unhealthy eating aspect of these verses. The cholesterol in animal flesh kills millions of people every year, yet Christians deliberately *pollute their temple* with cholesterol-packed, animal flesh food choices. Think about it; People don't take medicine because they are healthy. If any Christian is taking a statin medication (Statins are drugs that lowers cholesterol levels in blood.) because their cholesterol levels are too high, they are not well. So, deliberately eating foods that caused this illness (such as cholesterol-filled animal flesh) would be purposely sinning against the Holy Spirit. Christians willfully taking part in an ongoing activity (eating animals) that induces harm to their temple is being brought under the power of gluttony. Do my vegan readers see how good this can be for our activism?

1 Corinthians chapter 6 verse 20
For ye are bought with a price: therefore glorify God in your body, and in your spirit.

Does ingesting the flesh of tortured animals bring glory to God? Nope, it only satisfies human gluttonous cravings.

One last thought on health. Isn't it funny how eating plants cures many of the diseases eating meat causes?

Warning to my chubby vegan activist

Gluttony is good for vegan advocacy, but it's hard trying to dodge the battlefield of "Fat Shaming". To sidestep the political correctness of our time, I try to focus this discussion on the gluttonous sins that come from selfish indulgence.

If I talk to an overweight Christian, I have a hard time since I'm skinny. I keep my advocacy in the realm of questions like I posted above, or I get judged as a *fat shamer*, which blocks my advocacy. Warning to the activists; I get judged for being skinny, your weight will also be judged. If your BMI is pushing maximum density, you will lose vegan ground based on your waistline. It's not right, but maybe using Gluttony isn't for you.

Tumor test

If you're reading this and you eat animals, I want to tell you something sad and gross; animals get cancer. That is the sad part. Here comes the gross part. At the time of slaughter, many cows have massive, football-sized cancer tumors. At the slaughterhouse, the exploited factory workers don't cut those pus filled tumors out. So, along with miscellaneous body parts like eyes, lips, and buttholes, the tumors get ground up into your hamburger and sausages. So ya, carnists are eating pus-filled cancer tumors in their burgers. How does that make you a glutton? Even after reading this gross cancer tumor story, you're so addicted you will still eat a hamburger. Haha, and carnists think Tofu is gross.

How much is too much?

Just for giggles, I wondered just how much meat a person could eat before being labeled a glutton. Some Jewish history books allowed only 7 ounces of meat and one glass of wine. Next time you go to a restaurant and order that 16-ounce prime rib, think twice. That would've got you killed by public stoning. Also, one glass of wine can get you "stoned." Get it? Stoned—as in killed? Hahaha! My jokes just keep getting worse, don't they?

Wrap Up

OK, so I've given you some pretty good ways to connect gluttony to the eating of animal products. I've tried my best to avoid making it about obesity, but good luck with that. Just saying the word might end the conversation.

CHAPTER 15:
MEAT, MILK AND HONEY

*O*klah, "Minchah," "Anakeimai," "Meat."

When Christians hear the word *meat,* they think of burgers, steak, ribs, or any animal flesh. However, "Meat" can be translated as either plant food or animal flesh in the Bible. Sometimes it meant sitting down to a meal with other people. So how does an animal activist know when meat means animal flesh and when it doesn't?

5Ws

By using a concordance, I find over 200 verses in the King James Bible that translate Hebrew and Greek words that mean any kind of food to the single word *meat.* Unfortunately, through our 21st-century eyes, the word *meat* is only animal flesh. This mistakenly leads readers to think Bible people ate meat at every meal. Quite the contrary, the people of that time were poor. Many could only afford meat at religious festivals or special occasions, like maybe 5-6 times a year.

Let's review verses with the word meat. I will prove that meat doesn't always mean animal flesh. I'll put commentary after them, and I'll show how to use this information with vegan outreach.

Genesis chapter 1 verse 29
Behold, I have given you every herb bearing seed, which is upon the face of the earth, and every tree, in which is the fruit of a tree yielding seed to you it shall be for meat (Oklah - food, eating)

Here we are with Genesis chapter 1 verse 29. I'm gonna be quoting this verse so much you'll have it memorized by the time you finish this book. Here we have a place in scripture where God says herbs and fruit are considered <u>meat</u>. It's kinda hard for a meat-eating Christian to argue this.

In verse 29, using The Orthodox Jewish Bible, translates it:

To you, it shall <u>be food.</u>

Now, if you compare that to the King James Version and it says:

To you, it shall be <u>for meat</u>.

With these examples from two different translations, it's easy to understand why Christians are confused.

The Strong's concordance reads the original Hebrew word as "Oklah" and defines it as *food of any kind*. The average Christian will not know this definition, but reading verse 29 should prove that this has nothing to do with animal flesh.

Leviticus chapter 2 verses 14 & 15
14- And if thou offer a meat (Minchah) *offering of thy firstfruits unto the Lord, thou shalt offer for the meat* (Minchah) *offering of thy firstfruits green ears of corn dried by the fire, even corn beaten out of full ears*
*   15- and Thou shalt put oil upon it and lay frankincense thereon: it is a meat* (Minchah) *offering.*

This time, the Hebrew word is "Minchah." Here we have the King James version wrongly translating the word (again) to be *meat*. The New International Version (NIV), English Standard Version (ESV), New American Standard Bible (NASB), and Holman Christian Standard Bible (HCSB) each translate Minchah as "<u>Grain.</u>" Pretty messed up, huh?

Strongs concordance defines Minchah: *a donation, a tribute, an offering.* What's really groovy is The Strong's definition says the offering is "<u>usually bloodless</u> and voluntary." That's a long way from animal flesh. It's no wonder the average Christian is so confused! It takes such a deep-dive to get a true understanding.

So, as frustrating as it can be, let's remember to go easy on them. I have books in front of me where we can research this. Typically, the average Christian has nothing more to go on than the King James Version and what their pastor tells them. Oh, and Facebook memes.

Isaiah chapter 65 verse 25
The wolf and the lamb shall feed together, and the lion shall eat straw like the bull, and the <u>dust shall be the serpent's meat</u> (Lechem)

This verse from the book of Isaiah uses the Hebrew word "*Lechem*" for meat. Once again, NIV, ESV, HCSB, and the NASB translate *Lechem* as *food*. The Strong's concordance definition for *Lechem* is *bread, food*.

A Hebrew and English Lexicon of the Old Testament known as Brown–Driver–Briggs goes further in its definition, adding *Lechem: bread, the ordinary food of early Hebrews*. But again, what the King James Version calls *meat* is better translated as just "food."

Let's pop into the New Testament for just one more peek at a use of the word meat.

Mathew chapter 9 verse 10
And it came to pass, as Jesus sat at meat (Anakeimai) *in the house.*

Mark chapter 16 verse 14
Afterword, he appeared unto the 11 as they sat at <u>*meat*</u> (Anakeimai)

Here, the word meat is translated from "Anakeimai." The definition in Strong's concordance is <u>*to recline as a corpse.*</u> So here again, the word meat has nothing to do with animal flesh. This was hanging out at a meal, or maybe you ate so much that you just had to lie down afterward and unbutton your pants. Ya, we've all been there.

On to the New Testament

I want to prepare you for many, many upcoming New Testament verses where eating meat is not about the actual item of food but with religious customs (sacrifice, washings or kosher) connected to the food item, be it meat or veggies.

Meat offered to false gods.

As we go through part 3 of this book, we will pick apart individual verses from the New Testament that contain meat. I will repeatedly teach of meat being offered to idols or fake gods. A few verses imply vegans shouldn't condemn individuals eating meat. Other verses imply people who don't eat meat are wimps.

Many of those verses have little to do with animal flesh. It is whether someone could eat *any food product* that wasn't prepared according to kosher laws or was possibly offered as a sacrifice to a false god. If any food item was used in sacrificial worship to an idol, they might consider it sinful to eat, while others felt it was of no concern. I will give more information later on. It comes up very often, especially in the writings of Paul.

Meat is added

Beware! Sometimes the word *meat* is added when neither food nor meat is in the original texts. Check out

KJV John chapter 4 verse 8
(For his disciples were gone away unto the city to buy meat.)

Notice the verse is in parentheses ( ), meaning the transcribers later added it. The other translations rolled with it but used food.
NIV *(His disciples had gone into the town to buy food.)*
ESV *(For his disciples had gone away into the city to buy food.)*

Now peek at the original Greek:

For his disciple went away into the city to buy.

That's it folks, the verse just ends with *to buy*. No food or meat mentioned.

Wrap up the meat

I hope I've been able to show that in the Bible, especially the King James Translation, the word meat doesn't always mean animal flesh. Typically, the original Hebrew and Greek words mean any food. So don't stress out right away when someone says meat, but try to be prepared. If you can, quote verses from other Bible translations. Also, it's easy to use the first mention of the word meat. In Genesis chapter 1 verse 29, God said plants, trees, and fruit are also called "meat." So if someone brings up a verse with meat and you don't know what to say, you can always bring them to verse 29, where God called plant food meat. Ask them to read the verse to you. Once you prove that meat could additionally mean plant food, they might understand the verse they're quoting differently.

Animal flesh

Let me address something that might be upsetting activists, my use of the word meat. I know full well it's the flesh of a once living, breathing, sentient creature of God. Calling it meat is an insult. I am choosing to start my conversations with meat-eating Christians on *their level*. If that bothers you, don't do it. No worries. When I open conversations on the carnist Christians level and make a connection, I find I have had better discussions. Eventually, I might move toward saying dead animal flesh, but not until I feel its impact will be beneficial. You might remember me using this style of advocacy in my chapter on the word "murder".

Milk and honey ain't vegan

Abraham and his descendants (Israel) are promised a land (Canaan) of "milk and honey," otherwise identified as "the promised land." Unfortunately, that sounds like a land of actual bovine secretions and bee vomit, otherwise known as milk and honey.

As with the word meat, the term "land of milk and honey", is not always a reference to food products. Nor is it meant to be taken literally as a land made of milk and honey; that would be very squishy and sticky. Instead, this term is a figure of speech to describe a fertile, lush valley. I will first give their (Israel) cultural understanding of *Milk and Honey* for your activism and then hit you with scriptural back-up.

Milk

To the people of Israel, milk symbolizes fertility. These people understood God's original commands for humanity was to be fruitful and multiply. Milk equals lots of children, and there you are, being fruitful and multiplying.

Honey

God's other command back in Genesis was to enjoy eating the many delicious plants he made. Well, where there are bees, there are plants growing (bees are how plants have sex), and the people of Israel understood this "honey" term to mean an end to hunger because lots of plants are growing. Vegan win for an un-vegan expression.

5Ws

We get this milk and honey term from

Exodus chapter 3 verse 8
And I am come down to deliver them out of the hand of the Egyptians, and to bring them up out of that land unto a good land and a large, unto a land flowing with milk and honey;

We read in Exodus the (first generation) Israelites are promised a land of milk and honey. But they did bad pagan stuff, and God punished them to wander in the desert for 40 years, never to see the promised land. Harsh. Jump ahead 40 years, and this first generation of Israel is dying out. Their kids (next generation) are the new Israel. We will read about them in the book of Numbers as they enter the promised land of milk and honey.

But before this NextGen group enters, they decide they want to double-check and see if this land is as incredible as their parents told them. Joshua, Caleb, and a bunch of spies get sent out ahead of the entire group to retrieve evidence from this *milk and honey land.*

Numbers, chapter 13 verse 20, starts when the kids are camped just outside this promised land. I am quoting the NIV here.

20- How is the soil? Is it fertile or poor? Are there trees in it or not? Do your best to bring back some of the fruit of the land. (It was the season for the first ripe grapes.)

Their concerns are of the soil and trees in the promised land. They are not interested in actual cow's milk. They tell the spies to bring back grapes, not milk or honey. But wait, there's more!

23-When they reached the Valley of Eshkol, they cut off a branch bearing a single cluster of grapes. Two of them carried it on a pole between them, along with pomegranates and figs.

When the spies entered the land of milk and honey, they didn't milk any cows or catch any bees; they cut off a cluster of grapes. They scarfed up figs and pomegranates.

The spies were gone for 40 days. On their return, they reported back to Moses:

27- They (the spies) *gave Moses this account: "We went into the land to which you sent us, and it does flow with milk and honey! Here is its fruit."*

There you have it, the spies themselves said, here is the fruit. They confirm this was never about cow's milk or bee's honey. This spy mission was to confirm there was fertile land to grow food and sustain the people.

Free range honey

A side note here on how honey is collected in Bible times. It wasn't done as today's beekeepers do on bee farms. There was no sexual manipulation of insects. They did not take the bee's food (honey) and replace it with sugar water for the bees to eat. There was no killing of any bees. They place a bowl underneath a beehive, and whatever honey dripped out, they ate. If you're going to eat honey, you can't get much more "humane" than that. But it's still bug vomit. Yuck!

CHAPTER 16:
IS VEGANISM A CULT?

Veganism: diet or religion

To the average carnist person, veganism is nothing more than a diet choice. But for Christians, many consider veganism as a religious cult. Veganism is neither a cult nor a diet. It is a rejection of violence and a call to compassion. Both attributes are totally Christian.

When I get accused of being a cult member, I fight by comparing common cult activities to Christianity. In doing so, Christians become aware their religious lifestyle is more cult-like than veganism.

Christian: one who professes belief in the teachings of Jesus Christ.

Veganism: a way of living which seeks to exclude, as far as possible and practicable, all forms of exploitation of, and cruelty to, animals for food, clothing, or any other purpose.

Religion: the service and worship of God or the supernatural

Reading those definitions, I see nothing keeping a Christian from going vegan any more than a Christian going Gluten-Free.

Veganism is an ignored, yet essential component of Christianity. Veganism is not of human origin, but God's ordered way to eat (Genesis 1:29 & 30). It calls Christians to apply their moral ethics to their diets, clothing choices and entertainment.

Let the comparisons begin!

Cults sacrifice animals.

Do vegans purposely kill innocent creatures? Oh, heck no! Satanic cults do, Judaism did, many religions still do. However, Christians needlessly kill innocent creatures every time they purchase meat. Let's not forget the animal sacrifice that many Christians do for religious holidays. Oh, they don't think of their Easter ham or Christmas duck as a sacrifice, but blessings and prayers are performed while holding hands over the body of a dead animal. I'd say those Christian rituals are cult-like activities.

Leaders

Cults have a leader that they follow. Many think of Charles Manson, David Koresh, and Jim Jones. There are leaders in Christianity, too. Christians follow Popes, Bishops, pastors, preachers, tele-evangelists. They don't worship those leaders, but criticize any of them and watch their devotees come to their defense. Do Vegans follow a leader? Nope.

Excommunicated

Cults do not allow disagreement with their leaders. Christians can get booted out of their denomination if they disagree. Mainstream Christians don't accept Catholics, Mormons or Westboro Baptists and the list goes on. Vegans welcome everyone. Vegans can be straight, gay, black, white, male, female, trans, Mormon, Muslim, Buddhist, liberal, conservative, have bad breath and disagree with everyone around them. The only requirement to be vegan is you must stop hurting animals.

Money

Cult members raise money to support their organizations. Likewise, Christians raise money through a 10% tithe of their income. Christians have bake sales, church bingo, and fundraisers to support their leaders and institutions. Vegans are not required to financially support anyone.

Rituals

Cults practice rituals and ceremonies.
Christians also practice rituals and ceremonies. They do baptisms, communion, marriage and burial rites, laying on of hands and anointing in oil, to name a few. Many still keep the Sabbath. Vegans do not practice rituals...unless you consider tree-hugging a ritual.

So tell me, who belongs to the cult?

Veganism is not a cult. We have no leaders; no holy books or special days of worship. Vegans have no obligation to attend meetings or perform rituals. The uniting goal of vegans is stopping animal cruelty. Why isn't that a Christian fundamental?
You might get challenged on:

Romans chapter 1 verse 25
Who changed the truth of God into a lie and worshipped and

served the creature more than the Creator, who is blessed forever. Amen.

It's not unusual (that was not a Tom Jones song cue) for a Christian to accuse vegans of worshiping the creature more than the God that created the creatures. Thus, using this verse to put the SmackDown on veganism. Not true. The context of Romans 1:25 is concerns of idol worship. There were idols of animal forms, but many images were human form. Just back up a couple of verses to verse 23.

23 - And changed the glory of the incorruptible God into an image made like to corruptible man, and to birds, and four-footed beasts, and creeping things.

The apostle Paul is addressing idol worship of any kind regardless of what the statue is copying, be it animal or human. Vegans don't worship animals; we just want people to stop hurting them. Don't let Christians step on you with this one. It shows their Bible ignorance. It's an attempt to twist scripture to support their gluttony.

Christians and the Cult of Carnism

We've all heard this rebuttal.
Humans have always eaten meat.
Hit them back saying "that shows cult mentality". I use two verses to establish that;

Exodus chapter 23 verse 2
Thou shalt not follow a multitude to do evil.

Even if billions of people (multitudes) do an evil thing, believers should not follow them in those evil actions. Indiscriminately following the multitudes into the evils of animal abuse is not a representation of God's love but a cult-like obligation.

Romans chapter 12 verse 2
Do not be conformed to this world but be transformed by the renewing of your mind that you may prove what is good and acceptable and perfect will of God.

Paul's instructions are, Christians should not conform to the world's merciless habits. Christians are called to be examples of God's love in this fallen world. Sadly, Christians have accepted the cult of carnism into their faith. Blind from seeing how their carnism prevails over God's desires for a merciful humanity. Don't we worship a God of love and mercy? Christianity is not compassionate if it allows killing for no reason but a fleeting moment of taste pleasure in their mouths. Christians can be and should be vegan. Just ask God. This verse in Romans destroys Christians that say "we've always eaten meat".

Vegans can't be Christians.

Large numbers of vegans insist *they can't be Christian* because of Biblical directions to kill animals. I get that, but those laws are not for modern day believers. Moses gave those commands to a single pocket of people (Israel) moving into the city of Canaan. As dreadful as the Levitical laws were, they were an improvement over the sacrificial system in Canaan. The new restrictions stopped a tremendous amount of sacrificial death. The laws were for a specific time and a specific purpose; that time and purpose are done. Further discussion of this in upcoming chapters, but know this: eating animals was not God's original plan.

PART THREE:

VERSUS THE VERSES

CHAPTER 17:
GENESIS 1 – AND GOD SAW THAT IT WAS GROOVY

Anything less is animal abuse

The first chapter of Genesis is a goldmine for vegan advocacy because it establishes how God designed life to be before humans trashed everything. Consider chapters 1 & 2 of Genesis as God's perfect blueprint. As we progress through the Bible, we will see humanity drift away from that blueprint, followed by God's effort to return us.

Let's open this up.

Genesis chapter 1 verse 10
And God called the dry land Earth, and the gathering together of the waters called the Seas and <u>God saw that it was good.</u>

Verse 12
And the earth brought forth grass, herb yielding seed after his kind, and the tree yielding fruit, whose seed was in itself, after his kind: and <u>God saw that it was good.</u>

Verses 17 & 18
And God set them in the firmament of the heaven to give light upon the earth, and to rule over the day and over the night, and to divide the light from the darkness: and <u>God saw that it was good.</u>

Verse 21
And God created the great sea-monsters, and every living creature that moveth, wherewith the waters swarmed, after their kind, and every winged bird after its kind: and God saw that it was good.

Verse 25
And God made the beast of the earth after his kind, and cattle after their kind, and everything that creepeth upon the earth after his kind: and God saw that it was good.

So what's my point?

Here we have God creating everything and repeating the phrase, *it was good.* This is important because, in Genesis, we learn precisely how God designed everything and what *His* concept of good is.

God created the earth, the sky, the water, the light, the grass, sea creatures, cattle, and it was good…just as is. But did you notice humans were not created yet? I betcha didn't.

Something commonly missed is, creation was declared good apart from humans. The earth *didn't need* mankind to be good, and the animals *did not need* mankind to be good. God made animals good, independently, as they are, and apart from humans.

We are looking at the only place in bible history where everything is the way God wanted, and it was vegan (Genesis chapter 1 verses 29 & 30)

I encourage activists to use this as a measuring point on how Christians should care for the earth, each other, and the animals.

This is a HUGE win regarding animals having their own importance outside of their relationship to mankind. Christians can't claim animals are here for human desires, because humans did not exist yet.

Man overriding God's original intent is Animal Abuse.

I'm going to unpack this part of Genesis a bit further, and give one of my best arguments on how God wants animals to be treated. *Anything less than God's plan for the animals is animal abuse.*

The scene is this: God purposely created the animals the way they are. It was not an accident that God gave them eyes to see, ears to hear, noses to smell. God made animals with the attributes He wanted them to have. God made animals with instincts to do specific behaviors that are unique to their species. God created some to enjoy lying in the sun, others find joy to snuffle in the forest leaves or dig in the dirt. God created some creatures to run in a pack, providing healthy interaction with their own species and others to flourish in solitude.

Here is the key vegan argument to present: For a carnist Christian to deny animals every natural behavior God wanted the animals to experience, is animal abuse.

Ask the Christian carnist this and stop; just wait for an answer. They will try to sidestep but don't allow it. Hold their balls to the fire on this one and don't let them wiggle away. Ask, *"since God created animals with instinctual desires, why do Christians override God's natural design for the animals"?* To deny these instinctual needs is to block God's desires for His creation. That is absolutely animal abuse. And blocking God's plan is NOT living in God's image.

Let's compare

God gave humans the physical abilities and intelligence needed for human survival, human happiness, and human service to God. Humans are made with just the right measure of intelligence, the right number of legs, eyes, and hands as God sees fit for humans to have. God does not make mistakes.

Similarly, when God made fish, he gave them the ability to swim and the intelligence that fish need for their happiness and survival. Fish, as they are, have the attributes needed to bring glory to God.

Similarly, when God made birds, He gave them the abilities to fly and the intelligence birds need for their happiness and survival. Birds. as they are, have the attributes needed to bring glory to God.

Similarly, when God made the cattle and the beasts, He gave them the abilities and intelligence needed for their happiness and survival. Cattle, as they are, have the attributes needed to bring glory to God.

Forgive the repetition but I am saying God made zillions of animals with 100% of the abilities and intelligence they need to survive and enjoy the life God gave them. Each animal God *called good, just as they are.*

In comparison, even if their God-given abilities are lesser to human abilities, it doesn't matter. God designed them as He deemed appropriate. No Christian can call them inferior without insulting God's design. Not as smart? Maybe. Not able to write symphonies? Apparently not, but that does not make them inferior. God wanted them the way they are and they are perfect.

Today's Christians disregard all God called good by saying animals are inferior. They do this to justify killing them for nothing more than momentary taste pleasure.

Characteristics

Not all animals are clean. Not all are considered intelligent, but the Christian might need reminding, God wanted them that way. When a Christian meat-eater calls a chicken stupid or says "dirty filthy pig," do they understand what they are claiming? Those Christians are saying, *"Hey God, you didn't make pigs up to my standards of clean"* or *"Hey God, you didn't make chickens as smart as I would have made them."* Think about it, Christians are telling God that he could have done better! How insane is that?

Is correcting God carrying on in God's image? Heck no, it was <u>God's plan for animals to be as they are</u>. Animals meet God's standards to the level where God calls them good. No need to be smarter, cleaner, or smell better. Animals are not in competition with humans. God does not judge them by human standards, nor should we.

For his pleasure

Humans want to believe they are the center of everything, but they forget everything was created for God's pleasure, not humans.

Revelation chapter 4 verse 11
You are worthy, O Lord to receive glory and honor and power for <u>you have created all things and for your pleasure</u> they are and were created.

Simply because animals were not *made in God's image* does not mean they are meaningless. They bring God pleasure as they are. This works as a defense against those calling animals dumb, making them unworthy of consideration.

Finally, humans declared good.

From the beginning of their Christian walk, churches taught believers humans are good and animals, eh, not as good. The Bible has something to say about that. Let's look:

Verse 27
God created man in His own image, in the image of God He created him; male and female He created them

When we finally get to humans being created, absent is the comment, *"and it was good."* Next, in verses 29 and 30, humans get instructions to eat only plants. Then, verse 31 says:

31- And God saw every thing that He had made, and, behold, it was very good.

Interestingly, we finally get humans, but they are not called good *independently* as the animals were. Humans are only part of the "every thing" that was good. It took animals and humans living together, in peace, and eating plants to be called *very good*. How cool is that?

As you can see, the first chapter of Genesis is solid Vegan Gold. I skipped the parts of being made in God's image and dominion. They're coming up in the following chapters.

CHAPTER 18:
GENESIS 1:26 – MADE
IN GOD'S IMAGE

H*ey, meat-eaters, unless God works in a slaughterhouse, you're not an image of him.*

Genesis chapter 1 verse 26
And God said, Let us make man in our image, after our likeness:

What does this image thing mean? Does it mean physical image? Possibly. In Exodus, God has a face. In Psalms, God is seated on a throne, so maybe God has a butt? My jokes will get worse.

God is not physical, but spirit.

Christianity teaches God is spirit and humans are physical beings. The average Christian claims that *in His Image* means Christians display God's nature, morals, and justice in their lives. Additionally, God bestows only humans with a sense of reason, conscience, and rationality that animals do not carry. So, only humans are worthy of moral consideration, animals are not.

OK, that's some crazy talk, but I can prepare you to work within that mentality by focusing on what God's image is and how eating meat is falling short of His Image.

See me, see God.

A Christian, being made in God's image, should reveal the essential attributes of God in their lifestyle. What does that look like?

Colossians chapter 3 verse 14
Therefore, as God's chosen people, holy and dearly loved, clothe yourselves with compassion, kindness, humility, gentleness and patience.

When looking at a Christian, people should see God's character of love, compassion, kindness, humility, gentleness and patience. The carnist Christian will agree with that.

Here is where the carnist Christian disagrees with veganism. A Christian should mirror God's mercy in their food choices, the clothing they wear, and the entertainment they seek. I submit, God does not abuse animals. He does not hang innocent creatures upside-down, and while they are screaming in pain, begging for mercy, pay someone to cut their throats. His attributes cannot be found in a slaughterhouse. Unbelievers should observe kindness, mercy and compassion in the diet of a Christian, so no, eating meat is not fulfilling our duty of living in God's image.

With this verse in mind, ask a Christian meat-eater, "are you God's image bearer by supporting the selfish killing of God's creation?" Or wearing fur? Or going to a bullfight or rodeo? Heck no.

Let's consider what God expected from humans that were made in His image.

27- So God created man in his own image, in the image of God created he him; male and female created He them.
28- And God blessed them: and God said unto them, Be fruitful, and multiply, and replenish the earth, and subdue it; and have dominion over the fish of the sea, and over the birds of the heavens, and over every living thing that moveth upon the earth

Got it; verse 28 says that while humans are in his image, we have the duty to be fruitful and multiply. That means our first instruction is to make babies. We are to create, just as He did, got it.

Next, verse 28 adds instruction to replenish the earth and (here it comes) rule over the animals. Is this where God says can eat them? Nope. Regardless of what anyone thinks, God tells the humans (that are made in his image) to eat plants; check it out in verse 29:

And God said, Behold, I have given you every herb yielding seed, which is upon the face of all the earth, and every tree, in which is the fruit of a tree yielding seed; to you it shall be for food
30- and to every beast of the earth, and to every bird of the heavens, and to every thing that creepeth upon the earth, wherein there is life, I have given every green herb for food: and it was so.

In verse 29, God commands Adam and Eve to eat plants, and verse 30 reconfirms veganism for humans and animals. Whatever Christians think *Image* means, it can not be permission to eat animals. Simply put, Image was given alongside instruction to eat plants.

There were no chapters or verse when Moses wrote this. We are reading one continuous thought. It's misleading to pick one sentence in verse 28 and not include the entire passage (verses 24-31). It's as if God's intruction to eat plants is stated twice to make sure we don't take this image/dominion thing out of God's vegan context.

God's hobby

God is into creation, not destruction. At this point in the Bible, we know God's hobby is creating life, not death. This adds to our vegan defense. God created a place full of life (Garden of Eden), where there was no death. After the Garden, God created animals with life. Then He gave the animals and humans directives to create more life (fruitful and multiply) and govern the land (garden, harvest, replenish) by creating plant foods.

It's reasonable to say, if we are made in God's image, we should be creating, not killing. Somehow, today's Christian twist this verse to justify violence. Apparently, they see the image of God as a slaughterhouse worker they must emulate.

Women's rights and human rights

There's another reason to believe the term *in his image* has no connection to eating animals. We need to read this from the viewpoint of those this was written to in Egypt. Moses wrote this passage for a group of pagan slaves. These people believed pagan gods created humans to be their slaves. So, when Moses proclaims humans were made in God's image, it was elevating humanity. For the first time, slaves were given human rights!

These people were not interested in getting permission to eat animals, they were already doing that. It thrilled them to hear they had rights, and if we look, it wasn't just the male slaves that were being liberated. It says God made *male and female* in His Image. Did you notice that? This upgrades women's rights too! These verses were written in a culture where women and slaves were disposable property, but when God says both sexes are made *in His Image*, it elevates and liberates everyone of them. This was originally understood as human liberation.

Aside from liberation, this was also a criticism. At the time before the Exodus, the slaves were eating meat in Egypt. Now; they hear God intended them to eat only plants. In upcoming chapters, you'll see they obeyed and adopted a vegan diet during the Exodus.

Adam's Image

I have another angle to this Image thingy, so let's mess with them just for giggles.

Carnist Christians say, "humans are above the animals because only humans are made in God's image." My fun reply is, "no we are not." Well, not entirely, I will explain.

Look at:

Genesis chapter 5 verse 3
And Adam lived an hundred and thirty years, and begat a son in his own likeness, and after his image; and called his name Seth

Ask yourself, was Seth created in the image of God? From this verse, the answer is nope. Reread it. This verse says Adam had a son in his likeness and his image. Seth was begat (begat means you had a child) of Adam's likeness and Adam's image, not God's. Did you catch that? Wonder why? Well, things have changed drastically in the Garden of Eden since they ate that apple. In the beginning, Adam was in the image of God, immortal and sinless. Adam's son Seth could not be born immortal and sinless because *sin entered the world* through Adam. (Try to phrase it that way; Christians know this phrase from Romans 5:12) Seth is not immortal because through Adam's sin; death has entered the world. Likewise, we are not created sinless or immortal, as were Adam and Eve. We are now in Adam's image, born in sin and doomed to die a physical death. Death and sin are not part of God's image, are they? Nope.

Did you see the change? Humans have been knocked down a notch or two. That puts us lower than when God originally made Adam. Regardless of being made in God's Image or Adam's image, both Adam and his son Seth were vegan.

One last thing we can grab from this.

Lions tho...

Made in God's image gives activists a great rebuttal when Christians use the popular "Lions tho" argument. Their reasoning is, if animals eat each other, humans can too. To combat this, I agree with their superiority view and use it against them.

Carnist Christian: *Lions eat animals so we can.*

Vegan: *But you were made in God's image. You are above the animals. Why reject the supremacy God gave you and lower yourself to the level of an animal?*

See what I did there? Try it, it works well.

I'll give one more shot for the *Lions Tho* people. Let them know, in the beginning, God made the lions to eat plants:

Genesis chapter 1 verse 30
And to every beast of the earth, (including lions) and to every fowl of the air, and to every thing that creepeth upon the earth, wherein

there is life, I have given every green herb for meat: and it was so.

Fast-Forward to when everything ends. The lions in Heaven will be back to eating plants.

Isaiah chapter 11 verse 7
And the cow and the bear shall feed; their young ones shall lie down together: and the lion shall eat straw like the ox.

Lions started off vegan and return to vegan for eternity. These two verses make it so obvious God wants us eating veggies.

Note: This might have sounded choppy as I purposely avoid commenting on "dominion." That will be discussed in the next chapter. I don't want to repeat myself and make you all crazy.

CHAPTER 19: GENESIS 1:28 – DOMINION, GOD'S PROPERTY MANAGERS

F*orget kindness; God gave us Dominion, so let's kill defenseless animals!*

Genesis 1:28
And God blessed them, and God said unto them, Be fruitful, and multiply, and replenish the earth, and subdue it: and have dominion over the fish of the sea, and over the fowl of the air, and over every living thing that moveth upon the earth.

The Bible says God gave humans dominion over the animals. Somehow, Christians twist "dominion" to allow them unrestricted permission to hurt animals, eat animals, wear animals, and do any painful thing they want to do to animals as long as it benefits humans. Wrong!

God gave humanity dominion to govern creation *the way God would*. That is why he made us in His own image and not the Devil's. As God's "Image bearers" we are to rule with selflessness, kindness, and mercy. Jesus showed dominion in action, not by domination, but with servanthood. He washed feet (John 13), he cared for the least of us (Matthew 25:40), he would break laws to save an animal in need (Luke 14:5). Oh my, how humanity has messed up the idea of dominion. Let's get into this one.

5Ws

Having the Bible broken up into chapters and verses creates a problem. Moses (and God) never meant for verse 28 to be a stand-alone statement. It is only part of the entire narrative given in Genesis chapter one, particularly verses 26-31.

God gives humans dominion in verse 28, no argument there, but in the same statement giving man dominion, God *immediately gives vegan boundaries* for that dominion in verse 29. Have a look-see.

Verse 29
And God said, Behold, I have given you every herb bearing seed, which is upon the face of all the earth, and every tree, in the which is the fruit of a tree yielding seed; to you it shall be for meat (food).
    30- and to every beast of the earth into every fowl of the air and to everything the creepeth upon the earth wherein there is life, I have given every green herb for meat (food) *and it was so*
    31- and God saw everything that He had made and behold it was very good.

Upon reading the entire narrative (verses 24–31), it's as if God wanted to make sure we understood that the *Dominion* He gives comprises *eating plants only!* Somehow, today's Christians twist their God-given dominion in verse 28 to allow for death and violence while in a world that God made free of death and violence. It makes no sense.

We have another vegan win when we consider one of our 5Ws and ask Who this is about. This is dealing with Adam and Eve, and no way would they consider killing an animal at that point in time. They had no idea what death was. Death didn't even exist yet. Nothing around them was dying, and the rest of Eden (the animals) was eating plants. Eating animals was not something Adam could comprehend. To see Dominion as approval to kill animals is reading a 21st century understanding into year one of existence.

That should give you a good idea of how to squelch this dominion thingy, but I've got more for you.

Two accounts of creation

We have two accounts of the creation story in the book of Genesis. Chapter 1 tells of the beginning of creation, and so does chapter 2, starting in verse 4. Common Christian teaching is that chapter 1 gives us an overview while chapter 2 repeats it with a bit more in-depth detail. So please pay attention to what chapter I'm quoting as I pop back and forth. Using these two accounts will give activists more to prove Dominion is not tyranny.

In a Garden

Take a peek at Genesis chapter 2 verse 15. You'll get added details to creation.

15- And Jehovah God took the man and put him into the Garden of Eden to <u>dress it</u> and to <u>keep it</u>

There you go. It says God put man in the garden to dress it and keep it. It's self-explanatory. God didn't put a man in the garden of Eden to build a slaughterhouse. God instructed him to be a gardener. No need to question if humans are hunters or gatherers. God made you a gatherer.

In the original Hebrew text, the word *keep* is *"Shamar,"* and it means: *to keep, guard, observe, give heed.*

So Adam (humans) is to guard, protect, and care for creation, including the animals. Dominion did not hand over unlimited right to destroy or kill but to defend and preserve.

Now dig this, God ordered Adam to care for the garden (earth), which is the sole source of food for humans and animals. God did not tell the animals to tend the garden, only Adam. This means feeding animals is partially human responsibility. Get that? Humanity was not meant to *eat animals* but to *feed animals!* Vegan win again!

To recap: Adam's dominion requires him to make babies, keep the garden orderly, feed the animals, and eat veggies only. Such a simple gospel to preach, huh? To use Dominion as a justification for killing is a perversion of God's gift of Dominion.

Let's pop into the New Testament for a moment and consider how Jesus looked at Dominion.

Matthew chapter 20 verse 25-28
25- But Jesus called them over and said, "You know that the rulers of the Gentiles dominate them, and the men of high position exercise power over them"

26- "<u>it must not be like that among you.</u> On the contrary, whoever wants to become great among you must be your servant,"

Jesus is slamming those who use their dominance to exercise power over the lesser people. Jesus warns his disciples not to be that way, but to be servants to the lesser people.

27- "and whoever wants to be first among you must be your slave;
28- just as the Son of Man did not come to be served, but to serve, and to give His life—a ransom for many."

Jesus had dominion over everything. He used that dominance to serve, not to force his way on anyone. If that is how Jesus uses his position of dominance, so should we Christians.

Hop back to Genesis chapter 2 now.

We get another example of what having dominion over the animals means when God presented them to Adam:

Verse 19
And out of the ground the LORD God formed every beast of the field, and every fowl of the air; and <u>brought them unto Adam to see what he would call them:</u> and whatsoever Adam called every living creature, that was the name thereof.

When God presented the animals to Adam, He didn't ask Adam if he wanted to eat them; He instructed Adam to name them. Adam had dominion, so he could call them whatever he wanted.

Extra credit

If you want extra credit, go online, use your favorite Bible website and search the word Dominion. I found Dominion listed many times but noticed no reference connected to eating animals. They usually connect dominion to kings ruling over other people. For example. In **Psalm 72:8,** we have a righteous king that has dominion overall. Let's learn what that *dominion* looks like from a *righteous king,* starting in verse:

12- For he shall <u>deliver the needy</u> when he crieth; the poor also, and him that hath no helper
13 - He shall spare the poor and needy, and shall save the souls of the needy.
14 - He shall redeem their soul from deceit and violence: and <u>precious shall their blood</u> be in his sight.

This good king will use his dominion to help the poor and the needy. Their lives will be precious to him. He understood that his superior position was best used to help others, not to satisfy his own gluttonous desires.

SUBDUE

There is still more of this Dominion situation that needs to be dealt with.

Genesis chapter 1 verse 28:
And God bless them, and God said until then, be fruitful, and multiply, and replenish the earth, and subdue (Kabash) it and have dominion (Radah) over the fish of the sea, over the fall of the air, and over every living thing that moves upon the earth.

"Radah" means to rule over. I don't know why Christians are so quick to think ruling over something has to involve meanness. Thankfully, when we see the word "radah" in **Leviticus chapter 25 verse 43,** its use commands kindness:

Thou shalt not rule (radah) *over him with rigour* (harshly or ruthless)

The other word, "Kabash," is the Hebrew word that is often translated subdue and usually means bring into bondage. Without knowing the **5Ws** of the verse, it can sound as if it's saying, *bring into bondage and rule* over the stuff God made. So these two words together sound pretty dang harsh unless you understand the religious culture of the people that heard those words.

The Enuma Elish.

Moses is believed to have written Genesis (maybe 1400 BC) during the Exodus. Genesis was written for the people he was leading to the promise land. These people were slaves to the Egyptians for hundreds of years. While they were slaves, they did not have the Book of Genesis; it wasn't written yet. They only had the Egyptian creation stories of their pagan religions. They trusted in the Babylonian account of creation called *The Enuma Elish.*

The Enuma what?

Quick version, the Enuma Elish, is another creation story of the world. It features a violent and bloody fight among the "gods," resulting in humans as slaves on earth. These pagan gods ruled (radah and kabash) over the planet in any cruel way they pleased because they had *"dominion."*

Now, the God of Moses beats up these gods of Egypt (with the 10 plagues). He takes their dominion of the earth and gives it to the slaves/humans. This was mind-blowing! These slaves can now *"subdue and have dominion"* over a planet that was the property of the gods who dominated and kept them subdued. Get it? This verse brings *liberation* to enslaved people.

Remember the timing of this. This message is delivered to a group of people wandering the wildness and only eating a bread-like substance called "Manna." They would not have understood "dominion" as unrestricted permission to eat animals from a deity that had told them only to eat plants and is only feeding them bread (Manna). See why these **5Ws** are so crucial to understanding? Knowing the When, the Who, the Where, and the Why can radically change our understanding of past situations.

Moses used familiar language and stories to convey a new message of liberation to the slaves. These slaves are made in the image of the real God that just beat up the Egyptian gods and delivered them from generations of captivity. The earth is for them to rule; they are no longer slaves. Now they have Dominion along with the *vegan command* in verse 29. They were also being fed vegan food from God in the wilderness.

Recap: They got vegan restrictions on their Dominion and free vegan manna food from God. There is no way they would perceive Dominion as a permission to eat animals. Actually, later on in Exodus chapter 16, they sinfully complained they don't have meat to eat. Reconfirming vegan was their diet.

Humans are only property managers

Psalm chapter 24 verse 1
The earth is the LORD's, and everything in it, the world, and all who live in it;

Even though God gave humankind dominion over the earth; humans don't own it. God still does; check out Exodus 19:5, Deuteronomy 10:14, Job 41:11, Psalm 24:1, Psalm 50:12, 1st Corinthians 6:19 & 10:26, 1st Timothy 6:7, and a bunch more. Humans are only property managers. Everything humans do with our "dominionship" is subject to God's intentions for us. So if a Christian's food choice is destroying God's earth, oceans, and billions of innocent animals, it's selfish and wrong.

So keep this on the back shelf should someone want to dig deeper into the word Subdue. It can be an exciting study, but Genesis chapter 1:29 and chapter 2:15, as I discussed above, will still be the better answer, as most Christians have never learned of these non-biblical creation stories.

Another Dominion misunderstanding

Too often, Christians assume the earth, animals and everything else was created specifically for humans—wrong!

Proverbs chapter 16 verse 4
The Lord has made everything for its purpose.

Everything, even the animals, had their own purpose. Have you got that? Animals have their own purpose in God's vegan world, and it's not human food!

So why was anything made?

Colossians chapter 1 verse 16
For by him were all things created, that are in heaven, and that are in earth, visible and invisible, whether they be thrones, or dominions, or principalities, or powers: all things were created by him, and for him:

All was created for God, not humans. Humans may be uniquely made, but the world doesn't revolve around humans. Everything (animals included) is for God.

Revelation chapter 4 verse 11

Thou are worthy, O Lord, to receive glory and honor and power: for thou hast created <u>all things,</u> and <u>for thy pleasure they are and were created.</u>

<u>Everything was created for His pleasure,</u> not human pleasures. God doesn't eat animals; He doesn't lock them in filthy factory farms; He doesn't subject his creation to sexual abuse. He enjoys seeing them do the things he made them to do. Think about it, don't you love seeing an eagle fly? See a dolphin swim or a puppy play? If we kill the animals, we are taking those pleasures away from God.

Geez, how did humanity become so selfish to assume everything was made for human pleasure? How arrogant of us! Especially for Christians, knowing everything was made for God's glory. Grabbing a piglet's back legs and slamming its head into the concrete so Christians can eat pork chops does not bring pleasure to the piglets creator.

Wrap up

The style of Dominion God grants humans has vegan boundaries. Dominion does not involve destroying the garden (earth, environment) but caring for it. Even in times of war, we are to care for the land (Deuteronomy 20:19), not destroy it. Ok, this cracks me up because people killing their enemy is okie-dokie, but don't hurt their trees. Hah, love it. But back to Dominion.

The dominion given was to rule over creation per God's will. God did not make everything with the intention of humans using dominion to destroy everything. Humans should be asking, "how do I use my Dominion to serve God?" not thinking "what selfish pleasures can I get away with".

God designed humans and animals with the ability to feel pain. Knowing full well humans and animals experience pain, He commands us to eat plants. Plants are the living things he created that do not experience pain. Isn't that freaking awesome?

Just me being a goof.

In Daniel (Dan 4:3) and Psalms (145:13), when it says God has dominion over humans, does that mean God may eat us? Or when the Bible states Jews have dominion over the gentiles (non-Jews), can the Jews eat non-Jewish people?

If they're killed kosher, I assume? Ya, I'm an idiot.

CHAPTER 20: GENESIS 2:7 – ANIMALS HAVE SOULS

Do animals have souls?

Current understanding of the Soul is a non-physical, spirit-like essence deep inside a person. God breathed this "soul thing" into human mortals, giving life. When we die, it leaves our bodies to be with God. Many Christians assume animals don't have souls. Or, the souls they have are lesser souls, void of reason or immortality. Somehow, that removes any moral responsibility, allowing humans to hurt animals with no concern of judgement. Geez, any excuse, huh? I disagree, animals do have souls. Souls of tremendous importance to God, even if they are different.

This study also has some help to offer those thinking plants are equal, so there is a lot here for vegan advocacy.

5Ws

The translation for the Hebrew word *Nephesh* is the English word *soul*. Soul translates differently in various ways and uses in the Bible. The Strong's Concordance says Nephesh (and its similar spellings) translates to *soul* over 400 times in the King James Version (KJV). Nephesh can also translate to the entire living being: self, life, creature, person, mind, passion, and more. If you were to read those 400 verses, you'd see Nephesh is often <u>equal between humans and animals</u>. Demonstrating an equality of the soul can be powerful to outreaching Christians. I will start this chapter by showing God gave (breathed) the exact same "Nephesh" or "Breath of

Life" into humans and animals alike.

Let's begin with humankind getting a soul in **Genesis chapter 2 verse 7** in the King James Version:

> *Then the Lord God formed a man from the dust of the ground and breathed into his nostrils the breath of life* (nishmat chaym) *and the man became a living soul* (nefesh chayyah).

God gave humans a soul. Souls are "Nefesh" Got it? Good.
Now, let's move to **verse 19.**

> *Now the Lord God had formed out of the ground all the wild animals and all the birds in the sky. He brought them to the man* (Adam) *to see what he would name them and whatever the man called each living creature* (nefesh chayyah/living soul) *that was its name.*

See the connection? God referred to both mankind and animals as Nefesh. God does so again in Genesis chapter 9.

Genesis chapter 9 verse 10
And with every living creature (nefesh chayyah = living creature or living soul) *that is with you, of the fowl, of the cattle, and of every beast of the earth with you; from all that go out of the ark, to every beast of the earth.*

Did you catch that? In Genesis 2:7, God referred to man as nefesh chayyah (living soul). Then, in Genesis 2:19 and Genesis 9:10, God referred to animals as nefesh chayyah (living soul). This shows no difference in the kind or the value of these souls. Both are living creatures made from the same substance and given the same "Nephesh" or "living soul".

King James Bible translators

When we compare the KJV translation done in the 1600s to the original Hebrew written thousands of years earlier, you will see "Nephesh" or "living soul" changed to "Creature." Why? I'm convinced this change was a result of the KJV Bible translators feeling guilt. In the year 1600, everyone was eating meat just like we are today. When the translators noticed God's original language for the soul applied to man and animal alike, they freaked and changed it to wording that implies a difference in soul value. This allowed the consumption of flesh to be unquestioned.

Can it be different souls?

After I slap carnists with how the word soul is used, they fight with a concept known as "Sensitive Soul". This idea agrees animals own a soul, but it's a lesser soul called a Sensitive Soul, while mortals own *"Rational Souls"*. Only Rational Souls are immortal or have value. Nice try meat-heads but King Solomon disagreed, saying human and animal souls are ultimately the same in **Ecclesiastes chapter 3 verse 19 -21**

> *19- For that which befalleth the sons of men befalleth beasts; even one thing befalleth them: as the one dieth, so dieth the other; yea, they have all one breath; so that a man hath no preeminence above a beast: for all is vanity.*

There is background needed to understand this verse deeper, but the wisest man in the Bible, King Solomon, says both humans and animals die a similar death. King Sol adds, death for humanity has no preeminence (importance, relevance, superiority) over death for animals (beasts).

> *20- All go unto one place; all are of the dust, and all turn to dust again.*
> *21- Who knoweth the spirit of man that goeth upward, and the spirit of the beast that goeth downward to the earth?*

There is no reason to think the souls are different when Solomon says the spirits of mortals and creatures could equally pass either way.

As a vegan activist, you can use this. Animals are created from the same earth as humans, given the same breath of life as humans, die similar deaths as humans, and go up or down as humans. From reading that, how does anyone defend the idea their souls are different? Good stuff huh?

Kvetch time

In my research for this book, I watched a zillion hours of online sermons from pastors, teachers, and apologists (a person who speaks or writes in defense of a faith, a cause, or an institution) that hold opposing views from me. I always learn more from those with whom I disagree. In looking for support of lesser souls, I came across a presentation by a wonderful apologist known for teaching faith is *reasonable* (yes, that is a hint). I have oodles of respect for him. His presentation taught that animals have a different threshold of pain, so the slaughterhouse experience is not as painful for animals as for humans. Wow, first lesser souls, now lesser pain receptors. That broke my heart because my hero allowed himself to be blinded by his gluttony. Dogs possess a higher sense of smell, eagles with their superior eyesight, animals with the ability to sense tornados, and on and on, yet this Bible teacher claimed their pain senses are on a lower scale. Here is how you deal with that.

Assuming this apologist is right and animals experience less suffering, how does that justify causing unnecessary pain at all? Let's put this in numbers with a pain scale of 1-10. If he is correct, what humans experience as a pain level of 10, a cow only experiences a level 7, or maybe a level 5. The question arises, how much suffering is this Christian teacher willing to force upon an animal for food he has no biological need? This is selfish gluttony.

That's just the physical aspect. Psychologically, pain may be more intense for animals. For example, because of my intelligence, I know that if I break my leg, it will heal and the pain will end. If a pig breaks a leg, he won't have the comfort of knowing his pain is temporary. Heck, without a doctor involved, maybe the pain will be permanent. I say mentally, animals suffer a lot more. Consider this: any animal stuck on a factory farm has the mental anguish of believing his torment may never end. Why is that? The animal might not be aware of what death is and assume the pain he feels daily will last forever. Does that sound like they suffer less? How sad.

This "Pain Level" reply is also a useful outreach tool for when showing an undercover farm video. Carnists may accuse you of only showing video featuring the worst of the worst situations. Activists can reply, "What level of suffering should I show? Maybe if I showed you a video of a piglet getting one testicle cut off instead of two, it would only be half as bad? Would that make it acceptable to show?" OK, I'm done complaining, and now back to our regularly scheduled program.

If animals do not possess souls, why are we instructed to preach them the Gospel?

Mark chapter 16 verse 15
And he said unto them, Go ye into all the world, and preach the gospel to <u>every creature.</u>

This is "The Great Commission". Every Christian should be familiar with this verse. But did they pay attention when Jesus says preach the gospel to <u>every creature</u>? I'm not suggesting we bust out a Bible in the middle of a pet shop and read 1st Corinthians to the puppies. I'm saying God sees animals on a higher level than Christians do.

Proverbs chapter 12 verse 10
A righteous man regardeth (cares) *for the life* (nephesh/soul) *of his beast: but the <u>tender mercies</u> of the wicked are cruel.*

Yet another verse showing beasts have souls with an added win for our side. It says to be "Righteous," humans are required to care for the animal's soul. Sending an innocent animal to a butcher is not caring for their soul. Putting gluttonous human desires before an animal's best interest is not righteous. Even though their "tender mercies" are to kill humanely, it's selfish, misguided mercy. Slaughter is still cruel to the beasts that only want to live.

Psalm chapter 150 verse 6
Let every thing that hath breath (nshamah= spirit soul) *praise the LORD. Praise ye the LORD.*

All animals and humans have breath so it would seem animals can praise God. Can soulless creatures Praise God? Nope.

Isaiah chapter 66 verse 23
And it shall come to pass, that from one new moon to another, and from one sabbath to another, shall all flesh (basar) *come to worship before me, saith the LORD.*

The Prophet says all flesh can worship God. The word for flesh is Basar, meaning animal and human flesh alike. Can soulless creatures worship? Nope.
Likewise in

Revelation chapter 5 verse 13
And every creature which is in heaven, and on the earth, and under the earth, and such as are in the sea, and all that are in them, heard I saying, Blessing, and honour, and glory, and power, be unto him that sitteth upon the throne, and unto the Lamb for ever and ever

This prophesy says every living thing, the swimmers, flyers and crawlers will be sing praises to the Lord. Why am I babbling about animals being able to praise? I am building up the foundation animals are not just low-level or soulless life forms, they can love and worship God. That's good vegan stuff for your advocacy.
But enough of that, jump over to **Revelation chapter 8 verse 9:**

And the third part of the creatures which were in the sea, and had life (psuché: breath, the soul), *died; and the third part of the ships were destroyed*

And

Revelation chapter 16 verse 3
And the second angel poured out his vial upon the sea; and it became as the blood of a dead man: and every living soul (psuché: breath, the soul) *died in the sea*

The book of Revelation can be confusing. It contains both literal and apocalyptic literature. The confusion comes in not knowing which is which. Nevertheless, this adds to the abundance of verses stating animals possess more of a soul than they teach in Sunday school.

Hey activists, we can use this soul stuff to fight back when Christians claim vegans murder plants or plants have rights too, etc.

It is really rare that I get a Christian saying vegans murder plants. But sometimes, they throw it out there. This Soul argument offers an excellent defense. Let's get to the Biblical rebuttal.

Genesis chapter 1 verses 29 & 30
29- and God said, behold, I have given you (humans) every herb bearing seed, which is upon the face of all the earth, and every tree, in which is the fruit of a tree yielding seed; to you it shall be for (food) meat.

30- And to every beast of the earth, and to every fowl of the air, and to everything that creepeth upon the earth, wherein there is life (nefesh/soul), I have given every green herb for meat: and it was so.

In verse 30, God includes humans, beasts, and birds in his list of creations "*Wherein there is (nefesh/soul) life,*" but God leaves plants out of this list. So, according to the Bible, plants do not possess *life* (nefesh/soul) like humans and animals have. That means we can stop a plant's existence but not "kill" them in the same sense as humans and animals can be killed. If a carnist Christian accuses vegans of murdering plants, you can tell them God doesn't agree. God excludes plants from his creation having "life", which is precisely why He commanded plants to be our only food source. Let's add more Bible muscle to this "Plant/Life" reply with another look at:

Genesis chapter 2 verse 19
Now the Lord God had formed out of the ground all the wild animals and all the birds in the sky. He brought them to the man to see what he would name them and whatever the man called each living creature (nefesh chayyah/living soul) that was its name.

Wild animals and birds of the sky were formed from the ground as were humans, and God calls them living creatures (nefesh chayyah/living soul). Notice, no mention of plants as living creatures containing "Nefesh" or anything similar to what humans and animals have. Plants may be alive but not a soul life, if that makes sense.

No death in Eden

There was no death in the garden of Eden. If plants were "alive" then there would be death in the garden of Eden. Christians know that's not possible because of Romans chapter 5.

Romans chapter 5 verse 12
Wherefore, as by one man sin entered into the world, and death by sin; and so death passed upon all men.

When Adam sinned, death entered the world, but the human species was eating plants before Adam sinned. Got that? God instructed man to eat plants. Therefore, God didn't consider plants able to die. Plants are alive but don't have *nefesh/living soul* kind of life.

Word games

When I was at a cattle ranch protesting, a rancher corrected me, saying he was sending cattle off for "harvesting," not to slaughter. Wow! Such insane lingual gymnastics being used to protect their Carnism. Instead of harvesting plants, ranchers are now harvesting animals while accusing vegans of murdering plants.
Harvesting: *the process of gathering from the fields.*
Kill: *to cause death.*
Slaughter: *the act of killing, specifically the butchering of life stock for market.*
I combined these definitions with this next verse to overcome his objection. I think you might like it.

Isaiah chapter 5 verse 20
Woe to those who call evil good and good evil will substitute darkness for light and light for darkness,

This cattle rancher is calling that which is good (harvesting plants), evil (killing plants), and that which is evil (killing animals) good (harvesting animals).
It seems meat-eaters are fulfilling Isaiah's prophecy.

CHAPTER 21: GENESIS 2:18 – GOD MADE ANIMALS FOR FOOD

G *od made animals for food."*

Well, actually no, no, he didn't. He created animals for companionship.

Let's get some background first, then verses supporting God's reasons for creating animals.

5Ws

I will start with the 2nd creation narrative in Genesis chapter 2. God made everything. A week goes by, and the universe is running smoothly. Or is it?

Genesis chapter 2 verse 18
And the LORD God said, It is not good that the man should be alone; I will make him an _help meet_ for him.

OK, so it's not all peachy-neato in Eden. God sees the man is alone and alone is a major bummer. To fix this loneliness, God declares man needs something specific; a "Helpmeet." What the heck is a helpmeet?

Helpmeet

"Helpmeet" isn't a word used today, and it wasn't a word they used in the original Hebrew Bible. Webster's Dictionary says Helpmeet didn't pop into use until 1673. Helpmeet is a word invented by Bible translators during a male dominated era in a meat eating culture. Keep that in mind.

The original Hebrew words are "ezer" and 'k'enegdo." The translators blended them and created an English translation of Helpmeet.

In a quick read, Helpmeet sounds like an inferior helper to assist the needs of a superior. Helpmeet ended up being Woman. Coincidence that a group of Men made that happen? Since then, Helpmeet has given Bible believers the idea a woman's purpose is to help man. I say not so. A deeper study of "ezer" and "k'enegdo" will move us to a better understanding of woman as equals and animals as companions.

EZER

They translated Ezer as a helper, but it has more profound uses in the Bible days. The Bible has Ezer in it over 20 times. Many times, it referred to the help we get from God as a savior. That is a long way from the current Christian understanding of Helpmeet as a 2nd level, inferior person. They likewise used ezer as a warrior protector. A warrior protector does not sound like an inferior. Actually, if they can protect you, that would make them superior.

When God and Warriors can be "Ezers," we know it has something more profound to teach us than a simple assistant. Let's check out the second word.

K'enegdo

K'enegdo is the other part of Helpmeet. The Strong's Concordance says K'enegdo means "In front of" or "opposite to." How's that work? Imagine looking at yourself in a mirror. The image is opposite but equal. As long as you're admiring yourself in the mirror, check out your arms. The left and right are opposite yet equal. Are you getting the idea for the word yet?

Back to Helpmeet

We read Adam was alone. God said alone sucks, and he made a helpmeet. Someone there for him as an equal yet opposite (K'enegdo), and a powerful (Ezer) companion to cure the loneliness. We now know what a helpmeet is. Phew!

Now dig what God says in the following verses, and you'll see how this knowledge of helpmeet assists with understanding God's purpose of animals.

Genesis chapter 2 verses

18- And the LORD God said, <u>It is not good that the man should be alone</u>; I will make him an help meet for him.

19- and out of the ground, the LORD <u>God formed every beast of the field and every fowl of the air</u>; and brought them unto Adam to see what he would call them: and whatsoever Adam called every living creature, that was the name thereof.

20- And Adam gave names to all cattle, and to the fowl of the air, and to every beast of the field; but for Adam there was not found a <u>help meet</u> for him.

Did you catch that? God saw Adam was alone (verse 18), and alone = not good. So what does God create? <u>He makes animals first!</u> Not a woman! Doesn't that just blow your mind? Ya, ya, I know there's more to it, and I'll get there, but I want this to sink in and take root. Animals were created for companionship, not consumption! God's purpose for animals is companionship and any of us with a doggie knows the immense love and companionship animals can bring.

In the garden, God was Adam's BFF. They would walk and talk together in the cool of the day (Genesis 3:8). But according to God, that relationship wasn't quite right. God's first effort to relieve Adam's loneliness (verse 19) was animals. This is not something taught in a meat obsessed society.

Name game

19- And out of the ground the LORD God formed every beast of the field, and every fowl of the air; and brought them unto Adam to see what he would call them: and <u>whatsoever Adam called every living creature, that was the name</u> thereof.

Now Adam is naming the animals. How cool is that, huh? There is a significance to *naming* an animal. God wanted us to bond through the naming process. Christians will claim, when Adam was instructed to name the animals, God was giving humankind unrestricted power over animals through the naming process. Huh? I don't know how they reach that conclusion. When I was a kid, we got a dog. My dad let me name him, but I never assumed dad gave me authority to cut his throat so I could eat him.

Working on a farm, kids are often forbidden to name animals. Naming creates a bond, making it emotionally harder to slaughter. Giving Adam the ability to name must have done the same bonding thing. Adam never saw this naming process as permission to eat animals. It drew him closer to the animals.

Adam could snuggle with lions and pet elephants while he named them. Again, how cool is that? Note, Adam had no perception of death in the Garden, so eating animals wasn't even on his radar. Oh, and I'm sure

Adam was high when he named the platypus.

Woman

> *21- And the LORD God caused a deep sleep to fall upon Adam,
> and he slept: and he took one of his ribs, and closed up the flesh
> instead thereof;*
> *22- And the rib, which the LORD God had taken from man,
> made he a woman, and brought her unto the man.*
> *23- and Adam said, This is now bone of my bones, and flesh
> of my flesh: she shall be called Woman, because she was taken
> out of Man.*

God gave Adam these companions (helpmeets), but none were suitable for Adam. Young's literal translation of the Bible says, *"man hath not been found an helper—as his counterpart."* Whichever version you read, it has God almighty looking at the animals and saying their purpose was companionship, not food.

Finally, Adam gets his perfect helpmeet, a woman. An opposite, yet equal and powerful helper. The animals came from the dust of the earth just as Adam did, but Eve came from his rib. Jewish tradition says his complete side. Regardless, Eve is physically suited for Adam as a partner, but the animals are companions, still not food.

Adam is still in the name game and calls her woman. Notice, just like the animals, Adam has the "dominion" power to name Eve but does not eat her. So, God made animals as helpmeets but differently than he made woman as helpmeet. The similarity is, both were intended as companions. God's original plan was man and animals share a connected and benevolent relationship. This point of view also works well with Christians who would not eat a dog because they consider dogs companion animals. Here in Genesis, all animals were companion animals. That takes every creature off the menu. Before I end this chapter, let's circle back to the "companion" part because it may sound like:

Exploitation

This "companion" point of view will differ from mainline veganism by accepting the idea God allowed people to enjoy animals as pets. At that time, things were different. Companionship was conducted with more of a mutual give-and-take. Animals were free roaming creatures, some choosing of their own to be companions. They had freedom to leave, they were not captives.

What's the diff?

This is not a necessary discussion for this book's subject, but since I brought it up, I better discuss it. I agree with animals as companions today.

But with *love* as my guideline, there are restrictions to companionship.

An example might look like this: imagine an elderly person, perhaps lonely, ill, or both. A dog companion is within the boundaries of a human mental health need. With the shelters full of animals looking for homes, it could be mutually beneficial and loving to give the animal a better living situation while offering comfort to the human.

A negative example could be a healthy, able-bodied person who owns a horse for personal riding pleasure. Riding a horse is not a *need* for any horse. It is not a need for human wellbeing; it is an unnecessary *greed* use of an animal.

What is mutually beneficial varies from species to species. A negative of keeping dogs is when done with neglect of the dog's needs. Dogs are pack animals who bond with their "human." A negative example: is the doggie alone when you leave for work? Then maybe you're not properly set up to have a companion dog. Or, better to rescue two little doggies, so they have company while you're gone.

Please do not write to me thinking I approve of breeding for the pet trade. That's a solid NO. This is about finding homes for the millions in shelters, care for birds with broken wings or a lost forest critter in need of its mother that may be dead. OK, you get the idea.

CHAPTER 22:
GENESIS 3 – THE FALL

God's good garden goes to crap.

We all know the talking snake story; the newlyweds ate an apple, sin and death entered the garden. This action is often called "*The Fall.*" Many Christians believe, since *The Fall* allowed death to enter existence, it's OK to kill animals. As if sin and death are a positive thing. Ya, I know, Christians will search for any excuse to eat animal flesh, but no worry. God nipped that in the bud.

Genesis chapter 3
2- And the woman said unto the serpent, <u>We may eat of the fruit of the trees</u> of the garden

When I deal with this viewpoint from a carnist Christian, I like to start in verse 2. Eve reconfirms she knows food to be the fruit of the trees. Adam and Eve had no idea of eating animals at this time.

3- But of the fruit of the tree which is in the midst of the garden, God hath said, Ye shall not eat of it, neither shall ye touch it, lest ye die.

They had one rule, that's it, but what did these crazy kids do? Have a look at verse 6.

6- And when the woman saw that the tree was good for food, and that it was pleasant to the eyes, and a tree to be desired to make one wise, she took of the fruit thereof, and did eat, and gave also unto her husband with her; and he did eat.

Eating the fruit of the forbidden tree was an act of rebellion and disobedience that allowed sin and death to enter existence. Now that there is such a thing as death, the assumption is animals can be eaten. Wrong! The Scriptures will not allow that understanding.

> *17- And unto Adam he* (God) *said, Because thou hast hearkened unto the voice of thy wife, and hast eaten of the tree, of which I commanded thee, saying, Thou shalt not eat of it: cursed is the ground for thy sake; in sorrow <u>shalt thou eat of it</u>* (the ground) <u>*all the days of thy life;*</u>

After the fall, God instructs Adam to eat from the ground (plants). No approval to kill or eat animals.

> *18- thorns also and thistles shall it bring forth to thee, and <u>thou shall eat the herb of the field</u>*

Again, after the fall, Adam is told to eat the herbs of the field. Not animals.

> *19- in the sweat of that face shat <u>thou eat bread till thou return unto the ground</u>* (dies) *for out of it wast thou taken for dust thou art and unto dust shalt thou return.*

For the 3rd time in a row, Adam has instructions to eat bread. This time, until he dies. Still no approval to eat animals.

A little more Dominion talk

These verses confirm after Adam was given dominion, he did not understand eating animals as a part of his dominion. If you get a carnist Christian that thinks Adam did, you can see God squashed that option when He instructs Adam only eat plants and bread.

Wrap up

The Fall is no excuse to eat animals. Christians are called to turn from sin. Appealing to the fallen state of humanity as a justification to eat animals is the opposite of Christian ethics. In verses 17 thru 19, Adam is directed to be vegan after he brought sin into the world. Adam is told to eat what grows from the ground in verse 18 and God reconfirms bread to be food in verse 19. Add to that; God tells Adam to eat plants until he physically dies and returns to the ground himself.

CHAPTER 23: GENESIS 3:21 – DID GOD MAKE THE FIRST SACRIFICE?

God never made fur coats.

The current assumption is, God made the first animal sacrifice when he covered Adam and Eve with animal skins.

Genesis chapter 3 verse 21
Unto Adam also and to his wife did the LORD God make coats of skins (o'wr), and clothed them.

This verse is also used to support God is giving the OK to kill an animal for clothing.

I'll offer vegan replies designed to work within the current understanding. My favorite defense is, the coats of skin are human skin covering their bodies of light. Sounds totally Sci-Fi, I know but you'll love it.

Parts of this might seem wishy-washy until you learn of Cain and Abel's sacrifices in the next chapter. I hope you have the time to read both in one sitting (maybe 20 minutes total). Let's go.

Is it animal skin *"owr"* mortal human skin?

Verse 21 does not say animal skin in the KJV, NIV, ESV, NASB, HCSB or any of the older Literal Bible translations I know. Bibles using the term *animal skins* are recent editions known as "Dynamic Equivalent Translations." The New Living Translation, Amplified Bible, Contemporary English Version, Good News Translation, etc. The Dynamic Equivalent is a *thought for thought* version allowing the opinions of the guys doing the translating to have influence in the translation of the words and meanings.

O'wr or Or

Look at the underline I did in verse 21. The Hebrew word *o'wr* (pronounced or) means skin. Yep, that's it, not necessarily animal skin, just skin. The translator chooses which skin they assumed it was. If translation was done in an era where coats are commonly made of fur or leather, they are likely to insert animal flesh into the idea of a coat in this verse.

Let me give a couple other uses of o'wr to prove it can mean human skin.

Job chapter 10 verse 11
Thou hast clothed me with skin (o'wr) *and flesh, and hast fenced me with bones and sinews.*

Same word o'wr, but obviously, not animal skin.

Exodus chapter 34 verse 35
That the skin (o'wr) *of Moses' face shone: and Moses put the vail upon his face again,*

Same word again, but absolutely not animal skin.

Ezekiel chapter 37 verse 6
And I will lay sinews upon you, and will bring up flesh upon you, and cover you with skin (o'wr), *and put breath in you, and ye shall live;*

Absolutely not animal skin. There are many more verses. Do you see how misleading translations can be?

Death in the Garden?

Most Christians agree there was no death in the Garden of Eden. If the covering was actual animal skin, you can question the carnists on how death happened in the Garden of Eden. That usually stumps them.

As for Adam's death, Christianity teaches Adam only died a "spiritual" death the moment he ate from the tree. Adam was kicked out of the garden long before his physical death happened over 900 years later, so again, no death in the Garden of Eden.

From where did the coats come?

I'll first suggest the simple meaning of the text. If it says God made coats of skin, then he actually made coats of skin. It doesn't say he took skin from an animal and made coats. It just says God made it. God has no need for raw materials to create things. He can create something from nothing. No animals died.

When I presented this argument, I've had Christians fight the idea God can make skins out of nothing. Two chapters earlier, God spoke an *entire freaking universe* into existence, but He can't speak coats into existence without killing an animal? God can give sight to the blind, make the lame walk and raise the dead, but nope, his super-powers stop with making coats!?! Carnism and Christianity combined make believers think kooky things.

Now let's go look at the idea their bodies were made of light and the skin they got was actually human skin.

Skins of light

Some Jewish traditions teach before "The Fall," Adam and Eve were luminous creatures with immortal and glorified bodies, *"clothed in light"* because they are made in God's image (1st John 1:5). They lost their glorified bodies when they ate from the tree. When God returned for his daily walk with them, He would notice they were no longer luminescent, meaning they are now creatures of sin. Adam and Eve tried to hide that from God by covering themselves with fig leaves. That didn't work. God covered their corruptible mortal bodies with flesh, just as we possess today. If you get any pushback on people actually glowing, remind them of the time Moses came down from Mt. Sanai.

Exodus chapter 34 verses 29-35
29- When Moses came down from Mount Sinai with the two tablets of the covenant law in his hands, he was not aware that his face (o'wr) was radiant because he had spoken with the Lord.

30- when Aaron and all the Israelites saw Moses, his face (o'wr) was radiant, and they were afraid to come near him.

And in verse **35**:
They saw his face (o'wr) was radiant. Then Moses would put the veil back over his face until he went in to speak with the Lord.

A bunch more verses saying God is light:

Revelation chapter 21 verse 23
And the city had no need of the sun, neither the moon, to shine in it for the glory of God did lighten it and the lamb is the light there off.

Isaiah chapter 60 verse 19-20
No longer will you have the sun for light by day, nor for brightness of the moon give you light, but <u>you will have the Lord for an everlasting light</u>, and your God for your glory. Your sun will no longer set nor will your moon wane; for you will have the <u>Lord for an everlasting light</u>, and the days of your morning will be over

And Jesus in **Mathew chapter 17 verse 2**
There he was transfigured before them. His face shown like the sun, and his clothes became as white as the light.

1st John chapter 1 verse 5:
this then is the message which we have heard of him, and declare unto you, that <u>God is light</u>, and in him is no darkness at all.

Psalm chapter 104 verse 2
Who coverest thyself with <u>light as with a garment</u>: who stretchest out the heavens like a curtain

We've got a God who radiates light. We got Moses, who came in contact with God, and he himself radiated light. So it's not outrageous to say while Adam and Eve were sinless, immortal, and made in God's likeness, they share a radiance of their own.

Skins of flesh

So the verse says: *and the Lord God made garments of skins,* ask the 5Ws. "Who wrote it"? Answer - Moses. To whom did he write it? Israel. And how did Israel understand it? Recognizing the Jewish traditions, they knew the skin of Adam and Eve was luminescent. So, after sinning, God clothed them in *garments of skin,* normal, common, human skin. <u>The same flesh that we carry now</u>. If we were still sinless and living in the Garden of Eden, we might radiate light. Imagine the savings on our electric bills!

So, in Eden, Adam and Eve lost the radiance that came along with their innocence before eating that stupid apple. God covered their bodies with flesh He created. God changed them from immortal bodies of light to mortal bodies of flesh.

But what if?

For the sake of argument, let's go with the current carnist Christian understanding. When the Bible says skins, it means animal skins because most Christians (erroneously) maintain there had to be blood to cover sin. OK, if it was true, vegans can ask, "when was that law started"? *Adam and Eve existed hundreds of years before Moses and the Law.* The sacrificial system wasn't established until long after the Garden of Eden. God saved people *without sacrifice many,* many times *between Adam's sin and the law of Moses. Adam* and Eve were not under the Law, so they didn't need a sin sacrifice.

You might need proof Adam and Eve had no idea of animal sacrifice. Offer verse 7

Genesis chapter 3 verse 7
And they sewed fig leaves together and made themselves aprons

If the sacrificial system was a thing, why did Adam cover himself in fig leaves instead of making a sacrifice? This shows he knew nothing about sacrifice for sin.

Here is a fun, unrelated thought. Many people accept the fruit being spoken of as a fig because of this verse. I mean, if fig leaves were available to make an apron, it wouldn't be a stretch of the imagination as they ate a fig. Ya, more Bible geek stuff and I really like figs.

But what if #2?

My next *What if* option: "What if you're wrong Steve?" OK, I can still defend veganism with the current understanding.

Let's say God killed an animal, skinned it, and put the bloody skins on Adam and Eve. Here we have Adam, a guy who named and bonded with the animals one on one. Adam is living at perfect peace with the animals, so much so, he could walk up to a lion and pet it on the head and say, here, kitty-kitty. Heck, he could play and snuggle with any animal in the world, from a giant elephant to the smallest mouse. They were to Adam what a puppy dog is to us today. Imagine, if this were true, right there in Eden, God killed one of Adam's pet companions. Imagine how horrible was that for Adam to witness? Seeing actual death for the very first time, only to have God slap that bloody skin on Adam, signifying this was his fault for disobeying.

This must have scared the crap out of Adam. I'm not too sure he would love God after seeing something so horrible. Adam would have lived in daily fear this could happen to him. Any act of service to God is no longer from a place of love but of fear the next violent death could be his! I say this is not how it happened, its result is counterproductive.

If this *"What If"* is used as a justification for wearing leather, then the carnist Christian is missing the point. Do they think Adam watched this slaughter and said, *"Oh, killing animals isn't so bad. Let's sin again and get a* nice pair of boots"! No way.

Suppose we continue with the idea God killed because of His need for a blood sacrifice (ugh). There is no text showing God wanted Adam to continue on with sacrifices after this incident. Actually, the contrary:

Genesis chapter 3 verse 19

In the sweat of thy face shalt thou eat bread, till thou return onto the ground.

Here we are in verse 19. Are we to conclude Adam did not sin again? Now that God gave Adam a killing demo, wouldn't God give sacrificial instruction for Adam's next sin? Instead, we get verse 19 *reaffirming* Adam *is to eat bread*, no death of animals required or implied.

One more thing, step back a few verses and see what happened after Adam sinned.

Genesis 3 verse 8.

8- And they heard the voice of the LORD God walking in the garden in the cool of the day.

9- And the LORD God called unto Adam, and said unto him, Where art thou?

I never got the idea God is mad, He seemed hurt. God knew they sinned, but what was his action? He didn't come in with anger or wrath, demanding a blood sacrifice. Instead, God calmly came for his daily walk with Adam. In the following verses, God told them the consequences of their sins.

Second sin

The stupidest action is next. After the first sin, God came to hang out/talk with Adam. God asked what happened, even tho God knew. Here comes the sad part. <u>Adam blamed Eve and God</u> for what he did; check it out:

Genesis chapter 3 verse19

And the man (Adam) *said, The woman <u>whom thou gavest to be with me</u>, she gave me of the tree, and I did eat.*

Do you see the second sin? Adam went so far as to blame God for giving him Eve. Adam was busted, and he is like, *"hey God, you made her so it's your fault I ate the apple, not mine."* Adam pushing the blame was another sin but notice, there was not another sacrifice. I say God did not kill an animal for the first sin or even the second. This is not the beginning of animal sacrifices.

Wrap up

I've given a few different options on how to handle the *coats of skin* ordeal. I've used each in my vegan outreach but had the most success with my last option because I put the context of Adam's relationship with animals, as their relationship is to pets.

Sadly, so many Christians today don't understand God's forgiveness and love. They live with 1 foot in the law of Moses, the other foot in the Grace of Jesus Christ, thus spending most of their lives in confusion and fear. But these verses can teach us about atonement. They show it was God who provided the covering, God who provided the forgiveness, and God who continued on in relationship with humankind even after humans disobeyed. That's love.

CHAPTER 24: GENESIS 4 – CAIN'S GRAINS

ain and Abel

C We got two brothers, Cain and Abel. Cain was a gardener. Abel was a shepherd that cared for animals. Their story goes, Able offered an animal sacrifice to God while Cain offered grain. God accepted the animal sacrifice, but God didn't accept Cain's grains. Hey, that rhymes: *Cain's Grains*, haha.

Genesis chapter 4
4- And Abel, he also brought of the firstlings of his flock and of the fat thereof. And the LORD had respect unto Abel and to his offering:
5- But unto Cain and to his offering he had not respect.

Given only that much of the story in Sunday school, the average Christian gets the idea an animal sacrifice is better than a grain offering. As with so many stories in the Bible, you need to read the entire passage to understand the scene. So get your Hebrew lexicon open and let's look at various ideas on why the rejection of grains.

5Ws

Let's start with the "Where". There are two locations that are important to understanding this story. I'm sure you're familiar with the Garden of Eden, but there's mention of another place, another city east of Eden called the

Land Of Nod (Genesis 4:16). Got it? Good, I will return to this.

Now I ask the "Why". Like, "why were the brothers doing offerings and sacrifices"? They had no command of God asking for sacrifice, so what gave them the idea? The Bible does not say why but, we can try to piece it together. I have a theory. It's weak, but no less legit than anyone else's guess. I'll get to that soon.

Were grains bad?

Why was Cain's offering rejected? The problem wasn't that grains are inferior. Cain is doing exactly what God commanded in Genesis chapter 2 verse 15.

> *15- And Jehovah God took the man and put him into the Garden of Eden to <u>dress it</u> and to <u>keep it</u>*

So if God ordered man to be a gardener, why do Christians assume God preferred an animal offering? That makes no sense.

Next, sacrifice does not always mean animals. The Hebrew word for offering/sacrifice used is *Minchah*. My Lexicon tells me:

Minchah is a gift, tribute, offering, present, oblation, sacrifice, or meat offering.

It can be any offering, be it grain or animal. Leviticus chapter 2 verses 1-16 offers a long list of how to do grain offerings, so *grains are acceptable.* So again, why the rejection?

Quality of the offering

In the descriptions of the offerings, the wording shows a plausible reason for the grains' rejection.

> *4- Abel, he also brought of the <u>firstlings</u> of his flock and of the fat thereof. And the LORD had respect unto Abel and to his offering:*

The word <u>firstling</u> implies it was the best of the best Abel had. Now compare the wording of Cain's offering:

> *3- That Cain brought of the fruit of the ground an offering unto the LORD*

Abel's offering had "firstlings" as a qualifier for the quality of his offering. There is no such qualifier for what Cain brought. It might imply that Cain only brought whatever he had. Not the special stuff as Abel did. This view shows a reason for the rejection to be in the item's quality, not that meat is preferred over grain.

By Faith

A peek into the New Testament book of Hebrews gives more insight. The verse of interest for this discussion is:

Hebrews chapter 11 verse 4,
By faith Abel offered unto God a more excellent sacrifice than Cain, by which he obtained witness that he was righteous, God testifying of his gifts.

We learn the rejection of Cain's offering was an issue of faith. God was more concerned by what was in Cain's heart when he made the offering. It wasn't the product being offered. If Cain had made the animal sacrifice, it also would have been rejected because his heart was not right. This is not a matter of animal sacrifice being preferred by God over a grain offering.

Another way to go

If you're a Bible junkie, you might enjoy this pet theory of mine.
This is the first official sacrifice (if it was a sacrifice—stay tuned) listed in the Bible. Since we don't have any commands to make sacrifice, why did the boys want to sacrifice? Like, where did they get this idea they had to perform sacrifices? The Bible does not give a source, but I got this crazy idea when I read these verses about that other location, the Land of Nod.

16-And Cain went out from the presence of the Lord and dwelt in the Land of Nod on the east of Eden
17- and Cain knew his wife and she conceived and barebore Enoch and he build a city and called the name of the city after the name of his son Enoch

My "Uhhh? #1" is where did this Land of Nod come from? Aren't we dealing with the first family? My "Uhhh? #2" is Cain knew his wife. Was Cain married at the time of this sacrifice ordeal? Who were her parents?
Also, in Genesis chapter 4, God puts a mark on Cain to protect him from *other people*. OK, our next ask is, where did these *other people* originate? Is it possible God gave an account of only the first family but still made others? Did God take a break (day 7) from creating, and sometime later, created more people not recorded in scripture?

Land of Nod

A Jewish historian named Josephus (in his writings called The Antiquities Of The Jews) wrote the Land of Nod was a place of violence, robbery, and all sorts of evil stuff. Josephus was not alone in his feelings regarding the

Land of Nod. Clement of Alexandria, St. Augustine, and Origin (3 big-time church dudes) felt that way too. With Nod being such a terrible place, the people might have been doing pagan rituals, such as animal sacrifice. Could it be that Cain visited the Land of Nod before killing his brother? Remember earlier when I said many years (verse 3) passed? These guys could be in their 30s. 40s or older, we are not sure. However, enough time passed that entire cities were populated.

Maybe Cain picked up his wife on a weekend drinking party in this miserable pagan Land of Nod. Then, he brought her back home *along with the pagan customs* of Nod, such as animal sacrifice. See where this is going?

There are stories where good men of God were advised not to marry women of other faiths (Deuteronomy 7:3-4 & Deuteronomy 17:17 & Nehemiah 13:26 & 1 kings 11:2 & 1 Kings 16:31 & 2 Corinthians 6:14) because they will bring along their false gods and their pagan traditions. Like animal sacrifices! It's possible the brothers got the idea of making sacrifices from the ladies they hooked-up with during their vacations in Nod.

None of this theory is provable. I am reading this concept into the silence of scripture. I will trash this theory anytime, but isn't it fun?

But maybe it wasn't a sacrifice.

We're not done yet. There's another fascinating theory on this. Part of our problem is, 21st-century Christians are firm in believing God needs blood sacrifices to forgive sin. I disagree with that, but should it be true, we don't know that Cain and Abel committed any specific sin that required a blood sacrifice. Maybe they were just nice guys taking it upon themselves to offer a gift (bloodless) to God. So in verse 3, the word "Minchah" (Minchah: donation; euphemistically, tribute; specifically a sacrificial offering, usually bloodless and voluntary) is used. This could have been just a gift for no reason. Haven't you given gifts to your parents simply for the love of giving?

No such thing as animal sacrifice

Adam and Eve were vegan. Cain and Abel were vegan. Until Noah's time (Genesis chapter 9), God instructed everyone to be vegan. Never in their minds could Cain and Abel consider killing an animal to please a vegan God. God gave them instructions to care for the *animals*. The killing of animals is not an act of care, especially while being made in the image of (a vegan) God.

Are fat and meat the same?

"Now hold on there, ya hippie!"
    It says in verse 4,

And Abel, he also brought of the firstlings of his flock and of <u>the</u> <u>*fat*</u> (CHLB) *thereof.*

If they're offering fat, they had to kill it. Or didn't they?

I say no animal was killed. We have translation issues at play. The Hebrew word being used for fat is CHLB. Hebrew has no vowels. Its meaning is determined when the translator chooses what vowel to insert. It could be CHeLeB, meaning the fat of the animal, or CHaLaB, meaning milk or cheese. It's a matter of one vowel chosen by the translators. Check out Genesis 18:8, Exodus 3:8, Judges 5:25, and 1 Samuel 17:18. The word is: *chalab = milk, sour milk, cheese.*

Milk (chalab) makes more sense, as Cain and Abel did not eat animals (Genesis 1:29). The brothers could not imagine the fat from a dead animal as a thing to eat for themselves or God. Milk or cheese being offered has legit reasons. An offering has no value when there is no loss by the offerer. Able no longer has that milk to consume himself.

There is another reason to reject the idea of death. If this was a sin offering, why offer God *fat* and not the *blood*? There are a bunch of sacrifice laws requiring the blood to be given back to God. Just more reasons this word *fat*, as we understand it today, makes little sense. I see it as a poor translation. This defense works well.

Scapegoat

If they didn't kill it, how did they offer a live animal to God? In Leviticus chapter 16, we learn of "scapegoating." Two goats are used. They kill one and the other goes free. The freed goat has the ritualistic responsibility of carrying away the peoples' sins into the wilderness and releasing them of guilt.

When Abel offered his goat (or whatever the heck it was) to God, he just let it go into the wilderness. This fits with having a right heart before God, as Abel offered a sincere sacrifice. Abel gave up his access to wool or milk from the animal for his personal comforts. In this story, sacrifice is giving up stuff. Sacrifice is not always about killing.

Or maybe it was ox or bull that he let go into the wilderness in his efforts to give something back to God. Cattle were used in helping plow the land and grow food. Giving up something such as an ox is a genuine sacrifice. It leaves Able to do the plowing by hand himself. But, again, sacrifice is not always killing.

CHAPTER 25: GENESIS 6:5–7 – NOAH'S FLOOD

Earth's reboot.

We all know the story. Earth is messed up and the only fix is a total reboot. God sends a flood and destroys the earth and its inhabitants, that includes animals.

Personally, I don't accept this one. I believe Moses presented this story as a *polemic* to attack their current religious belief (Epic of Gilgamesh) of the flood. Heresy you say? I know and I accept I could be wrong. Regardless of my stance, most fundamental Christians view the flood/ark report as a fact. So, I'll give replies based on the fundamentalist view of Noah's Ark being a real, historical event.

The flood story, as is, will show eating animals is wicked enough for God to kill everything. To a fundamentalist, this is a kick in the naughty bits. Many carnists have crawled away questioning their meat eating beliefs. Enjoy!

5Ws

Eight hundred to 1000 years passed since the Noachian flood. Moses is giving his version to Israel to correct their misunderstanding of the world-wide deluge they were taught. There are many underlying principles in this story relating to God's forgiveness, His redemption of man, His want to restore goodness to His creation, and more. We are going to skip that. I am not saying it's unimportant, but not needed for vegan activism. I'll begin with what was bad enough to cause this flood.

Genesis chapter 6
*5- And God saw that the <u>wickedness</u> of man was great in the earth,
and that every imagination of the thoughts of <u>his heart was only
evil continually.</u>*

*6- And it repented the LORD that he had made man on the
earth, and it grieved him at his heart.*

*7- And the LORD said, I will destroy man whom I have
created from the face of the earth; <u>both man, and beast,</u> and
creeping things, and fowls of the air; for it repenteth me that I
have made them*

Wickedness

OK, I got it, wickedness. God killed every living thing because of
wickedness. Geez, this must have been some serious kind of wickedness.
God said humans are wicked and verse 7 implies the animals (*<u>both man
and beast</u>*) are wicked too. Huh? Wait a minute, how could animals be evil?
More on that later.

Only a few chapters earlier (1200-1500 years actually), God called
everything good. Now, it's messed up to where every intention of man is
continuous evil. What the heck is so evil? Was it Child sacrifice? No. Was
it murder? No. Pineapple on pizza? Hmmm, no.

I get clues to these evils in the New Testament books of Mathew and
Luke. We read Jesus is warning people of the wicked bad stuff they were
into, and it reminds him of the wicked bad stuff humans did back in Noah's
day. Check it out.

Luke chapter 17
*26- Just as it was in the days of Noah, so too it will be in the days
of the Son of Man.*

*27- <u>People were eating,</u> they were drinking, they were
marrying, they were being given in marriage—right up to the day
Noah entered the ark. Then the flood came and destroyed them
all.*

And in

Matthew chapter 24
*37- but as the days of Noah were, so shall also the coming of the
son of man be.*

*38- For as in the days which were before the flood <u>they were
eating</u> and drinking, marrying and giving in marriage, until the
day that Noah entered into the ark*

Now we have more info on the *<u>evil and wickedness</u>*. Jesus says <u>eating,</u>
drinking, and giving in marriage. Now that caught my attention because

eating, drinking, and getting married weren't evil. Somehow, humans were eating, drinking, and getting married *in an evil way*. OK, how did they do that?

Marriage

The marriage part could be humans marrying angels (implied in Genesis 6:1&2) or marrying animals (beastiality). OK, that takes care of an evil way to do marriage, but what about evil eating?

Eating

How can eating be evil? Well, gluttony comes to mind, but further down, chapter 6 tells us.

Genesis chapter 6
11- The earth also was corrupt before God, and the earth was <u>filled with violence</u>.
    13- And God said unto Noah, The end of all flesh is come before me; for the earth is <u>filled with violence</u> through them; and, behold, I will destroy them with the earth

Got it, violence. This "evil eating" involves violence. So again, I ask, what would violent evil eating look like?

I say cannibalism is violent eating, so I researched it, and yep, cannibalism was a thing before the flood. I trust I don't need to detail why people munching on people is evil.

How else can eating be a violent form of evil?

At this point in history, eating animals was still a no-no. Mankind was vegan over 1500 years (in Genesis 1:29 through Genesis chapter 9). It wasn't until Genesis chapter 9 when God gave Noah minimal permission to eat specific animals. Thus, if people were eating animals before the flood, they disobeyed God.

So, I propose this *"Violent Evil Eating"* is eating animals. I say this for two reasons. One, because God forbade it, and two, people can't eat animal flesh without violence against the animal being eaten. They had to kill it, to eat it. Eating animals is intrinsically violent. This fits the idea of evil eating.

Animals ate animals

Carnist Christians may argue back, saying animals ate animals. Yep, and they weren't supposed to, so animals were also doing wrong. God's earlier command was animals and humans were to eat plants (Genesis 1:30). By violating that command, people and animals were doing wrong. That's why there was a punishing flood that included animals.

Dinner on the ark

Here is an interesting vegan thingy. The animals Noah saved on the ark *ate only plants*.

Genesis chapter 6 verse 21
And take thou unto thee of all food that is eaten, and gather it to thee; and it shall be for food for thee, and for them

The food for Noah (thee) was plants, so the food for the animals (them) must have been plants. This order was before the meat-eating permission in chapter 9. The food must have been plants only as it was for the last 1500 years since Adam and Eve.

My wild last thought

Here in the flood story, where billions of animals are killed and we can still get a vegan message. Dontcha just love it :-)

CHAPTER 26: GENESIS 6:7 – MORAL AGENCY?

Did God give animals morals?

This is one big, crazy thought experiment you might enjoy it. Or, this will be fodder for my haters on YouTube.

Meat-eating Christians (and many vegans) say no, animals are incapable of moral decisions. I'm not convinced it was always so. I will present scripture that supports the view at one time, animals *may have had moral agency*. Maybe not a morality equal to humans, but animals don't need to have the same level of morality to deserve kindness from "morally superior" human beings.

Why spend time on this theory? If I'm wrong, you wasted 8 minutes reading this chapter. But, if God gave animals morals, then animals matter morally. And if animals matter morally, Christians can not use them for food, clothing, entertainment, research or any purpose. Am I nuts? Probably, but if God can change a lion from an herbivore to a carnivore, removing morals is not that much of a stretch.

Moral Agency is an individual's ability to make judgments based on a notion of right and wrong.

Bad kitty!

Now let's consider that definition to our current understanding with a story many know of. The year is 2003, the place, Las Vegas. Magician Roy Horn of Siegfried & Roy fame got attacked by Montecore, a white tiger. They did not punish the tiger for attacking Roy. Montecore died of natural causes in 2014. Montecore was not held responsible because he's a tiger doing what tigers do when cruelly exploited day after day in a magic show. Montecore did not act immorally because today, we hold that tigers have no moral agency. But that was not always so. If this were the Old Testament, they would have put Montecore to death.

That's not fair!

In my previous chapter, I listed scriptures implying animals are capable of doing wrong. The challenge is, if animals lack morals, they can't be judged for doing wrong. Yet in the Bible, it seems animals had moral agency or God is not playing fair:

Genesis chapter 6 verses 7 through 12:
7- And the LORD said, I will destroy man whom I have created from the face of the earth; <u>both man, and beast,</u> and the <u>creeping thing</u>, and the <u>fowls of the air</u>; for it repenteth (sorry or regret) *me that I have made them.*

God is upset with His creation, both man and beast. You can be sure it means animals because it breaks the animals into their categories. There is no escaping animals were included in this judgement.
(The next few verses are boring genealogy stuff we can skip)

12- God looked on the earth, and behold, it was corrupt; for <u>all flesh had corrupted</u> their way upon the earth.
13- And God said unto Noah, The end of <u>all flesh</u> is come before me; for the earth is filled <u>with violence</u> through them; and, behold, I will destroy them with the earth

God is saying <u>all flesh</u> had corrupted their way with violence. That means animals too, because <u>all flesh</u> means <u>all flesh</u>. There's no mistake. These verses show humans and animals were doing wrong and needed to be wiped out. If animals were amoral, they couldn't be judged as corrupted or wrong.
Amoral = *lacking a moral sense, unconcerned with the rightness or wrongness of something.*
This alone is not proof positive, but it presents the possibility that animals had a degree of moral agency before the flood. Maybe not identical to human morality, but enough that God included animals in his judgments, covenants and rules. It is hard for me to accept my conclusion, but if animals did not have moral accountability, was God fair when billions were killed in Noah's flood? Tuff concept, I know.
Let's read about animals and morals after the flood.

Genesis chapter 9
5- And surely your blood, the blood of your lives, will I require; at the hand of <u>every beast</u> will I require it: and at the hand of man, even at the hand of every man's brother, will I require the life of man.

6- Whoever sheds man's blood, by man shall his blood be shed: for in the image of God made he man

God is saying, if a human murders a human, capital punishment is justified. OK, you might not roll with that, but capital punishment doesn't need to be debated right now. Fundamentalist Christian understanding is, they got the OK to execute a guilty murderer. Activists can use this because this law is not restricted to human life. Verse 5 says, if an animal (beast) kills a human, its life is required as payment. If you read it as written, we see an implication animal life provides equal justice for punishment. If an animal had *no moral agency*, any punishment ordered from God is unjust.

Can animals be evil?

They sure can. Have a look at these verses.

Ezekiel chapter 34 verse 25
And I will make with them a covenant of peace, and will cause the <u>evil beasts</u> (rā·'āh: bad, evil) *to cease out of the land:*

Yep, that's the same word for evil as used in Genesis for the tree of good and evil.

Leviticus chapter 26 verse 6
And I will rid <u>evil beasts</u> out of the land,

It's the same evil word again.

Ezekiel chapter 5 verse 17
So will I send upon you famine and <u>evil beasts</u>, and they shall bereave thee (leave them childless).

In this verse, the animals are so evil they will kill children. Since we have verses saying animals can be evil, it's reasonable to think they have morals.

Eye for Eye

This next part is a little weak, but let's kick it around. In Exodus chapter 21, the *life for life* example of justice includes animals.

23- But if any harm follow, then thou shalt give life for life,

24- eye for eye, tooth for tooth, hand for hand, foot for foot,
25- burning for burning, wound for wound, stripe for stripe.

We learn equal punishment for the crime is fair. Let's move up 3 verses:

28- If an ox gores a man or a woman so that either dies, then <u>the ox must surely be stoned</u> (killed) *and its flesh must not be eaten, but the owner of the ox will be acquitted*

Scripture said, eye for an eye and tooth for tooth, is equal and fair. OK, cool beans, but how do we accept verse 28 if animals are not accountable in a moral way?

Verse 28 says animal life is being valued just as human life. Punishment is fair only with creatures of moral agency. God does not spare animals from responsibility for their deeds. I found this a confusing, but powerful way to show animals had moral accountability.

Stoning

Stoning is exactly as it sounds. People pick up rocks and throw them at a guilty offender until death. Stoning is a slow, painful way to die. The purpose of public stoning was justice delivered by the shared hand of the community. When people witnessed the death of criminals via stoning, it sent a message of retributive justice to all watching.

Stoning of animals is evidence animals had some level of moral agency. Why? Unless animals had intelligence and moral agency, a wild beast couldn't understand the retributive justice of public stoning. Stoning violates Jewish laws of cruelty unless animals have moral accountability. Also, the people doing the stoning became guilty of animal abuse if animals had no morals.

There could be an argument saying a vicious animal needs to be eliminated for future safety. But that does not work when punishment is death by stones. If an animal is executed so it won't hurt anyone else, why the slow, painful death of stoning? Nope, stoning had a moral reason. Either animals had moral agency or stoning an animal is cruelty.

Animals can lie

In Genesis chapter 3 verse 1, He called the serpent in the garden *Arum,* which means crafty, cunning, wise. Serpents can tell a lie. Remember the apple in the garden ordeal? Only creatures with moral capacity can lie. Ok, I admit, that's a stupid one.

Beastiality

Here's sex stuff for perking up the ears. Animals were morally responsible for their actions in sexual issues. Leviticus chapter 20 verses 15 & 16 says if anyone has sex with an animal, the person <u>and animals</u> are punished by death. Think about this the next time a dog humps your leg.

Animals can be sad.

Take a look in the book of Jonah, chapter 3. The city of Nineveh was bummed out for the way they behaved, so they dressed themselves in sackcloth. Sackcloth is an itchy fabric worn to signify a rejection of comfort for a particular reason, such as mourning a death. Well, Nineveh even dressed their animals in this itchy sackcloth.

> *8- But let man <u>and beast</u> be covered with sackcloth and cry mightily to God. Yes, let them turn every one from <u>their evil way</u> and from the violence that is in their hands.*

In verse 8, beasts can turn (repent) from evil deeds and violence, proving they are not irrational creatures. In addition, animals are taking part in a mourning ritual and animals can cry out to God.

Animals can fear.

Habakkuk chapter 2 verse 17
For the violence of Lebanon shall cover thee, and the spoil of beasts, <u>which made them afraid</u>.

Ever question if an animal can experience fear? This verse says they can.

Animals can reason

Numbers chapter 22 verse 30
And the donkey said to Balaam, "Am I not your donkey, on which you have ridden all your life long to this day? Is it my habit to treat you this way?" And he said, "No."

We have a donkey trying to reason with his owner named Balaam. This led to the donkey saving Balaam's life.

Human moral responsibility to animals

Christians have a moral responsibility to animals.

Exodus chapter 23 verse 5
If you see the donkey of <u>someone who hates</u> you lying helpless under its load, and you want to refrain from helping it, <u>you must help</u> with it.

Vegans Vs. The Verses

I love this verse! Even if the pet's owner is your enemy and he hates you, even if you don't want to help the donkey because it will help his owner, you must! For the sake of the animal, Christians are required to help. It's a Law! The donkey isn't an enemy. It's an innocent victim of an immoral guy that loaded it up with too much weight to carry. As God's image bearer, Christians must step in and relive that suffering.

Talk about a *call to activism*! You see an animal in need. God wants you to step in and relieve suffering. That's literally what activists do when they liberate animals!

Hmmm, did I just say God approves the ALF?

Deuteronomy chapter 25 verse 4
Thou shalt not muzzle the ox when he treadeth out the corn.

We are to be kind and feed the animal as they want, even a working animal. Earlier, in chapter 11:15, this need to care goes a step farther and says we are to feed the animal before we feed ourselves.

Genesis chapter 49 verse 6
For they have killed men in their anger and hamstrung (crippled) *oxen as they pleased*
    7- cursed be their anger, so fierce, and their fury, so cruel!

In this verse, killing men due to anger is a moral evil right alongside hurting an animal (ox). Notice, killing a human and crippling an animal are considered cruelty on a similar level. That's a big deal when a carnist Christian claims we are so superior.

Consider what they did to the ox. These awful guys broke the legs of an ox for pleasure. Can you think of anybody else who hurts animals for their pleasure/entertainment? Yes, I'm looking at you hunters, bullfighting and rodeo fans. This condemnation also applies to carnist Christians because the eating of meat is done only for human pleasure (taste). Eating animal flesh is not a necessity for human survival, thus making it a choice, a cruel, unnecessary choice.

Wrap up

The Bible implies animals had morals. They held animals accountable for murder. Animals told lies, experienced fear, cried in regret, and much more.

Humans are morally accountable to animals. We are to feed and provide for those in our care. We are judged for hurting them and we are good if we care for them.

I know it's a big "if" but if we can convince Christians, God originally gave animals morals, then animals matter morally. We cannot use them for food, clothing, entertainment, research or any purpose.

CHAPTER 27: GENESIS 8:20 – NOAH WAS CLUELESS

Noah was clueless

After the whole flood ordeal, Noah built an altar and sacrificed animals. Assumably, God was pleased. Eh, not so fast there sparky. God had some pretty harsh criticism of this.

Genesis chapter 8 verses 20–21
20- And Noah builded an altar unto Jehovah (God)*, and took of every clean beast, and of every clean bird, and offered burnt-offerings on the altar.*
21- And Jehovah smelled the sweet savor;

We will discuss verse 21 with God smelling a "pleasing aroma" or "sweet savor" in the next chapter. There will be repeating as they blend together. Just roll with it, you'll get a better understanding when done.

5Ws

Noah comes from an idolatrous society that taught sacrifices were required to please, appease, or receive favors from their pagan gods. Well, old habits are hard to break. When Noah got off the ark, he immediately went back to the sacrificial customs of his idolatrous society. Noah may be a Bible hero, but he didn't have a clue. Let's read chapter 8, starting when Noah, his family, and the animals get off the ark.

15- And God spake unto Noah, saying.

16- Go forth from the ark, thou, and thy wife, and thy sons, and thy sons' wives with thee.

17- Bring forth with thee every living thing that is with thee of all flesh, both birds, and cattle, and every creeping thing that creepeth upon the earth; that they may breed abundantly in the earth, and be fruitful, and multiply upon the earth.

Noah and his family are getting off the ark, and God says, bring the animals with. The first instruction was to allow the animals to breed abundantly. That is all God instructed of Noah, but what does he end up doing? Noah was clueless; he took it upon himself to repeat the same violence that was happening before the flood; he made violent sacrifices.

20- Noah built an altar unto Jehovah, and took of every clean beast, and of every clean bird, and offered burnt-offerings on the altar.

Notice God did not command this sacrifice; it is of Noah's own initiative. Noah builds an altar to kill at least one of every clean beast and bird. Didn't Noah understand God saved the animals to repopulate the world? Maybe burning them up isn't a good idea dude!

Keep the pagan fires burning

Ignoring God's lesson of the flood, Noah reestablished the ritual of the pagan religions by building an altar. This is the first mention of any alters in the Bible. God did not order this alter/ritual. This sacrifice was 100% Noah's idea brought over from idolatry. Are you seeing how these pagan practices are sneaking back into humanity's reboot?

We are reading of God accepting the evil flaws of humanity because He knows humans are imperfect creatures from the start.

Genesis chapter 8 verse 21
For the imagination of man's heart is evil from his youth;

God sees before the flood, the human heart is not naturally inclined for good behavior. Doing good (kindness, justice, mercy, etc.) are not in the heart of man. Humans have a self love that is too strong for them to overcome on their own. After the flood, the human heart hasn't changed. It was evil before the flood (see Genesis 6:5), and evil after, as demonstrated by Noah's sacrifice. You know what? It still is today.

Bring clean and unclean

Hey Steve, didn't God specifically tell Noah to bring clean animals? Wouldn't that imply they were for sacrifice?

Nope, God said to keep the clean and unclean animals alive.

Genesis chapter 6 verses
*19- And of every living thing of all flesh, <u>you shall bring two of</u>
<u>every kind into the ark, to keep them alive with you;</u> they shall be
male and female.*

*20- Of the birds after their kind, and of the animals after their
kind, of every creeping thing of the ground after its kind, two of
every kind <u>will come to you to keep them alive.</u>*

You might get the argument this instruction was only for the sets of 2
unclean animals. God told Noah to take 7 of the clean animals so there
would be plenty to sacrifice. Chapter 7 says differently.

Genesis chapter 7 verse 2
*Of every clean beast thou shalt take to thee by sevens, the male
and his female: and of beasts that are not clean by two, the male
and his female.*

*3- Of fowls also of the air by sevens, the male and the female;
<u>to keep seed alive upon the face of all the earth</u>.*

Like I said, Noah was clueless.

Mud pies

I've got a silly story (don't I always?) for bringing this acceptance action
of God into current understanding. It works half the time.

God was accepting man's desire to please Him, even though it was not
as God wanted. Very much as a parent will receive a worthless gift from
their <u>adolescent child.</u> Think of it like a 5-year-old kid giving his Mom a
"Mud Pie" he made from dirt in the backyard. Not exactly a pie Mom can
eat. Sure, it's fun to throw at his kid brother, but ya, not to eat. Now, if
your kid gave you a mud pie, would you chastise him? No. Could you eat
it? Of course not. No parent eats it; they accept it with love. I bet you'd tell
your kid, *"Mmmm, that smells wonderful."* You work with the young
child's good intentions. You know what else? Mud pies make a mess, and
who cleans up the mess? Mom does, and in this case, God does. To God,
it's the thought that counts.

Fast forward 20 years, and imagine that same child giving you a mud
pie. As a parent, you expect a mature, 25-year-old adult child will not to
offer such a thing. God expected Noah to exit the ark as a more mature
child, but sadly, Noah didn't grow up.

CHAPTER 28: GENESIS 8:21 – WHOEVER SMELT IT, DEALT IT

Holy nostrils

We just finished with clueless Noah doing the first post-flood sacrifice. I want to go farther with his use of the term "pleasing aroma". Let's look at the first part of verse 21.

21- And Jehovah smelled (Hebrew-Ruach; accept, smell, touch, make of quick understanding) *the sweet savor;*

God is a spirit. He does not *smell* stuff; that is a pagan idea. Even non-existent false gods used the pleasing aroma term (Ezekiel chapter 6:13).

Sadly, verse 21 contributes to the misunderstanding God wanted them to burn an animal. As if God smelled it and announced, *"Whoa! That smells great, so ya, I'll forgive them for murdering each other"*. Geez! I don't know where Christians get this goofy stuff. But, on the surface, it appears to say that. So how does an activist deal with it? By confirming who spoke it. When reading verse 21, I want to point out Noah is doing the talking. The *sweet smell* is only a poetic expression describing how *Noah felt about his offering* to God. God did not say He smelt or accepted the offering. *Noah said* God smelled it. *Noah said* it was sweet; we are reading Noah's view of the situation. We need to finish verse 21 to get God's point of view. When you do, you will see how God interpreted Noah's offering, and it's a vegan win.

> *21- And <u>Jehovah said in his heart,</u> I will not again curse the ground any more for man's sake, for that the imagination of <u>man's heart is evil</u> from his youth; neither will I again smite any more everything living, as I have done.*

This is no longer Noah speaking. The speaker transitions with "*<u>Jehovah said in his heart"</u>.* Now we read as God shares His thoughts of the offering. God is heartbroken when Noah makes this evil, pagan influenced sacrifice. Remember verse 17?

> *17- Bring forth with thee every living thing that is with thee, of all flesh, both of fowl, and of cattle, and of every creeping thing that creepeth upon the earth; <u>that they may breed abundantly</u> in the earth, and <u>be fruitful, and multiply</u> upon the earth.*

God's only order was to let the animals *breed abundantly* and *be fruitful, and multiply upon the earth.* Noah experienced this entire flood ordeal, yet he ignored God's direct order and chose the old pagan ways of violence and sacrifice. God, on seeing this sacrifice and calling man evil (*the imagination of <u>man's heart is evil</u> from his youth*), shows His displeasure at Noah's sacrifice. The smell did not please Him in any way. This is God's criticism. When God order Noah to let the animals be "fruitful and multiply" it was a call-back to the Garden of Eden (vegan may I remind you). God intended the post flood world to be as it was when He declared "*it was good*". I guess Noah didn't get the memo.

Poetic smell

I've got another possible rebuttal for ya. Let's consider some proof it's not a literal smelling but a poetic use of the word by looking at Ezekiel.

Ezekiel chapter 6 verse 13
Where they offered pleasing aromas to <u>all their idols</u>.

The same "pleasing" term is used for false idols, but we know from Psalms, false idols can't smell, see, or touch things.

Psalm chapter 115 verse 6
They have ears, but they hear not: noses have they, but they smell not:

So no, this is not about God's need to sniff burning flesh to clam Him down. If He wanted to burn something, He could do it Himself. God has no anger that needs to be appeased by humans burning animal flesh. This whole smelly thing is from a human perspective, not God.

Alternate perspective

Not my favorite, but another theory why it says God found the aroma pleasing is because Israel switched their burnt offerings to Him and not other pagan gods. It wasn't the actual smoke of an animal on fire God found pleasing, but that His plan of moving people away from false pagan gods was working. They are now offering to Him, thus rejecting their pagan gods. This turning from other gods is what God found pleasing. Now that God has their trust, the next step is the end of animal sacrifices entirely.

One last whiff:

Ephesians chapter 5 verse 2
And walk in love, as Christ also hath loved us, and hath given himself for us an offering and a sacrifice to God for a sweet smelling aroma.

This verse from Ephesians likewise uses that sweet-smelling fragrance/aroma poetic kind of language. Please notice what this verse implies. For those who claim God actually does smell stuff, this verse says God enjoyed the sweet fragrance of human sacrifice when Jesus was crucified. Is God approving human sacrifice? Obviously, Jesus was not burned on the cross and no, God does not approve of Human sacrifice. This Ephesians verse proves the idea of "smelling" is a poetic license by the writer and does not necessarily reflect God's thoughts.

CHAPTER 29:
GENESIS 9:2 – EATING
ANIMALS IS A CURSE

Eating animals comes with a curse.
In Genesis, it seems God says we can eat animals.

Genesis Chapter 9 verse 3
Every moving thing that liveth shall be meat for you;

Before I destroy that in the next chapter, we need to understand **Genesis chapter 9 verse 2**. As an animal lover; I find this verse absolutely heartbreaking. Verse 2 sets the mood for verse 3 and you'll see eating animals comes with a huge negative. Humanity loses its harmonious relationship with animals. Essentially, verse 2 is a curse. The second element activists can grab from verse 2 is humanity loses its dominion over the animals. Sometimes, this verse comes in handy when arguing dominion, but it's not the key element that we will learn. Check it out:

Genesis chapter 9 verse 2
And the fear of you and the dread of you shall be upon every beast of the earth, and upon every fowl of the air, upon all that moveth upon the earth, and upon all the fishes of the sea; into your hand are they delivered.

Did you catch that? Re-read the first part where it says animals will *fear and dread* humans. That's pretty heavy. Remember what I said earlier regarding Adam and his peaceful relationship with animals? Humans and animals had no fear of one another, but now, they will. This is a negative response from God. Don't let the carnist twist *fear and dread* into a blessing because it leads to meat eating. God is separating humanity from their companions. It's a curse.

Prove it was a fearless relationship

If you get questioned on the harmonious relationship status, you can give them 2 clues.

First, if God had to *put fear and dread* into the animals, then fear and dread were not in the animals prior. Duh!

The second clue, the animals fearlessly went into and lived on the ark with Noah. No fear or dread noted. Millions of animals on one boat and not a single report of any fighting with each other. I'm sure God added miracle power to the animal parade because no way 8 people (Noah's family) could gather millions of animals on their own. Still, overall, an uneventful vacation cruise. If animals had "fear and dread", this peaceful round-up and co-existence could not happen. I say until verse 2, humans and animals are buddies that did not dread each other.

Dominion go bye-bye?

Activists can use this when you've got a dominion debate going on. I say verse 2 tells us things are not as they were. There is now a rift lessening the dominion humanity had. Man doesn't rule over animals as they once did. Animals now act on their own accord. Don't think so? Try to ride a horse without "Breaking" it first, or ask ten-thousand ants to leave your kitchen. Try getting two of every creature on an ark. Nope, dominion has taken a severe hit and has been replaced with domination by our strength. Sad that we have sunk so low just for a sandwich.

Curse

Once they disembark the ark (hey, that rhymes!), God will say Noah can eat specific animals, but reading verse 2 has me asking, "at what price"?

Remember, God's intention for the flood was to wipe out all violence in the world, kind of a reinstatement of the Garden of Eden. Same blessings and all, but in chapter 8, Noah brought violence right back into the world when he did an animal sacrifice. That put the kibosh on God's intention for people and animals to live harmoniously. That window is closed. No longer can people and animals run and play together, coexist in peace, or just calmly enter an ark. Animals know humans might kill and eat them. God has to put the fear of humans into animals so they may protect themselves. Our mutually loving relationship with the animals has changed for the worse. Imagine your family pet lives in constant fear you might eat it. Yep, that's what happened in verse 2, and to me, it sounds like a curse.

CHAPTER 30: GENESIS 9:3 – PERMISSION TO EAT ANIMALS

P ermission to eat (some) animals.

Genesis chapter 9 verse 3
Every <u>moving thing</u> that liveth shall be meat for you; even as the green herb have I given you all things.

This is the *Meat-Eaters Clobber verse* used against veganism. It is the first time the Bible says humans can eat animals. But it says a lot more when taught in its entirety. This study is tedious with lots of repetition, but the creepy outcome is worth it for grossing out carnists. This is not a slam-dunk for carnism. I'd say it's more a 80% win for vegans. Let's jump in.

5Ws

After 1600 years of vegan living, did God change his mind about eating animals? Nope. This story starts with a drunk guy named Noah getting the heads up from God that the earth needs to be wiped clean of the horrible violence going down. God saves Noah so life may restart after the flood. Noah gets instructions to build an ark to save his family and animals from a watery death.

Personally, I see a lot of trouble with the flood story, but that's for another book. The average Christian accepts every detail of the flood as fact, so that is how I will present my vegan arguments. Remember, we work with the carnist where they are at, with what they can handle. This will take a few miles of Bible study, so here goes.

MOVING THING

In Genesis chapter 9, God gives Noah permission to eat _Moving Things._ We need to start way back in Genesis chapter 1 to understand what "_Moving Things_" are. Please pay extra attention to the repetition of the parts I underline.

Genesis chapter 1
24- And God said, Let the earth bring forth the living creature after his kind, cattle, and creeping thing, and beast of the earth after his kind: and it was so.

25- And God made the beast of the earth after his kind, and cattle after their kind, and everything that creepeth upon the earth after his kind: and God saw that it was good.

26- And God said, Let us make man in our image, after our likeness: and let them have dominion over the fish of the sea, and over the fowl of the air, and over the cattle, and overall the earth, and over every creeping thing that creepeth upon the earth.

Let me ask, did you notice anything strange? Like, in these verses, God has Moses list the _kinds of creatures,_ not just once or twice, but three times. He called some of them cattle 3 times; he called other animals beasts twice; he called some of them creeping things 3 times and called another group of creatures, fish. I'm told Moses had a stutter but come on, wouldn't just saying animals get the point across?

Ya, it would, but God has a reason for the specific separations of species listed, so stay tuned; it will make more sense soon.

Genesis chapter 2
19- And out of the ground the Lord God formed every beast of the field, and every fowl of the air;

20- And Adam gave names to all cattle, and to the fowl of the air, and to every beast of the field;

Yep, there again, God is separating the distinct kinds of animals. I want you to notice that He is not using just one umbrella term for every animal. Are you catching that?

He does it repeatedly in **Genesis Chapter 6**.

7- And the Lord said, I will destroy man whom I have created from the face of the earth; both man, and beast, and the creeping thing, and the fowls of the air;

And further:

20- Of fowls after their kind, and of cattle after their kind, of every creeping thing of the earth after his kind,

Are you now seeing what I see? God is keeping his description of the animals distinctively different. You're thinking yes, I get it. Birds are not cattle, and cattle are not fowl, and fowl are not creeping things, and the creeping things are not fish, so yes, I get it.

But wait! There's more!

Genesis chapter 7 verse 8
Of clean beasts, and of beasts that are not clean, and of fowls, and of everything that creepeth upon the earth,

And again:

14- And every beast after his kind, and all the cattle after their kind, and every creeping thing that creepeth upon the earth after his kind, and every fowl after his kind, every bird of every sort.

And again:

21- And all flesh died that moved upon the earth, both of fowl, and of cattle, and of beast, and of every creeping thing that creepeth upon the earth, and every man:

And again:

23- And every living substance was destroyed which was upon the face of the ground, both man, and cattle, and the creeping things, and the fowl of the heaven;

Hey, wake up! We haven't even got to chapter 9 with the permission to eat animals verse yet. Monotonous, I know, but we see God is continuously distinguishing between the kinds of animals He made. God never just says "animals." He always separates them by species. For example, the animals of the air or animals of land or sea. And what's with these "creeping things"? Let's look at more:

Genesis chapter 8 verse 17
Bring forth with thee every living thing that is with thee, of all flesh, both of fowl, and of cattle, and of every creeping thing that creepeth upon the earth;

And:

19- Every <u>beast</u>, every <u>creeping thing</u>, and every <u>fowl</u>, and whatsoever creepeth upon the earth, after their kinds, went forth out of the ark.

We are only 8 chapters in, and we see over and over (and over and over and over) again God describes animals, not in a single, all-encompassing word, but in several, very separate terms. Cattle are cattle, fish are fish, and these creeping things are creeping things. By the way, humanity is still under the vegan rule from the Garden of Eden (Genesis 1:29).

For further distinctions, God adds whether the animals fly, swim or are of the field. I say God has reasons for such precise separation of each species. Now we move on (finally) to that "Clobber" verse. Or is it?

3- Every <u>moving thing</u> that liveth shall be food for you; as the green herb have I given you all.

Huh? Wait, what?

Every moving thing…that's it?

Almost a dozen times, God breaks the animals into species, kinds, or categories, but now, this one time, God is using a single, all-encompassing term when He said every moving thing? Well, Golly Gee Whiz, humans are listed as moving things in chapter 7:21. Can we eat humans? Oh, chill out, I know it doesn't mean humans, but why no distinction of kinds here? Is it just a matter of translation? Did God mean cattle, fish, and birds were to be food, or did God mean precisely what He said when He said *moving things*? Could it be that God gave permission to *only* eat the moving things that are mentioned independently from cattle, fowl, and beasts? Hmmm?

Remes

Are you starting to wonder what this <u>moving thing</u> was? Like, I know cattle, fowl, and fish can "move," but are they part of the *Moving Things* category? I'd say no because *moving things* are listed separately, apart from cows, sheep, birds, and fish.

I need to see if I can determine what these moving things are. Time to bust out my Hebrew Interlinear and Lexicon.

School time: A lexicon or interlinear helps you interpret a word for its meaning based on its intended use at the time and in the culture it was written.

My lexicon and interlinear tell me *moving things* was the Hebrew word "<u>Remes</u>" (pronounced reh'-mes). The Jewish Orthodox Bible translates verse 3 this way:

Every <u>remes</u> that liveth shall be food for you; even as the yarok esev (green plant) *have I given you all.*

We reached chapter 9, verse 3, the "Clobber Verse," and God gives Noah permission to only eat <u>Remes</u>. But what the heck is *Remes* if not cows, birds, fish, or bacon?

I have a Jewish family, it took me one phone call to find out that Remes was a word to describe—are you ready? Are you sitting down? Remes are reptiles, worms, or swarming insects. Ewww!

I bet you didn't see that coming, and you know what? Neither does any Christian I speak with.

The King James Bible translates Remes as "<u>creeping things.</u>" If you need more info, grab a Hebrew lexicon and look up *Remes*. *Remes* is used 17 times in the Old Testament, and here is the kicker. *Remes* is always and only "<u>creeping things.</u>" God never ever gave Noah permission to eat cows, pigs, or chickens, <u>just the creeping things</u>. So whatcha gonna do with that, huh, Mr. Meat-eater? BOOM! (Steven Lee August drops the mic)

Now let's tie this up nice and tight. First, we learn *Remes* is not cattle, as cattle were mentioned separately from *Remes* when God described them.

We recognize *Remes* is not birds because fowl of the air were mentioned independently of *Remes* when God described them.

We perceive *Remes* is not beasts either, because God mentions beasts separately from *Remes*.

Therefore, when God gave permission to eat *Remes*, he was only giving Noah permission to eat bugs, not cows, pigs, or chickens. This verse can be a big - big - BIG win for our activism.

Back to Noah.

Silly side thought

With only 2 (or 7) of each animal, how could they repopulate if they were being eaten by Noah and his family. And a big boat with thousands of newly turned carnivorous animals? Nah, it makes little sense to think they were chowing down on each other, but bugs, well, they multiply like crazy. Interestingly, there are entomologists (scientists who study insects) who believe many insects do not feel pain. Insects do not have pain receptors as vertebrates do. They can sense damage to their bodies, but it's still in debate if it's pain as we know it.

Remes or Every Living Thing

Various translations of the Bible use the term "every living thing" or "every living creature" or "everything that moves." Since few Christians will look at the original Hebrew text and see "living' things" is a poor translation, you will have to work with that. But have a little fun. Point out permission to eat *every living creature,* includes permission to:

Eat people?

It will sound crazy, but note the word "flesh." Flesh is a blanket term for all life, which means animal *and human* life. Look to before Noah got on the ark.

Genesis chapter 6 verses 12 &13
12- And God looked upon the earth, and, behold, it was corrupt for all flesh (basar= all life, human or animal) *had corrupted his way upon the earth.*
        13- and God said unto Noah, the end of all flesh (basar= all life, human or animal) *is come before me.*

Now connect this with **Genesis chapter 9:4** when Noah gets off the ark.

But flesh (basar = all life, human or animal) *with the life thereof, which is the blood thereof, shall ye not eat.*

In those verses, the word *flesh* (basar) includes humans. If this verse gives permission to kill/eat animals, then this verse gives permission to kill/eat humans too. If meat-eaters are holding to "every living thing" or "every living creature" or "everything that moves" is food, then God is granting permission for cannibalism. Obviously, that's not true, so creeping things (Remes) makes much more sense.

"Husbandman"

Before we exit this chapter, something interesting is starting in verse 20 that adds more vegan kick to the sauce. Just for fun, try to catch it before you read my thoughts on it:

20- And Noah began to be a husbandman and planted a vineyard
        21- and he drank of the wine, and was drunken. And he was uncovered within his tent.

We got another one of those words we don't use today, "Husbandman." The dictionary says Husbandman: *a person who cultivates the land; a farmer.*
        Are you thinking what I am thinking? Noah gets permission to eat animals, and what does he do? He plants a vineyard and grows plants. If you read the original Hebrew, it says:

And began Noah a man of the soil and he planted a vineyard.

Notice this: Noah, the guy who got direct permission from God to (assumably) eat animals, doesn't start a slaughterhouse to become a butcher. Nope, he becomes a man of the soil. The way I read it, a man of the soil does not plant roast beef, does he? Nope. That's pretty heavy *vegan* stuff for a non-vegan chapter.

Did God give Noah temporary permission?

I trust you got a good grip on this verse, and from my experiences, you are a hundred miles ahead of most meat-eating Christians. But I'm not done yet.

There are well-meaning Christian vegans on YouTube and speaking at vegan festivals, teaching that God gave Noah only <u>temporary</u> approval to eat animals because there was <u>no vegetation</u> available after the flood. I encourage you to pass on that one, it's a dead end. There was plenty of food growing. I think that rebuttal was one of those things a random activist said, and the rest were like, *"Eh, ya, it sounds good, let's go with it."* Also, it's easier than the 3000-word study I just dumped on you. It might work on most Christians, but I am not a fan. Let's consider why it's a bad vegan argument.

There were plenty of Num-Nums after the flood.

Millions of animals and 8 people lived on an ark for over a year. That required a year of food, duh. Since animals and humans were herbivorous (plant eaters), I'd say there were gardens on the ark to regrow the food supplies for that year. Those gardens would still be available after the flood.

Time for timeline discussion

Another reason the no vegetation theory won't work is in Genesis chapter 7. Noah gets on the ark, and it rains for 40 days. In chapter 8, Noah sends out a dove that brings back an olive branch. Noah does it a second time, and the dove does not return. So far, it's estimated at 274 days.

> *13- And it came to pass in the six hundred and first year, in the first month, the first day of the month, the waters were dried up from off the earth: and Noah removed the covering of the ark, and looked, and, behold, the face of the ground was dried*
>
> *14- And in the <u>second month</u>, on the seven and twentieth day of the month, was the earth dry.*
>
> *15- And God spoke unto Noah, saying,*
>
> *16- Go out from the ark, you, and your wife, and your sons, and thy sons' wives with thee.*

Now the land is dry. But Noah does not get off the ark for another *two months!* Consider the condition here. The earth was flooded, and the water was dissipated. That would leave a climate replicating a giant greenhouse.

Nature can easily grow food in such a humid environment. There would be plenty of vegetation grown in the additional months for Noah to eat. Also, God's not an idiot. I'd say He planned this greenhouse climate knowing it wasn't just 8 humans to feed; there was a boatload of herbivorous animals that needed food. Want a small piece of biblical evidence that plants were growing?

Genesis chapter 8 verse 11
And the dove came in to him in the evening; and, lo, in her mouth was an olive leaf pluckt off: so Noah knew that the waters were abated from off the earth.

Food was already was growing. We see an olive tree was ready to bring forth fruit, and they didn't exit the boat for a long while after that. There was plenty of time (estimated 150 days) for food to regrow. Besides, if no food was available, God could send *"Manna"* as described in the books of Numbers and Exodus (We will get to that soon).

So, that *Temporary Permission* excuse to eat animals because of no vegetation is not likely.

Ok, class, you are now armed with the basics to debunk the Christian meat-eater on Genesis chapter 9 verse 3, but ohhh my, my, my, this Noah story has much more to offer us in defensive of veganism, and this is just the tip of the iceberg. Or should I say, the tip of the iceberg lettuce? Hah, I made another vegan joke.

Carnist Christian: *God gave us permission to eat animals.*

My rude Back-Slap reply: *I see that permission in Genesis chapter 9, but in Genesis chapter 1 God originally said we should only eat plants. So are you saying God made a mistake and changed his mind? Maybe God thinks a better food source is food that can feel pain and suffer? Did God finally realize He was wrong commanding us to eat the cruelty-free healthy food from plants?*

I'll leave this chapter with this last one;

Meat-Eating Christian: *God said we can eat animals.*

Activist: *Sure we can, but how much needless suffering should an animal have to endure before a Christian shows mercy and stops?*

CHAPTER 31:
GENESIS 9:4 – LIFE IS IN
THE BLOOD

The Blood

We discussed animals having souls back in Genesis chapter 2. Here in chapter 9 we see the soul is in "The Blood."

Genesis chapter 9 verse 4

But <u>flesh</u> (basar = all life, human or animal) *with the life* (nephesh = soul) *thereof, which is the blood thereof, shall ye not eat*

In verse 4, God says humans can not eat *living* creatures. Vegan win #1. The second thing to note, God says animals have souls. Vegan Win #2. This verse tells Noah not to eat a living animal, as living animals still have their souls. It does not say to kill anything.

5Ws

About one minute ago (verse 3), Noah lived a vegan lifestyle. So, killing an animal is not how I see a vegan Noah understanding this blood command. Literally, Noah is commanded not to eat animals until their life (souls) has left their bodies. Nowhere does the verse say *"kill, kill, kill drain blood, eat."* So my takeaway is, when an animal's soul leaves its body (like, when it dies of natural causes), I can eat it. I am sure Noah, coming from a vegan life, thought similarly.

CowLand

How does verse 4 work? Imagine I am in a place called, ohhh, let's say, "Cowland." A place where cows live their full lives, enjoying the natural behaviors that God gave them. Should I stumble across a cow that died of natural causes, then ya, cut it up and throw it on the BBQ. Its life (soul/nephesh) has left its body through a natural death. Nowhere do I see this verse as an order or permission to kill an animal and drain its blood just to eat the animal. Noah would have to read "kill" into the verse because it's just not there.

Also, this idea of waiting for a natural death fits better with verse 7 when God commands the animals to repopulate (be fruitful and multiply) the earth. If Noah and his family started munching on the few "clean" animals available, how long before they wiped a species out? But if Noah waits for them to pass naturally, then all is groovy. The animals had a long, fun life of reproducing until old age takes its course.

Possible pushback on corpse munching

As silly as my CowLand theory sounds, it often works because you won't be arguing against eating animals, you will make the carnist aware that God's permission comes with acts of self-control. I am sure you will have success using it. But, there is possible push-back with two verses. Let's peek at those:

Deuteronomy chapter 14 verse 21
You shall not eat anything which dies of itself. You may give it to the alien who is in your town, so that he may eat it, or you may sell it to a foreigner (visitor), *for you are a holy* (separate or unique) *people to the LORD your God.*

In this verse, "holy" does not mean sinless. Holy is separate or unique. Israel is a group of people chosen by God to be separate from others. God is telling only Israel (see Deuteronomy 21:2) to display their separateness, they can't eat animals that die naturally. However, they can give (or sell) the flesh to their visitors (foreigners), which is what we are today. So yes, anyone today could eat "CowLand" meat.

Leviticus chapter 22 verse 8
He shall not eat an animal which dies or is torn by beasts, becoming unclean by it; I am the LORD.

This was only for the people of Israel (Leviticus 22:2). We get this warning twice and both times it's directed entirely to Israel. Why is that important to the CowLand defense? Because these laws weren't given to Noah. My CowLand defense was during the time of Noah, which is hundreds of years before Moses and Israel were told not to eat already dead animals. It does not apply to any of us living today.

Restricting Israel from eating animals that were found dead forced them to deal directly with their part in the violence, suffering and death of God's animals. Just like the other restrictions, this rule inspires Israel to control their lust for meat.

I like the CowLand theory. So I've got one more use for ya. If you get a Christian who really, really, really wants to fight my CowLand theory, you can beat them by agreeing with them. Because, if they are correct with quoting Leviticus 22:8, that would also stop them from eating any animal foods they buy in the grocery store, restaurants or fast-food joint. The law said you cannot eat anything that is already dead. OK, all those body parts wrapped up in the grocery store or served in their favorite restaurant have been dead for several weeks. You were told not to eat anything that died, so go find a live cow and sink your giant human canine teeth into its throat and start chowing away while it's still alive. Obviously, I'm being sarcastic, but the point is, every carnist is eating meat that is from an animal that has been dead for quite some time.

Controversy

There is controversy regarding the term clean or unclean. Earlier on (Genesis 7), it says Noah took "clean and unclean" creatures on the ark. The *mistake* is the timing of the laws. It wasn't until many years later (Leviticus chapter 11) when Moses established which animals are clean or unclean.

I sound mean writing this, but I can't begin to count how many Christians I spoke with that don't understand; *Noah did not write the story of Noah's ark.*

Moses (assumably) wrote it hundreds and hundreds of years *after Noah* was dead and gone. Moses was using *his cultural* understanding (about 1400 BC) to describe what was going on with Noah hundreds of years before him.

The difference

In the time of Moses, it was the law to drain animal blood to pour on the altar as a way of giving life back to God. However, Noah had no idea of this blood ritual. The rules haven't been written yet. Noah was not a Jew under Torah legislation. Heck, Judaism (or Jews) didn't even exist yet, but Noah gets Jewish Torah instruction. Do you see the controversy?

Don't eat living animals.

Another look at this verse builds off the idea that people are eating animals while still alive. Gross as it sounds, they were. Here is the deal. There was no way to preserve a dead, rotting carcass of an animal in those days. If someone was to eat an animal, they cut the leg off, pack the wound with salt or dirt to save the animal from bleeding to death. They could eat the leg they cut off, thus, eat a living animal. This allowed them to cut off the remaining legs for another meal, another time. Verse 4 is to eliminate that style of cruelty.

As I look into the next verse, this can have another interpretation.

An eye for an eye

Moving into verse 5, I see another time God values animals much higher than Christians currently do.

Genesis chapter 9 verse 5
And surely your blood of your lives will I require; at the hand of every beast will I require it, and at the hand of man

When Moses wrote this, these people got their understanding of justice from a legal system known as "The Code of Hammurabi." It was an *eye for an eye* style of punishment. Verse 5 says the punishment for killing a human is *a life for a life*. Got that? Good. Now verse 5 also says if a beast kills a human, the animal's life is sufficient payment for justice. See the vegan punch there? Animal life is being put on a level equal to human life. If not, how can an animal's life be matching payment for human life? I talked more in-depth on this in my chapter about animals having moral agency.

Paraphrase verses 3, 4 & 5

If I had to paraphrase this, I might come away with God saying:
All right, Noah, have it your way. You can eat animals, but you gotta wait for them to die naturally. Eat them if you choose, but if you kill any of them, well, I'm gonna demand your life for killing them just like I will require their lives if they kill you because it's only fair, a life for a life.

Activists Fail

There are Christian vegans using only the last part of this verse: *the blood thereof, shall ye not eat.*

A popular Christian vegan claim is, you can not drain *every drop of blood* from an animal, so this was God's way of saying you can't eat animals at all. Like this is a silly prank God plays on Noah:

God: *Hey Noah, you can eat animals now, but you got to drain ALL their blood.*

Noah: *But that's not possible!*

God: *Hah, Gotcha! Nah, you can't eat 'em at all.*

I'm not too happy with that one. I've never used it and I can't say if it's effective or not, but I wouldn't use it for 2 reasons. First, the people reading this would not understand the verse as a literal draining of every single drop of blood. They needed to drain whatever blood came out so they may offer it to God, as required in sacrificial laws.

Second was the possible connection to a pagan ritual of drinking blood. This prohibition will connect to why certain animals were unclean in Leviticus. For example, eating pigs and drinking their blood was used in the pagan worship of other gods. So ya, I don't like that one.

So now we've got a couple of different ways to handle this. Pick one you like and let me know how it works for you. Oh, we are not done with Noah yet. There is still more ground to cover. So much more, the Atheists are going to be praying for it to end! Haha! My jokes just get worse :-)

CHAPTER 32:
GENESIS 9 –
COVENANTS

Let's make a deal

Covenants are promises, deals, or contracts. In this chapter, I will show God makes covenant promises with humans and animals alike. This can be a tool when a carnist Christian claims animals are not worthy of consideration equal to humans.

Genesis chapter 9 verses 9-12

9- I now establish my covenant with you and with your descendants after you

10- And with every living creature that is with you, of the fowl, of the cattle, and of every beast of the earth with you; from all that go out of the ark to every beast of the earth.

God is making a covenant with Noah, his children, and every animal. God breaks down the creatures into their categories, such as birds, livestock and wild animals. There is no doubt this covenant includes animals.

Here is more:

11- I establish my covenant with you never again will all life be destroyed by the waters of a flood, never again will there be a flood destroy the earth

12 - and God said this is the sign of the covenant I am making between me and you and every living creature with you, a covenant for all generations to come.

Repeatedly, God says the covenant is with Noah *and every living creature,* human and animals.

Then again, we've got God's repeated emphasis on this agreement with animals in **verses 15-17**:

> **15-** *And I will remember my covenant, which is between me and you <u>and every living creature</u> of all flesh; and the waters shall no more become a flood to destroy all flesh.*
>
> **16-** *And the bow shall be in the cloud; and I will look upon it, that I may remember the everlasting <u>covenant between God and every living creature</u> of all flesh that is upon the earth.*
>
> **17-** *And God said unto Noah, This is the token of the covenant, which I have established <u>between me and all flesh</u> that is upon the earth.*

It's 5 times now God includes the animals in his promises.

The timing here is important. This covenant was said only a few sentences after Noah got permission to eat animals (verse 3). These covenants wouldn't make sense if animals were given a status of nothing more than food. Ask yourself, would God promise to protect animals from floods but not our forks? This is excellent vegan evidence God sees animals as more than a menu item. So should we.

We have additional covenants regarding the safety of animals if we pop over to:

Hosea chapter 2 verse 18:
In that day I will <u>make a covenant</u> for them with the <u>beasts of the field</u>, the <u>birds</u> in the sky and the <u>creeping things</u> that move along the ground. Bow and sword and battle I will abolish from the land, so all may lay down safely.

So we've got safety for the animals. And did you notice the animals are still broken down into categories? Creeping things is still different from the beasts, the birds and things that move along the ground?

God includes animals in Sabbath covenants. Look in:

Deuteronomy chapter 5 verse 14
But the seventh day is the Sabbath of the LORD thy God: in it thou shalt not do any work, thou, nor thy son, nor thy daughter, nor thy manservant, nor thy maidservant, nor thine <u>ox</u>, nor thine <u>donkey</u>, nor any of thy <u>cattle</u>, nor thy stranger that is within thy gates; that thy manservant and thy maidservant may rest as well as thou.

And again in:

Exodus chapter 20 verse 10
But the seventh day is the Sabbath of the LORD thy God: in it thou shalt not do any work, thou, nor thy son, nor thy daughter, thy manservant, nor thy maidservant, nor thy <u>cattle</u>, nor thy stranger that is within thy gates:

To a Jew, the Sabbath was a huge commitment back then, and still is today. Heck, even my refrigerator has a Sabbath mode. I digress. This command specifies animals right alongside the humans as equals in need of rest. These are huge vegan wins!

In **Matthew chapter 12 verse 11,** Jesus talks of breaking the Sabbath law to help an animal in need.

And he said unto them, What man shall there be among you, that shall have one sheep, and if it fall into a pit on the sabbath day, will he not lay hold on it, and lift it out?

Again, in Luke chapter 14 verse 5, (The NIV, ESV, and several other translations):

If one of you has a child or an ox that falls into a well on the Sabbath day, will you not immediately pull it out?

Did you catch the addition of "a child"? Jesus is giving approval to break the Sabbath to rescue an animal and or a human child. This suggests a level of equality far beyond what carnist Christians offer animals today. God is treating animals equal to humans regarding deals and covenants and the value of their lives. I mean, God is not making covenants with trees or plants now, is He?

This is something to consider when a Christian meat-eater says animals are lower than humans or of lesser consideration. You can come back with confidence that God feels differently.

Scripture repeatedly shows animals can love, know, and believe in God. That alone may not put animals on the same level as humans, but it definitely doesn't put them at a level where humans can cut their throats just for a sandwich.

Speculation

This is a guess, but there could be a difference in animals before the flood compared to how they are now. Keep in mind, eating in the future *kingdom* will be a copy of eating in the Garden of Eden. Animals might return to a place where they will have much more accountability, morals, and rationality than they have today. Wouldn't that be cool?

CHAPTER 33: GENESIS 15 – COVENANT OF PIECES

Covenant of pieces...gross!

Back in my chapter on animal sacrifice, I spoke of how messed up people were during the Bronze Age. Well, I've got another example of that craziness with how they made contracts. They cut animals in half to confirm their agreement. In an agreement with Abraham, God took part in this animal splitting ritual. Carnist will present as proof God doesn't care much for animals. Heck, I would too, but I know this isn't God's idea.

My vegan approach, God, is working within human customs because that's what humans want. In one verse, Abraham trusted God completely, but then, Abe wanted human-styled proof. If Abraham had taken God at His word (trusted) both times, nothing would have died.

5Ws

Abram and Sarai are an old married couple. Most Christians will know them by the names Abraham and Sarah, so I'll use those. They were monolatrous (believed in many gods but worshipped only one) pagans that lived in a city called Ur of the Chaldeans.

God made two promises to Abraham. First is the promise of a child and countless descendants. Those kids will become the Hebrews, Israelites or Jews. They will be a holy nation of priests. And don't go making the common Christian mistake and think holy means they are some kind of sinless, perfect people. Holy, just means they are separate or set apart for the service of God. They are screw-ups just as much as you and I.

Second, God confirms He will give Abraham the land of Canaan (Genesis 12), often called the Promised Land.

Kids, kids and more kids.

In this culture, having children was a big deal. Abraham and his wife Sarah didn't have any kids. Lots of teachings say it was because of Abraham being 80-90 years old. I don't buy that. Abraham was elderly, but certainly able to get it up since he got his female slave pregnant (see Genesis 16:4), so the blame goes to Sarah's age.

Cutting a deal

The Canaanite culture of the time had a nasty custom that involves cutting animals in half to solidify a deal. Obviously, there wasn't a vegan lawyer around to suggest a humane way, but that's what you get when dealing with pagan customs.

They place each half of the animal across from the other half, and in a row. Both parties involved walk through the blood pooling between the halves. The walk signifies both parties accept the same horrible punishment (see Jeremiah 34:18,19) of being cut in half if they break the deal. Harsh times.

Abraham and God are having a chit-chat. We eavesdrop on this conversation in verse 3.

> *And Abram said, Behold, to me thou hast given no seed* (children)*: and, lo, one born in my house* (Eliezer of Damascus) *is mine heir.*

Abraham says God hasn't given him any children, so this guy named Eliezer of Damascus is his only potential successor. Eliezer is not his kid.

> *4- And, behold, the word of the LORD came unto him, saying, This* (Eliezer of Damascus) *shall not be thine heir; but he that shall come forth out of thine own bowels* (body) *shall be thine heir.*

God corrects Abraham and tells him that the child will come from his sperm.

> *5- And he* (God) *brought Abraham forth abroad* (outside)*, and said, Look now toward heaven, and tell the stars, if thou be able to number them: and he said unto him, So shall thy seed be.*

This is a serious promise from God. He's going to give Abraham more descendants than the stars in the sky. So many he won't be able to count them.

6- *And he* (Abraham) *believed in the LORD; and he counted it to him for righteousness.*

Verse 6 is essential in understanding this situation. God promised Abraham will have lots of kids. Abraham only had to trust in God's promise. That's it, only trust. For this unquestioning trust/believing, Abraham was declared righteous. No rituals of cutting animals needed. Abraham did nothing but put total trust in God, take God at his word. For this alone, Abraham was declared righteous. Got that?

7- *And He* (God) *said unto him, I am the LORD that brought thee out of Ur of the Chaldees, to give thee this land to inherit it.*

Now we are at a second promise where God tells Abraham he will get the promise land. Look at my first underline. In the middle of this conversation, God re-confirms who He is to Abraham. He says *I am the LORD.* Why is that important for our vegan defense? God is saying he can do these things. He is all powerful. God is not a liar, He will do what he says. The importance of this will make more sense shortly.

8- *But he* (Abraham) *said, "Lord GOD, how can I know that I will possess it?"*

Nooooooo! Abraham just blew-it, big time. Only one sentence ago, Abraham had totally trusted in God's promise about having many children. He did not question God's power or abilities to do the supernatural. Then, in verse 8, Abraham is asking, *"oh yeah, how will I know I'm gonna possess the promise land? I need some confirmation".* What happened to Abrahams faith that was strong enough to make him righteous in verse 6? Poof! All gone!

Abraham's request for earthly verification broke God's heart. James chapter 2 tells us Abraham was known as *a friend to God.*

James chapter 2 verse 23
And the scripture was fulfilled which saith, Abraham believed God, and it was imputed unto him for righteousness: and he was called the Friend of God.

Just one sentence ago, God made an unbelievable promise, giving Abe countless descendants/children. Abraham believed it, no proof needed because that's what friends do. Contracts aren't necessary between close friends. God was giving blessings of children and land to Abraham, but Abraham started treating it as if they were doing a business deal.

Overwhelmed with grief, God capitulates and uses the customs of the Abraham's culture to satisfy Abraham's insensitive request.

9- And He (God) *said unto him, Take me an heifer of three years old, and a she goat of three years old, and a ram of three years old, and a turtledove, and a young pigeon.*

God shouldn't have to lower Himself to human customs for humans to believe him. Knowing Abraham wanted earthly, customary proof, God told him to get the animals for the contract known as The Covenant of Pieces.

10- And he (Abraham) *took unto him all these, and divided them in the midst, and laid each piece one against another: but the birds divided he not.*

If you noticed, God did not cut the animals, Abraham did. Abraham didn't have power tools, so cutting up cows, goats and rams was a tremendous ordeal. God could've done this in the blink of an eye, but I see hesitancy in God's part in this custom. God may have surrendered to Abraham's request, but His lack of involvement speaks volumes.

11- And when the fowls came down upon the carcases, Abram drove them away.

These animals have been dead for so long, in verse 11, they are attracting scavengers. Again, God isn't very active in this process.

12- And when the sun was going down, a deep sleep fell upon Abram; and, lo, an horror of great darkness fell upon him.

It's sundown and only Abraham had done any killing. Apparently, God was not in a hurry to finish this. Abraham falls into a trance. In the next few verses, God tells of the future for his decedents and its bad. I understand verse 13 as punishment for Abe's mistrust.

13- And he (God) *said unto Abram, Know of a surety that thy seed* (Abe's descendants) *shall be a stranger in a land that is not theirs, and shall serve them; and they shall afflict them four hundred years;*

During his deep sleep of verses 12 and 13, Abraham is told his descendants will be slaves for 400 years. Again, this does not sound like God is a happy camper with this situation. In verse 17, we get the last part of this agreement:

17- And it came to pass, that, when the sun went down, and it was dark, behold a smoking furnace, and a burning lamp that passed between those pieces.

The smoking furnace and lamp represent God walking between the animals alone by Himself. This signifies God took responsibility to fulfill the agreement and Abraham was to do nothing. Just like the first promise. God only wanted Abraham to trust and believe He will do all the work. In this story, God acquiesced to the human level and gave into Abraham's request. But God killed nothing for this legal ritual.

The Covenant of Pieces resulted from Abraham not having faith. I am sure Abe realized his mistake when God did everything on his own without Abraham walking through the pieces. That first promise was the way things should have been for the second promise.

CHAPTER 34: GENESIS 22 – ABE KILLS A RAM

S on, today is your lucky day

Time to study the child sacrifice kerfuffle in Genesis chapter 22. Every Christian knows this story of Abraham offering his son Isaac as a sacrifice. There is a surprise twist: God ends up saving the kid, and Abraham sacrifices a ram instead. This switcheroo of victims leads Christians to assume God wanted this animal sacrifice. But it ain't so.

The way this story has been told is misleading. Consider the story of George Washington cutting down the cherry tree. George never did, but the story has been told so often people believe it's true. Christians are continuously told God provided the ram stuck in the bushes for sacrifice. Nope! That is only assumed and forced into the story. God never ordered the sacrifice of the ram. That was Abraham's idea.

5Ws

We observed Abraham's addiction to his culture back in Genesis chapter 15 with the Covenant of Pieces. Knowing old habits are hard to break, God used Abe's addiction to sacrifice and his community status to make a serious change.

About Abe

At one time, Abraham is monolatrous. That means he worshiped the one "Most High God" without the denial of other gods existing. Think about it, if there is a "Most High God" there must be other gods for the "Most High" to be above (Genesis 14:22).

Abraham is a rich guy that believed The Real God or these pagan gods blessed him with his riches. Abraham believed he needed to show thanks for his riches by doing sacrifices. Watch how this plays out.

Genesis chapter 22 verse 2

Take now thy son, thine only son Isaac, whom thou lovest, and get thee into the land of Moriah; and offer him there for a burnt offering upon one of the mountains which I will tell thee of.

That command sounds bat-poop crazy but God had a hidden plan. One of our 5Ws is the "When". This took place in the Bronze Age. People assumed the pagan gods expected human and animal sacrifices. So when the real and most high God says sacrifice your son, Abraham was like "OK" because sacrifice is normal for that culture.

Oh, wanna know something freaky? This is the first time God orders sacrifice, and it wasn't animal sacrifice, it was human!

Hair of the Dog

Have you ever heard of the expression "hair of the dog that bit you"? It would go like this, if you got drunk on whiskey Friday night and woke up Saturday morning with a hangover: You drink another shot of whiskey. God's plan was kind of like that. He's going to use child sacrifice to end child sacrifice.

But his own kid?

Know this, Abraham wasn't shy in his dealings with God. He could have argued to keep his boy, but he didn't. Yes, people can argue with God (Genesis 18, verses 16-33). Abraham talked God out of destroying Sodom to save his son-in-law. That's bold! Abe wasn't so bold with saving Isaac. Why? I say Abraham was expecting this call to sacrifice Isaac, and God is going to make use of that expectation.

Isaac isn't a kid

Let's get the idea that Isaac was a kid out of our minds. It seems every picture drawn of this event shows Isaac as a young boy. Being someone's son does not always mean you are a young child. Abraham was an old man, Isaac was probably in his 30s. If Isaac wanted to get away, he could easily punch out his old dad, but Isaac let himself be bound up (verse 9) for this sacrifice. Isaac was deceived at the start of this story (verse 8), but his willingness shows he expected this day to come.

Just kidding!

When Abraham and Isaac are ready to do the deed (verse 9), God stops Abraham. WTF (What the Fudge)? Was this a cruel joke?

Verse 12
And he said, <u>Lay not thine hand upon the lad</u>, neither do thou any thing unto him: <u>for now I know that thou fearest God</u>, seeing thou hast not withheld thy son, thine only son from me.

Kill the kid, then don't kill the kid. Why did God put Abe through this emotional roller coaster? Christians will claim it was a test of faith and ya, sure, it was. When the angel said *now I know that thou fearest God*, it confirms that Abe passed the test. The test is <u>now finished</u>. But there remains more to grab from this. We can see further when we ask why God used child sacrifice as a method for testing.

Go Viral

God wanted to end <u>sacrifices,</u> and Abraham was the vehicle to make this public. Abraham was a wealthy man, popular, envied, and respected. People paid attention to him then, as people follow celebrities today. A sacrifice like this would go viral (not a thing then, I know). To have the "Most High God" stop this live demonstration told everyone, this God of Abraham is not a god of sacrifice. By this presentation, God has wiped out the ritual of sacrifice using the cultural norms of that society in a way they can understand. Fundamental Christians accept this as an end to human sacrifice. Sadly, they draw the line at animal sacrifice because of the poor teaching of the story.

No rules yet.

Remember, our "When" needs to be taken into consideration. The nation of Israel has not started yet. The Levitical laws were not yet given. Sacrifice was man's invention and God is doing away with it using their customs and religious beliefs.

Abraham misses the point

You've got the groundwork for why God chose Abraham and the reason for requesting a child sacrifice. In the next verses are our vegan defenses regarding the animal part.

Genesis chapter 22 verse 13
And <u>Abraham lifted up his eyes, and looked,</u> and behold behind him a ram caught in a thicket by his horns: and <u>Abraham went and took the ram</u>, and offered him up for a burnt offering in the

stead of his son

Do you remember back when we read how Noah took it upon himself to do a sacrifice? Likewise, here. Abraham took it upon himself to continue the ritual with the sacrifice of a ram he saw stuck in nearby bushes. Re-read my underlines in verse 13. The scripture doesn't say that God provided the ram or wanted further sacrifice. The sacrifice is totally Abraham's idea. As far as God was concerned, this event is completed in verse 12 when the angel of the LORD said:

Now I know that thou fearest God, seeing thou hast not withheld thy son, thine only son from me.

Abraham already passed the test of faith with Isaac. There is no need for the sacrifice of a ram.

Christian understanding is God needs sacrifice, so they assume this ram must have been sent from God. That is a forced viewpoint. Further sacrifice was not needed. Remember, God declares Abraham as "righteous" in Genesis chapter 15 with no sacrifices back then, and he can do so now. In our vegan defense, we can say God never required a ram to be sacrificed. Consider what the Angel of the LORD said in verse:

16- Because thou hast done this thing, (willing to sacrifice his own son) *and hast not withheld thy son, thine only son:*

The angel said *because thou hast done this thing.* The angel is referring to the offering of Isaac as *this thing*, not the ram. Look at verse 17 for confirmation no animal sacrifice is ordered.

17- That in blessing I will bless thee, and in multiplying I will multiply thy seed as the stars of the heaven, and as the sand which is upon the sea shore; and thy seed shall possess the gate of his enemies;
18- And in thy seed shall all the nations of the earth be blessed; because thou hast obeyed my voice.

Abraham was blessed because Abraham obeyed. What did he obey? He tried to sacrifice his only son. That was the only test and Abe passed. He was rewarded for that, end of story. No ram is needed.

The result

The people got 1/2 the message: human sacrifice is over. Soon, animal sacrifice will end.

CHAPTER 35: EXODUS 20 – THE 4TH COMMANDMENT AND THE BEGINNING OF ANIMAL LIBERATION

nimal liberation starts

Abet everyone knows of the 10 Commandments. It's recorded twice in the Hebrew Bible (Old Testament), in the books of Exodus and Deuteronomy. The 3rd commandment is an order to rest, take a day off to just chill. But there is more to this commandment, and it's a vegan win.

5Ws

I'll start with the order of the 10 commandments. Depending on what religious tradition you follow, the order might vary. For example, commandment #3 might be considered #4. The order has nothing to do with vegan advocacy, so don't argue the order should a carnist Christian correct you. You may not want to quote the numbers at all. Maybe just say the verse or actual commandment, shalt not kill, shalt not covet, shalt not fart, and so on. OK, fart is not in there. I just wanted to make sure you're paying attention.

Let's start with the "Who" in this story. We read Moses came down Mount Sinai with the 10 Commandments for the slaves he freed from

Egypt. While captive in Egypt, these slaves were taught the "gods" created humans for work. The Egyptians forced these people to work seven days a week, under the threat of death. But their captivity has ended. They are now free people thanks to the God of Moses.

When Moses told them God is concerned for their rest (keep the Sabbath), it was liberating for these captives. What is fantastic for us vegan activists is this commandment includes rest for the animals right alongside humans. Check it out.

Exodus chapter 20 verse 8
Remember the sabbath day, to keep it holy.
    9- Six days shalt thou labour, and do all thy work
    10- But the seventh day is the sabbath of the LORD thy God: in it <u>thou shalt not do any work,</u> thou, nor thy <u>son,</u> nor thy <u>daughter,</u> thy <u>manservant,</u> nor thy <u>maidservant,</u> nor thy <u>cattle,</u> nor thy <u>stranger</u> that is within thy gates:

We have another record in the book of Deuteronomy:

Deuteronomy 5 verse 14
But the seventh day is the sabbath of the LORD thy God: in it thou <u>shalt not do any work,</u> thou, nor <u>thy son,</u> nor thy <u>daughter,</u> nor thy <u>manservant,</u> nor thy <u>maidservant,</u> nor thine <u>ox,</u> nor thine <u>donkey,</u> nor any of thy <u>cattle,</u> nor thy <u>stranger</u> that is within thy gates; that thy <u>manservant</u> and thy <u>maidservant</u> may rest as well as thou.

The Deuteronomy account has a more detailed listing of the animals. God is classifying the animals as equal recipients in this command. There is no wiggle-room here; the animals are on the same level of importance as sons, daughters, visitors, and human servants. If you're an activist into animal equality, memorize this verse.

Animal Rights

Many pastors preach this commandment is the start of human rights. The beginning of the end for slavery is here. It suggests sons (males) and daughters (females), maids and butlers and strangers who visit, no matter how rich or poor, no matter what color their skin, they should be allowed a day off for the Sabbath. It puts everyone on the same level in their need for rest.

    The messed-up part is preachers won't teach using the entirety of the verse. They claim God is ending slavery and racism while promoting women's rights. I agree, but their deep-rooted carnism shows when they neglect teaching the animals are included in this liberation.

If Christians can claim this commandment is the beginning of human rights, vegans can also claim this commandment is the beginning of animal rights. See how that works? Nice, huh?

More from the top ten.

We discussed keeping the Sabbath included animals. Christians can't give you an argument there. Now we consider the 10th commandment. It instructs people not to covet, and again, animals are included.

Exodus chapter 20 verse 17
Thou shalt not covet thy neighbour's house, thou shalt not covet thy neighbour's wife, nor his manservant, nor his maidservant, nor his ox, nor his donkey, nor any thing that is thy neighbour's.

God gave two commandments that include animals. Why is that good for veganism? We've got reason to claim the commandments are not meant for humans only. Establishing the possibility the 6th commandment, *thou shalt not kill,* might include animals.

Exodus chapter 20 verse 13
Thou shalt not kill (ratsach: to murder, slay).

The carnist Christian will often deflect with claiming a better translation is *Thou shall not murder.* That's fine. I have no problem with murder being a better translation. Be it *kill* or *murder*, there is a period after the word. The command itself doesn't state humans only. If 2 other commandments include animals, why assume this one is for humans only?

This also gives support to the idea that we can consider the killing of an animal as actual murder.

Have fun with this one :-)

CHAPTER 36: NUMBERS 11 – GOD GAVE US BIRDS TO EAT

Don't be such cry babies

It's rare Christians will quote me the Book of Numbers, unless they're trying to prove veganism wrong. But this definitely is not the verse to use.

Numbers chapter 11 verse 18
And say thou unto the people, Sanctify yourselves against tomorrow, and ye shall eat flesh: for ye have wept in the ears of the LORD, saying, Who shall give us flesh to eat? For it was well with us in Egypt: therefore the LORD will give you flesh, and ye shall   *eat.*

Carnist Christian says: "You see, you see! God gave them flesh to eat, so take that you vegan tree-hugger!"

On the surface, that verse sounds as if God heard the cries of the people and He happily gave them animal flesh to eat. By now, you know we can't read a single verse to get a complete understanding. To fight this, we need to start at the beginning. You'll be glad you did because even though animals are getting eaten, this can be a fantastic *vegan-ish* story.

5Ws

The Israelites are wandering the desert after the Exodus (the departure of the Israelite slaves from Egypt under the leadership of Moses). Their

source for food, water, safety and all their needs is God. He wanted it the
way. Let's start in verse four.

Numbers chapter 11 verse
*4- and the _mixt multitude_* (Rabble or Riff Raff) *that was among
them felt a _lusting_* (Hebrew; taavah: a greedy, gluttonous desire)*:
and the children of Israel also wept again, and said, Who shall
give us flesh (Basar) to eat?*

There was a *mixed multitude* of people. OK, let's get one of the 5Ws
answered. *Who* is this mixed multitude? It is the first generation of Israel,
their children, and other slaves escaping Egypt. Israel is God's peeps, and
the others are referred to as the *Rabble* or *Riff Raff.* Those distinctions of
groups are important to know.

Other Bible versions reveal these "Rabbles" are troublemakers,
pagans, and contemptible people. They were not good buddies to the
Israelites, but God (via Moses) saved everyone and allowed them to
accompany Israel to freedom. In the next verses, we hear them
complaining.

5- We (the mixed multitude) *remember the fish, which we did eat
in Egypt freely; cucumbers, and the melons, at the leeks, and the
onions, and the garlic:*
    *6- But now our soul is dried away: there is nothing at all,
beside this manna (a bread), *before our eyes.*

Manna and Lusting

During this time, God fed them all a bread-like substance made from seeds
called *manna*. Totally vegan and obviously nutritional if it's going to keep
thousands of people healthy while they wandered the desert for 40 years.
Some of these people (rabble, riff-raff) were unsatisfied with manna. Back
when they were slaves, the Egyptians fed them meat. In the King James
version, it adds the Rabble started lusting for animal flesh to eat.

When the Bible declares people were lusting (verse 4) for something,
it's pretty serious. The Hebrew word for lusting is *Taavh; a strong, lustful,
gluttonous, greedy desire*. This lust for meat is bad news and definitely not
pleasing to God.

Now that you know the set-up, let's revisit the situation. God makes a
bunch of crazy plagues, forcing Pharaoh to free every Egyptian slave from
a lifetime of bondage. Moses will lead them through the desert to The
Promise Land. During their wandering of the desert, God miraculously
feeds them healthy food (manna) from heaven. Sounds like God has it
under control, but is this *Riff Raff* grateful? Nope, they got the balls to say
they want more, specifically; they have a gluttonous lust for meat.

Exodus chapter 16 verse 3
And the children of Israel said unto them, Would to God we had died by the hand of the LORD in the land of Egypt, <u>when we sat by the flesh pots</u> (meat), and when we did eat bread to the full; for ye have brought us forth into this wilderness, to kill this whole assembly with hunger.

See how addictive animal flesh is? Finally freed from 400 years of enslavement, but they rather be slaves with "flesh pots" of meat. Insane, huh? Back to the book of Numbers and verse 14. Moses gets sick of their kvetching (complaining) and goes to God and says, "these people want to eat meat."

In verse 18, God acknowledges:

18- And say thou (Moses) unto the people, (riff-raff, Israel) sanctify yourself against tomorrow, and you shall eat flesh: for ye have wept (God is calling them cry-babies) in the ears of the LORD, saying, Who shall give us a flesh to eat? For it was well with us in Egypt; therefore the LORD will give you flesh, and you shall eat.

So ya, God agrees, but are you grasping this situation? God is not saying, "oh yeah, meat, that's a good idea Moses, what was I thinking with this stupid manna stuff? Hmmm, how about some quail? Would you guys like some yummy quail?"

No-No-No! God is hopping mad! He showed them miracles; He freed them from hundreds of years of slavery; He fed them healthy vegan food; He kept them safe, and these people still weren't satisfied. By verse18, God is ticked off! He is like, "*OK, you ingrates want meat? I'm gonna give you so much meat that comes out your nose"!* Totally serious, God says out their noses. Check it out:

19-You shall not eat one day, nor two days, nor five days, neither 10 days or 20 days;
*   20- but even a whole month <u>until it comes out of your nostrils</u>, and <u>it will be loathsome</u> onto you; because that <u>ye have despised</u> (ma'ac) the LORD which is among you, and you have wept before him, saying, Why came we fore out of Egypt?*

Does that sound like God *wanted* to give them meat? No way! God was mad. I don't know if the quail literally came out of their nostrils. That might have been an expression of anger, totally gross booger anger, but God's threat was obvious. Read on and notice the horrible finish in verse 33.

31- And there went forth a wind from the LORD, and brought quails from the sea, and let them fall by the camp, as it were a day's journey on this side, and as it were a day's journey on the other side, round about the camp, and as it were two cubits high upon the face of the earth.

32- And the people stood up all that day, and all that night, and all the next day, and they gathered the quails: he that gathered least gathered ten homers (a homer is a unit of measurement, about 55 gallons or so)*: and they spread them all abroad for themselves round about the camp.*

33 - And while the flesh was yet between their teeth, ere (before) *it was chewed, the wrath of the LORD was kindled against the people, and the <u>LORD smote</u>* (killed) *the people with a very great plague.*

Even if that nose comment was only an expression, this upset God enough that He killed them. Think about how you can use this for your vegan outreach. The Rabble/RiffRaff people didn't murder anyone; they didn't steal from anyone; they didn't worship false idols or lie or commit adultery; they wanted to eat meat. Talk about dying for a burger! It's fun to present it that way, but the full context is what I underlined back in verse 20. The word '<u>despised</u>' in Hebrew is *ma'ac* and translates as reject. When they complained like spoiled brats, God saw that as rejection (ma'ac) of Him and missing their old gods simply because of meat. Not good.

It's the same for us now. In Genesis chapter 1, God says He created plants for our food, yet today, we are arguing with Christians who continuously reject God's original intent and demand to eat meat. They will search the scriptures for any excuse and any reason to justify their gluttonous lust for animal flesh, and you know what? It may not be coming out of their noses, but considering the diseases associated with eating animal flesh, they're dying just as the Riff Raff did.

Kibrothhat taavah

34- and he called the name of the place Kibrothhat taavah: (translates as graves of lust/gluttony) *because there they buried the people that lusted.*

You might get the argument this was only about their rejection of God and had nothing to do with meat eating. Their rejection is only one part of a two-part problem. Look at verse 34 to reassure this happened because of their lust for animal flesh. God smote them dead, and they were buried in a place they called *Kibrothhat taavah*. That means graves of craving, lust or gluttony, not graves of rejection. Don't let them wiggle away on this one. It's a vegan win.

Livestock

There's a little more vegan stuff we can squeeze out of this. These people were traveling with livestock (Numbers 11:22). Cows, goats, and sheep were available, yet the people were not allowed to eat them. They could only eat the manna from heaven. Their livestock was not on the menu. I argue God is stepping in to reestablish plant-based food for humans. Ultimately, God had his vegan way when we read the conclusion in Exodus.

Exodus chapter 16 verse 35
And the children of Israel did eat manna forty years until they came to a land inhabited; they did eat manna,

This is a powerful verse for vegan advocacy. It's saying that humans (Children of Israel, slaves, people) can live without eating meat. I guess a carnist could argue back, *"Ya, but only for 40 years"*. I'd reply, *"OK, let's start your 40 years now please"*.

Dead Quail

The difficult *un-vegan* part is God allowed animals to die to make His point. God performed non-animal related miracles, yet they continuously rejected God's vegan way.

The quail was the last straw. The Exodus verse shows God had them eat manna after that, but it was under threat, I'm sure. God's first actions are to get the people to serve him for love, but this ended in their serving him out of fear. Not His first choice, but better than it was.

Makes me think of the people saying, *"If God would just show me a miracle I'd believe."* This Rabble/Riff Raff people experienced more miracles (plagues and parting of the Red Sea) than you or I could ever imagine, yet they turned their backs on God. I wonder if any of us would do the same if we witnessed genuine miracles. Sadly, for this group, it took the death of innocent animals. The bottom line, God was not giving them meat to please them, He did it out of anger.

Oh, do you get the idea their "manna" is our Tofu?

CHAPTER 37: DEUTERONOMY 12 – GIMME, GIMME, GIMME

S hut up, you whining little brats.

In the 12th chapter of Deuteronomy, Moses gives the nation of Israel procedures they must follow to eat meat. A carnist Christian may use those (or other) procedures to support their lust for meat. As we read these verses, please keep the words *lust* and *kill* running in your mind. The word *lust* is key to understanding these meat-eating allowances, and come on now, any Christian knows when we hear the word *lust*, we are in trouble.

Go ahead, say it to yourself over and over, *"Lust, kill, lust, kill, lust, kill."* Now you're ready for a Bible study.

Deuteronomy chapter 12 verse 15
Notwithstanding thou mayest kill and eat flesh in all thy gates, whatsoever thy soul lusteth after, according to the blessings of the LORD thy God which he hath given thee: the unclean and clean may eat thereof, as of the roebuck (Gazelle) *and as of the hart* (deer).

Did you notice lust and kill in that verse? Good, because we have more lusting coming up in verse 20.

20 - when the LORD thy God shall enlarge thy border, as he had promised thee, and thou shalt say, I will eat flesh because thy soul longeth to eat flesh; thou mayest eat flesh, whatsoever thy soul lusteth after

Again, this is about lust, It's not for nutrition or sustenance but because they lust for it. No bueno.

5Ws

The "Who" is Moses shortly before he dies. He is instructing the 2nd generation of Israel. The "When" is right before they cross the Jordan River and enter the Promised Land. The "Why" is because Moses feels the need to give them a last-minute reminder of the laws, so they don't screw up as the 1st generation (their parents) did. Remember the lust for quail ordeal in Numbers, chapter 11?

Additionally, we need to consider the "Where." God guaranteed his people a new territory with larger borders. There is a law saying Israel cannot eat animal flesh unless they bring it to the Temple altar for lots of *religious ritual stuff.* Once they are in the promised land, the borders will become so large they won't be able to travel back to their temple/altar to complete the *religious ritual stuff* and get the meat that they lust for.

OK, we know the problems from verses 15 & 20. Let me move back a few verses to establish the "Who" (no, not the band) they wrote this to. If a carnist uses these verses to argue that God allows us to eat meat as we want, you can always reply, "nope, He didn't allow us anything."

Deuteronomy chapter 12 verse 1
These are the statutes and judgments, which ye (Israel) *shall observe to do in the land,* (Canaan) *which the LORD God of thy fathers giveth thee to possess it, all the days that ye live upon the earth.*

These instructions were not given to us. They were given specifically to the people of Israel and only when they go into the promised land of Canaan, not to any Christians in any other part of the world.

If a 21st century Christian is using chapter 12 of Deuteronomy to support their desire to eat meat, try asking a few questions to help them realize none of this was meant for them.

Are Christians offering these animals as sacrifices? And only in a specific place, as instructed in verses 13 & 14?

13- Take heed to thyself that thou offer not thy burnt offerings in every place that thou seest:
14- But in the place which the LORD shall choose in one of thy tribes, there thou shalt offer thy burnt offerings, and there thou shalt do all that I command thee.

Carnist can't make offerings (such as meat) in any place they choose. It has to be where the LORD ordered it. And no, a fast-food drive-thru is not a place on God's list of approved altars. You can also ask, are today's Christians pouring the blood on the ground as instructed in verse:

16- Only ye shall not eat the blood; ye shall pour it upon the earth as water

And, are today's Christians taking over cities and destroying temples?

2- Ye shall utterly destroy all the places, wherein the nations which ye shall possess served their gods,

Look at that part in verse 2 about destroying other people's temples. Is that what Jesus wants us to do now? Are we ordered to destroy a Mormon or Buddhist temple just to have a salami sandwich? Heck no, we are supposed to love them and share the gospel of Grace with them. Don't let carnist Christians employ this chapter to defend meat-eating and ignore the full set requirements.

Lions tho

To use verses in this erroneous way reminds me of the "Lions Tho" reasoning meat-eaters employ against veganism. The argument is, since lions feed on animals, humans can too. The carnist Christian wants to imitate one trait and indiscriminately exclude other lion traits. Lions have been known to eat their young, sniff each other's butts, publicly poop. Don't let carnists quote a single meat-eating allowance while disregarding the other rules. It's a package deal. It's that way with the Bible. I repeat, carnist Christians can't pick one verse and ignore the surrounding verses. They've got to accept the entire passage.

Hunting to save animals.

Meat-eating away from the altar is allowed in this chapter. However, a new restriction is included to make it difficult.

Verse 22- Even as the roebuck (gazelle) and the hart (deer) is eaten, so thou shalt eat them: the unclean and clean shall eat of them alike

At this point, the city's (Canaan) borders are so big, people can't make it back to approved altars. The restriction of meat only at the temple is ended, people may eat wherever. Got it, but verse 22 says *it has to be the same way you eat gazelle and deer.* Huh?

Being told you can eat meat the way you eat a gazelle is a confusing thing to say in the 21st century. The people of Israel understood this was a restriction to only eat what they hunt. Deer and gazelles were not something the shepherds kept in their flocks. If you wanted a deer, you had to go hunting. Again, God accommodates man's gluttonous cravings for meat, but creates restrictions on their access to it. They couldn't grab a lamb from their flocks; they had to go out and hunt. These old guys were not about to go running around hunting gazelles and deers. So again, God always makes eating meat difficult, never easy.

I will go deeper into this hunting aspect later. But for now, let's continue chopping away at verse 20 and the lusting in their souls for meat.

Often, God associates the desire to eat meat with gluttony and lust. We can gather "a lust" for meat, is not a good thing, and in these verses, we got lots of lusting going on. Go back to the parts I underlined. We've got a group of people who are using animal sacrifice to satisfy their _lust_ for eating meat. God limits the allowance to eat animals by making it much more complicated than simply taking from the herd of cattle they have.

God says if they casually want meat, NO. But if their soul has an uncontrollable lust, they can. It shouldn't be a breakfast, lunch and dinner activity. It's only when their soul has an _uncontrollable lust,_ they can partake. Even then, God said to _go out and hunt for it_. This added effort curbs their lust and inhibits man from giving into gluttony. Taking into consideration these many extra efforts, does that sound as God wanted them (or us) to eat meat? Nahhhh.

I want what I want

I'm still bothered with verse 20: _I want flesh, my soul lusts for flesh."_

Am I the only one who catches this as the whining of a spoiled brat? These people are demanding, "_I want flesh,_" and God is saying, "_OK fine, just please shut up_"! Use this view in your activism, it's powerful.

Hunting

Since I brought hunting up, I want to share a couple of thoughts. First, every mention of hunters in the Bible is negative. My real-life experiences with hunters aren't much different. _"Kill their babies and watch the mommy animals cry"_ was shouted at me during a protest at a hunting expo. It saddens me how disconnected from compassion people (especially Christians) can be. The Bible echoes that attitude with hunters.

There are (possibly) 4 hunters in the Bible, Ishmael, Nimrod, Esau, and another in Revelation. Nimrod is the founder of the Babylonian empire. Babylon is the enemy of God. Next we've got Esau, who was called a godless (NASB), immoral (NIV), or a profane (KJV) person (see Hebrews 16:16). Heck, in Malachi chapter 1 and repeated in Romans chapter 9, it says God hated Esau. As reported in Galatians chapter 4, Ishmael wasn't looked at favorably. The rider on the white horse in Revelation chapter 6 is "ify" but many consider him a form of Anti-Christ, so ya, hunters aren't looked at well in the Bible.

Hunter makes a vegan

One last thought I want to share on hunting before I go. In part one of this book, do you remember how I felt my vegan turning point happened in a conversation with a hunter? We can look at it this way. We vegan activists know hunting is evil but, God used someone (a hunter) who did horrible things to animals as a tool to convert me to a vegan lifestyle. As a result, I have gone on to a life of activism and turned my wife vegan. And then many friends vegan. And then, through my speaking engagements, I watched many carnist Christians change to a diet of compassion. I don't mean to toot my own horn, but I want to point out that what we see as evil, God can use for mighty works of compassion. I hope that helps explain why sometimes God allows so many evil things to happen. He has a bigger plan. Those of us that have faith, we trust that somehow, God is working miracles.

CHAPTER 38: DEUTERONOMY 25:4 – DON'T MUZZLE A HUNGRY OX

Ox has got to eat too!

Vegan activists often use Deuteronomy chapter 25 verse 4 to prove God demands kindness to animals, and I agree. But be careful; this verse might come back and bite you because it involves exploiting animals for farm work.

I will give a defense for it, but if you haven't read my chapters on Jewish dietary laws or God's accommodation, it may appear as if I'm stepping in and out of a welfarist view.

Deuteronomy chapter 25 verse 4
Thou shalt not muzzle the ox when he treadeth out the corn.

5Ws

We can start with the "When & Who." The people of Israel are free from Egyptian slavery thanks to God, Moses, and the plagues. Moses leads them across the Red Sea and into the wilderness, where they wandered for 40 years. I imagine Moses' wife saying, *"Honey, just pull over and get directions."*

Directions wouldn't have helped; these people had a covenant (deal) with God promising to keep his laws. In turn, God will give them The Promise Land (Canaan). The people never kept their part of the covenant.

As punishment, God keeps them lost in the wilderness until the generation that broke the covenant dies out. Their children (2nd generation of Israel) will get to The Promise Land (Canaan) without their parents.

Before Moses gets these kids into the promised land, he gives them a speech. He reminds this new generation of Israel of the importance of following God's laws. If they obey, there will be blessings. If they disobey, it will bring misery, as it did for their parents. That is the "Why" for his speech.

As we approach verse 4, we catch Moses speaking of <u>fairness.</u> The order of the fairness rules is useable to prove animals are of high value and are not just items on a menu. Let me start with verse 1.

> *If there be a <u>controversy between men</u>, and they come unto judgment, that the judges may judge them; then they shall justify the righteous and condemn the wicked.*
>
> ***2-*** *And it shall be, if the wicked <u>man</u> be worthy to be beaten, that the judge shall cause him to lie down, and to be beaten before his face, <u>according to his fault,</u> by a certain number.*
>
> ***3-*** *Forty stripes he may give him, and not exceed: lest, if he should exceed, and beat him above these with many stripes, then thy brother should seem vile unto thee.*

Notice what I underlined. Moses is speaking of fairness in judgment and fairness of punishment for <u>human beings,</u> got it? I'll momentarily skip verse 4 and go to verse 5 because I want to establish a method being used. I will return to verse 4 after.

> ***5-*** <u>*If brethren*</u> (humans) *dwell together, and one of them die, and have no child, the wife of the dead shall not marry without unto a stranger: her husband's brother shall go in unto her, and take her to him to wife, and perform the duty of a husband's brother unto her.*

In verse 5, we have more <u>rules for human beings</u> concerning marriage and widowhood. By today's standards, this law makes many pastors blush. I can't wait to tell you more of that in my next book. What I want to point out now is, we have <u>human rules</u> demanding fairness to humans on each side of our *muzzle an ox* verse.

Now we can read verse 4.

> *Thou shalt not muzzle the ox when <u>he</u> treadeth out the corn.*

If animals are nothing more that food items, this verse does not fit. Think about it, Moses plops this command of kindness to animals (an ox) between fairness rules to humans for a reason. Consider the setup: we've got human rules, then more human rules, and then even more human rules.

Moses then says, *"Be kind to animals,"* and returns to human rules, human rules, and more human rules.

This might look odd in today's culture with its heartless opinion toward animals, but to God, the placement of this rule shows animal fairness is equally vital as human fairness. Vegan win!

He/She or it

Did you notice the King James Version calls the ox *"he"* and not an *"it"*? This is one time the KJV is on our side. The translation can legitimately be either *he* or *it*. Applying the translation *"it"* lowers the ox to the status of an object, and objects are unworthy of consideration. Since one does not show compassion to an *"it"*, using *"he"* is appropriate. Once again, the Bible elevates animals to a high level. If you feel so inclined, you can use this verse to defend the *He/She or It* discussion.

Let's discuss the "Ox" rule further.

"Tza'ar ba'alei chayim,"

This verse is the basis for a big law from the Jewish Talmud called "Tza'ar *ba'alei chayim*", which means *To Prevent the Suffering of Living Creatures.*

The Talmud is the central text of Rabbinic Judaism and a source of Jewish religious law. This law is pretty basic; it's wrong to cause unnecessary suffering. Because of this verse (and Deuteronomy 22:10), Jews received over 100 laws and rules about preparing food made from animals. Each rule reduces animal suffering.

Give yourself a few seconds to expand on that thought. They had over a hundred rules to lessen animal suffering. But today, factory farm animals are exempt from most animal cruelty laws. In 2019, they passed a law called the Preventing Animal Cruelty and Torture Act. (PACT). Sounds nice right? Well, it is, but the law does not apply to people who slaughter animals for food, farmers, or people that hunt and fish. Doesn't that tell you something? If hunting, fishing, and turning animals into food need to be exempt from a cruelty law, then those actions must be cruelty! Farming is a business like any business. A farm must make a profit. They display no consideration of the torment forced on God's innocent animals if it will affect profits. Big difference from Bible times, huh?

If someone comes back saying God instructed how to eat animals, just agree. Then hit them with, "There are many additional rules *connected* with God's allowance to eat animals. Any food from today's factory farms cannot meet the regulations God gave and, therefore, are off-limits." Activist can use this!

Donkeys too!

In **Deuteronomy chapter 22 verse 10**:

Thou shalt not plow with an ox and an ass together.

This is another one of those *Tza'ar ba'alei chayim* verses commanding the further care of animals. There is a considerable size difference between an ox and a donkey. To join them in a plow increases cruelty. The donkey would suffer physical stress trying to keep up with his big buddy. The ox works twice as hard to cover the donkey's weakness.

There is also mental stress for the donkey. The ox will always chew his cud, giving the donkey the impression he's eating. Poor little donkey guy will feel cheated thinking the ox has food, and he doesn't.

Many people today wouldn't care about mental stress to a donkey or any animal. I mention this to make a point. Back in Bible days, people were required to give the utmost concern for the physical <u>and mental well-being</u> of their farm animals. That's a huge vegan win.

Beast of Burden

Here is my warning: this verse assumes the exploitation of animals. The animals plow and tread. Plowing (breaking up the topsoil) and treading (to press out with the feet).

Even tho Moses says, don't be abusive, the ox is still being exploited. You say "OK Steve, I still want to use this verse, but how do I handle the welfarist attitude here?"

The "When" comes to your defense. Moses wrote this when using animals for plowing was of <u>necessity</u>. Today's farming has tractors and equipment run by machines. It has become 100% <u>unnecessary</u> to use an animal anymore. What we take away is God had concern about animal suffering on farms then, so we must accept He still cares for animals on farms now. Today's factory farms are non-stop suffering for the animals. Any food item from a factory farm is off limits to Christians. If the carnist you are speaking to continues with this verse as support for exploitation, challenge them on the activity.

I didn't feel exploited.

Think back to what the family life was in that age. Often, these farms fed one or a few extended families living communally. They weren't feeding millions of people. Based on the family or "tribe" size, working an ox might only require a couple of hours. Plus, the Ten Commandments orders days of absolute rest for the animals. If God is concerned with the care of an animal only working occasionally, you can imagine what He'd think of the non-stop suffering in today's factory farms. Activists can use this comparison.

This reminds me of when my dad had me mow the lawn for a couple of hours every week. I didn't feel exploited. I know it's different. The ox doesn't want to work at all, it's only doing this by force. The idea was, families, children and the animals worked together for mutual survival.

That is leaning towards a welfarist point of view, but it has helped me through some conversations where the carnist just couldn't see past their cognitive disconnect. I don't like it much, but, eh; it allowed me to further a vegan conversation.

Wrap up

These verses confirm humans are required to treat animals with compassion. There was an allowance to use animals if genuine <u>need</u>, but the invention of mechanical farm equipment changes things. Humans <u>no longer need</u> to burden any animal. With alternative methods available, using animals violates the boundaries God gave.

CHAPTER 39:
ISIAIAH 1:11 – FED UP
WITH SACRIFICE

Is God "fed-up" with sacrifices?

Today's carnist Christian uses animal sacrifice as God's approval to kill animals. Vegans often fight this by using the following verse from Isaiah. Sorry class, this is not the verse to prove that.

Isaiah chapter 1 verse 11
To what <u>purpose is the multitude</u> of your sacrifices unto me? Saith the LORD: I am full of the burnt offerings of rams, and the fat of fed beasts; and <u>I delight not in the blood of bullocks, or of lambs, or of he-goats.</u>

Quoting Isaiah 1:11 sends most meat-eating Christians into a state of panic. My experience is this verse will work 99% of the time to support God never wanted animal sacrifices. It works 99% of the time because 99% of Christians never read the Bible for context. If they did, they would know God isn't telling them *sacrifice is worthless*; He's saying He's fed up with *the way* they're making sacrifices. Big difference.

Don't freak out, I found some good vegan stuff here. The entire chapter brings us to an overall anti-sacrifice lesson from God. So let's look into the 5Ws and then discuss how to use this verse without scripture twisting.

5Ws

After King Solomon dies (around 900 BC), they divided the kingdom into two parts: Israel is the north and Judah is the south. It sounds like the Civil War, doesn't it? Oh well, Israel and Judah governed themselves in an ungodly way. They were pretty much idiots. If you think I'm rude for calling them idiots, check out verse 3 when Isaiah tells them donkeys are smarter than they are. Name-calling continues in verse 10 when Isaiah calls them *"rulers of Sodom"* and *"you people of Gomorrah."* That was harsh talk for those times.

The situation is this: Israel was doing what religious people were supposed to do, such as sacrifice and keeping the Sabbath day. The problem was, their worship was *insincere worship*; they were only going through the motions with no heartfelt repentance.

In verse 11, notice I underlined the word purpose. God is not telling them to stop animal sacrificing. He is criticizing their *intentions*. To understand why, we need to read on. Let's look at verses 12 &13.

12- When you come to appear before me who hath required this at your hand, to tread my courts?

13- Bring no more vain (futile, meaningless) *oblations* (offerings/sacrifices): *incense is an abomination unto me: the new moons and sabbaths, the calling of assemblies, I cannot away with, it is iniquity, even the solemn meeting*

Look at each underline in verse 13. God says He doesn't want vain offerings of any kind. That is the issue, the religious rituals were done in vain. It wasn't only animal sacrifice God rejected. He didn't want the incense they burned, or the special days they celebrated, or the meetings they attended. They were going through the religious motions without a fundamental change of heart regarding the evil they did.

A sacrifice is supposed to mean something serious. They are expected to be repenting of their wrongdoing, turning away from sin. These people hit a low point where they thought, "hey, I can steal", or "hey, I can slap my wife around, I can lie or cheat. All I need to do is kill an animal, and I'm good to go again!" That is not a genuine sacrifice at all. Get it?

Back to the verses:

14 - your new moons and your appointed feasts my soul hateth: they are a trouble unto me; I am weary to bear them.

15 - and when ye spread forth your hands, I will hide mine eyes from you: when ye make many prayers, I will not hear: your hands are full of blood.

Notice the activities underlined. These corrupt people did the religious rituals, did the correct feasts and made as many prayers as required, but they were empty of any heartfelt repentance. A person can do good and still be sinning.

So there's the context for verse 11. It is not exactly saying sacrifice is bad; it says meaningless, unrepentant, and self-serving sacrifices are unwanted by God.

Let's veganize this!

What makes this useable to vegan activism comes later when God tells *what He wants* to fix this specific situation. Guess what? There are NO animal sacrifices in the fixing!

16- Wash you, make you clean; put away (stop) *the evil of your doings from before mine eyes; cease to do evil;*

In verse 16, God is saying you can make yourself clean if you stop doing evil. What is that evil? It's listed in verse 17.

17- Learn to do well; seek judgment (justice), *relieve the oppressed, judge* (defend) *the fatherless, plead* (stand up for) *for the widow*

In verse 17, God says what upset him. They need to start:
1- Seeking justice
2- Helping the oppressed
3- Help the fatherless or help the widow

He didn't mention animal sacrifices or command religious rituals to clean up their mess. I repeat, to fix this mess, they gotta help the poor, serve the widows, seek justice. God says nothing about correcting insincere animal sacrifice methods. Our obedience is more important. So yes, ultimately, this passage shows God does not want or need animal sacrifice.

Forgiveness without blood is difficult for Christians to accept, but in verse 18, God can forgive without sacrifice

18- Though your sins be as scarlet, they shall be as white as snow.

Verse 18 says God will turn our red sins to white by *giving to the poor* and *being full of mercy*. Absolutely no animal sacrifice or blood required.

19- If ye be willing and obedient, ye shall eat the good of the land:

There is more fun vegan stuff in verse 19. God does not say they will eat the fatted calf or any Bible thingy meat-eaters expect, but they will eat the good of the land. That's veggies!

20- But to refuse and rebel you shall be devoured with the sword:

for the mouth of the LORD has spoken it

Verse 20 ends with a warning that if they refuse, they will die by the sword. Ouch! Seems harsh, but Isaiah warned them many times.

Another vegan tid-bit

Let's revisit verse 15:

> *And when ye spread forth your hands, I will hide mine eyes from you: when ye make many prayers, I will not hear: your hands are full of blood* (Hebrew: dahm = blood guiltiness).

Remember what I wrote about using the word *murder*? Once again, it applies here in verse 15. These people are not repentant when doing sacrifice. That turned the "proper killing" of an animal into the "murder" of an animal. God saying their hands are full of blood, meaning they are guilty of murder.

Wrap up

We see people doing the required religious rituals, such as animal sacrifice, keeping festivals and holidays, but they are not loving God with their whole hearts, so it meant nothing to God.

The vegan take away is animal sacrifice cannot fix a lack of love. God may have allowed and even accepted the sacrifice, but God's first choice was love over sacrifice.

God is way more concerned with people, love, and social justice than with ceremonial or organized religion. At one time, sacrifice was the "in thing," but no longer. As you read the Bible, you'll get more light shining on precisely how God's love and forgiveness works. You can see His continuous efforts to move us away from these legalistic religious activities.

CHAPTER 40: ISAIAH 11 & 65 –THE PEACEABLE KINGDOM

The wolf and the lamb become BFs

The 11th and 65th chapters of Isaiah offer activists great ammunition. The vast majority of Christians believe Isaiah is describing the Messiah's future kingdom, where everyone will live in harmony. It will be a time of peace and, you guessed it, veganism!

Every Christian accepts there will be no death or suffering in this kingdom, but they don't quite understand these verses apply to the animals, too. Activists can easily point that out. For most vegan outreach, verses 6-9 are enough to prove your point. But I will discuss extra in case you need it.

Isaiah chapter 11 verses 6-9

6- The wolf also shall dwell with the lamb, and the leopard shall lie down with the kid (young goat)*; and the calf and the young lion and the fatling* (cattle) *together; and a little child shall lead them*

Verse 6 tells us there will be peace by comparing the predators and prey hanging out together.

7- And the cow and the bear shall feed; their young ones shall lay down together: and the lion shall eat straw like the ox.

When we reach verse 7, it says the lion shall eat straw like the ox.

Strangely, carnist Christians often laugh at that. As if God can't transform carnivores into herbivores. Their denial is a display of their carnism taking over. They accept God turned herbivores into carnivores after sin enters the world, but somehow, He is limited and can't change them back.

You may need to remind them of Genesis chapter 1 verse 30. *"Everything that has the breath of life in it—I give every green plant for food."* Ya, that's an easy vegan win.

> *8- And the suckling child shall play on the hole of the asp and the weaned child shall put his hand on the snake's den.*

Verse 8 shows people not getting hurt by venomous creatures, making the point there is no death in the kingdom.

> *9- They shall not hurt or destroy* (death) *in my holy mountain: for the earth shall be full knowledge of the Lord, as the waters cover the sea*

Look at what I underlined in verse 9. You see an excellent defense for veganism. God's Millennial kingdom has no death, so no pork chops.
We get added vegan confirmation in the 65th chapter.

Isaiah chapter 65 verse 17
For, behold, I create new heavens and a new earth: and the former shall not be remembered, nor come into mind.

God is creating a new vegan world in which they won't remember eating meat. Share this with the carnist Christian. "You might not be vegan now, but God will make you vegan for eternity."

Verse 25
The wolf and the lamb shall feed together, and the lion shall eat straw like the bullock: and dust shall be the serpent's meat. They shall not hurt nor destroy in all my holy mountain, saith the LORD.

And verse 25 repeats the lion will eat straw transformation. We don't have to go into who, what, where, when, or why. These verses are so easy-to-understand. This is a grand slam home run for veganism.

Just for fun.

Another vegan thing is Isaiah speaks of Heaven and animals together. For those wondering if animals will be in Heaven. These verses give us a pretty good reason to say yes indeed!

CHAPTER 41: ISAIAH 66:3 – OX EQUALS HUMAN?

Does an ox equal a man?

Vegans are tempted to use this verse to establish equality between humans and animals. There are verses in the Bible that support that point of view, but this verse is not one. Vegans beware.

Isaiah chapter 66 Verse 3

He that killeth an ox is as if he slew a man; he that sacrificeth a lamb, as if he cut off (breaks) *a dog's neck; he that offereth an oblation, as if he offered swine's blood; he that burneth incense, as if he blessed an idol. Yea, they have chosen their own ways, and their soul delighteth in their abominations.*

A quick reading might sound as if killing an ox is equal to killing a man. That seems true on a surface reading, but this is one of those tricky verses. Sadly, this shows the killing of animals is acceptable. Isaiah is pointing out the similarities of unacceptable sacrifices from the unrepentant people of Israel to the unacceptable human sacrifices of pagan people. This is not vegan ammunition.

5Ws

Isaiah is an Old Testament prophet dude who had good and bad news to share with the corrupt rulers of Israel. These leaders were worshiping false gods and being cruel in the way they treated the poor. Isaiah tells them God will use bigger cities such as Assyria and Babylon to kick Israel's butts if they don't get their act in order.

Important side note: Pagan religious groups are sacrificing their children and "unclean" animals like pigs and dogs to their gods.

Back to Israel. Sacrifice was supposed to be a solemn expression of heart-felt repentance. People of Israel are misusing this ritual of sacrifice. When the people of Israel committed a sin worthy of their death, the death of an animal was a substitutionary payment for that sin. Consider it a last chance for the people who did wrong. It was an opportunity to turn from that sin and start anew. Sadly, sacrifice became corrupted and used like a loophole in the law.

They were making proper, clean animal sacrifices but have no actual "spirit" of repentance for their sins. They are like, "Hey, let's rip off the poor people. All we gotta do is sacrifice a few lambs for forgiveness." See what I mean? No genuine spirit of repentance and God knew that. So, if these guys kill an ox to be forgiven, that sacrifice has no value. It's as if they were making an unacceptable dog or human sacrifice, get it? The ox was an acceptable offering but because of the deceitful, empty nature of the guy performing the offering, it was as worthless. God saw it as presenting an abominable sacrifice such as a human sacrifice.

The verse goes on with comparing the sacrifice of the lamb and a dog. Lambs are clean and acceptable sacrifices, but dogs are not. With an unrepentant heart, the lamb (acceptable sacrifice) is as worthless as breaking a dog's (unacceptable pagan sacrifice) neck. This verse is not about lamb or dog, ox or human, but the attitude of Israel. See? God's concern is their shallow religious rituals, hypocrisy, arrogance, and evil. You will notice this problem a lot.

Don't be a jerk

If you talk to an average Christian meat-eater, chances are they don't know the background of this scripture. It's tempting to use this verse, and it usually works, but that's really disingenuous. Also, it can backfire. They may go back to their pastors and ask for clarification. Their pastor (hopefully) knows the proper context and will undo any vegan progress you might have made.

Be sure to read my chapter on animal sacrifice. Vegans don't have to hide from the subject of sacrifice. Ya, ya, ya, I know it's a long, confusing read, Sorry. But you need to get it in your head to do effective vegan outreach when sacrifices are a concern.

CHAPTER 42:
DANIEL 1:8 – DANIEL'S DIET WASN'T VEGAN

Pass me the veggies, hold the meat

I'm going to take another shot against the vegan activists claiming Daniel was vegan.

8- But Daniel proposed in his heart that he would not <u>defile himself</u> with the portion of the king's meat

Sounds vegan, huh? Not so fast. This story is not about veganism. There are many vegetable and meat comparisons in the Bible. Those comparisons are not concerned with the kind of food, be it vegetable or meat. Instead, the meaning is based on what each particular food represents in that culture.

I will show the Daniel diet was Daniel's attempt to keep pure before God, not veganism. Activists should be cautious using these verses. This study will also aid in understanding meat issues in the New Testament letters of the Apostle Paul. More on that later.

5Ws

To understand this, I've got to take you through the entire chapter. Relax, it will take less than 10 minutes.

1- in the third year of the reign of Jehoiakim king of Judah, came Nebuchadnezzar, king of Babylon onto Jerusalem, and <u>besieged</u>

it

According to 2nd Chronicles chapter 36, God repeatedly tried to get his people in Judah (southern Israel) to turn from their evil ways, but they didn't. God sent messengers and prophets, but Judah picked on them and rejected them! Totally rude. This resulted in God letting the king of Babylon conquer Judah.

2- and the Lord gave Jehoiakim king of Judah into his hand, with part of the vessels of the house of God: which he carried into the land of Shiner to the <u>house of his God</u>; and he brought the vessels into the <u>treasure house of his God</u>

In the first chapter of Daniel, God lets the king of Babylon, a guy named Nebuchadnezzar, kick Judah's butts and take prisoners. Daniel and 3 young friends are among those prisoners of war.

3- And the King spake unto Ashpenaz the master of his eunuchs, that he should bring certain of the children of Israel (Judah), *and of the King seed, and of the princes;*
   4- <u>Children</u> in whom was no blemish (healthy, good looking), *but well-favored, and skillful in all wisdom* (smart), *and cunning in knowledge, and understanding science, and such as had ability in them to stand in the Kings Palace, and whom they might <u>teach the learning and the tongue of the Chaldeans</u>* (Babylon)

After the conquest of Judah, the King has the brilliant, good-looking, and skilled children brought to the palace. Daniel and 3 friends are among those chosen.

The king knows he can train the youthful children to follow Babylonian ways much easier than old adults. The goal is to teach these kids the language, customs, and religions of the Chaldeans (the Babylonians). Then these brilliant, good-looking, and skilled children can be of service to the Chaldeans king and gods.

5- And the king appointed them a daily provision of the king's meat (Patbag = animal flesh or other delicacies), *and of the wine which he drank: so <u>nourishing them three years</u>, at the end thereof they might stand before the king.*

The king appoints teachers and gives them three years to educate Daniel and his buddies on the way of the Babylonians. The king wants the kids to be strong and healthy, so he orders they get the same food that he, the king, gets. Apparently, this king never saw *What The Health.*

6- Now among these were of the children of Judah (Israel),

Daniel, Hananiah, Mishael, and Azariah:

Name Game

These kids had Hebrew names, and those names had Hebrew meanings. This is important to understand the scene here.

Daniel means: God is my judge

Hananiah means: God has been gracious

Mishael means: Who is like God

Asariah means: God helps

In the next verse, there is an order for a name change. When we compare the alternative names for these four kids, you'll start to figure out Daniel's reluctance to the king's food. You see, the king is attempting to indoctrinate the kids into the Babylonian life, culture, and its worship of false gods.

7- unto whom the prince of the eunuchs gave names: for <u>he gave onto Daniel the name Belteshazzar</u>; and to Hananiah, of <u>Shadrach</u>; and to Mishael, of <u>Meshach</u>; and to Azariah, of <u>Abendnego</u>.

Look at the meaning of these new Babylonian names:

Belteshazzar means: <u>Bel </u>will protect.

Shadrach means: inspired of <u>Aku.</u>

Meshach means: Belonging to <u>Aku</u>.

Abendnego means: Servant of <u>Nego</u>.

See what the prince of the eunuchs is doing here? He is trying to wipe out any connection the kids had with their Hebrew God. "Bel" and "Aku" and "Nego" were Babylonian gods. The king's intention was to change their identities from being Hebrews that worshiped the God of Abraham, Isaac, and Jacob to followers of Babylonian gods. Pretty sneaky, huh? When I was a kid in church, I wasn't taught those crazy names had a religious meaning. Knowing that gives me a different perspective on the story than I once held. The Babylonians are preparing them for some major brainwashing.

Daniel figured out what was going down. Learning the language was a minor thing, no religious commitment needed for that. But changing their identity through their names set off red flags. Next, is changing them through the food they eat. That was going too far for Danny and the boys.

8- But Daniel proposed in his heart that he would not defile (pollute, desecrate, stain) *himself with the portion of the king's meat* (Patbag = animal flesh or other delicacies), *nor with the wine which he drank: therefore he requested of the prince of the eunuchs that he might not <u>defile himself.</u>*

Let's consider this "defile" term. It could mean Daniel didn't want to eat anything that wasn't kosher. Daniel, knowing he was in a pagan city, assumed this food might have been offered to a false god in a sacrificial ritual. Or perhaps the animal was strangled. Or maybe still had blood in it.

Now that you understand the attempted brainwashing going on behind the scenes, you can understand why I say these verses are not Daniel going vegan. His refusal to eat meat was putting a stop to the indoctrination into the Babylonian religions.

9- Now God had brought Daniel into favour and tender love (racham) *with the prince of the eunuchs*

Oh my, my, my. Yep, I checked up on the translation of the word *"racham"* and *tender love* it is between Danny and the Prince of eunuchs. Take that any way you want, but it was enough of this "tender love" (Boom Chicka Wah Wah!) to make the prince of eunuchs risk his life, allowing Daniel to request a food change.

10- And the prince of the eunuchs said unto Daniel, I fear my Lord the king, who had appointed your meat and your drink: for why should he <u>see your faces is worse</u> liking than the children which are of your sort? Then shall ye <u>make me in danger my head</u> to the king.

This verse cracked me up because it made me realize not much has changed. How many of my vegans reading this have friends and family concerned they would get sick if they stopped eating meat? Yep, they thought that stupid crap back then, too. The Prince of the eunuchs could not figure out how the boys could become healthier on vegetables than the kids eating meat. I intend to show their extreme positive health is God's miraculous intervening, not the veggies. Sorry.

11- Then said Daniel to Melzar, whom the prince of the eunuchs had set over Daniel, Hannah, Mishael, and Azariah,
        12- Prove they servants, I beseech thee, ten days; and let them give us pulse (vegetables) *to eat, and water to drink.*

Daniel pleads that they only get water and vegetables. So he offers a deal.

13- Let our countenances (appearance) *be looked upon before thee, and the countenances of the children that eat of the portion of the king's meat: and as they seest, deal with thy servants.*

Daniel cleverly proposed he and his buddies get vegetables and water only. After 10 days, compare them to the other kids eating the king's delicacies. It was only ten days, no one would die. Melzar (the dude in charge) was to make the determination. This allowed Melzar to be a judge and not appear to be giving in to the request of a slave.

14- So he consented to them in this matter, and proved them ten days

This Prince of eunuchs guy could force Daniel to eat the king's section of food. The king will cut off eunuch guy's head if the kids got sick. I'm thinking, getting your head cut off is pretty serious. Either God was at work in this Prince of eunuchs decision, or maybe that *tender love* thing was part of what convinced him to give Daniel a chance. Yep, these thoughts get me kicked out of respectable churches everywhere.

15- And at the end of 10 days their countenances (a person's face or facial expressions) *appeared fairer* (towb = good pleasant agreeable) *and fatter in flesh than all the children which did eat the portion of the king's meat.*

I know the health benefits of veganism are amazing. Still, there's no way 10 days on a vegan diet will *visually* be better than a meat-eater. They didn't have the ways to test our health as we scientifically do today. It was visual or sometimes by demonstration in athletic competitions. In this verse, their superior health was based on how they *appeared* to be fairer and fatter. Oh, and fatter? Are they nuts? I eat a ton of vegetables, and I cannot gain a pound. I'm not calling shenanigans here; I'm saying God miraculously intervened. God made them look healthier than the meat-eating kids. Not better because it was veggies but because Daniel rejected the (un-kosher or un-permissible) kingly Babylon diet and stayed true to the God of Israel. God rewarded the kids miraculously with a much healthier appearance.

16- Thus Melzar took away the portion of their meat, and the wine that they should drink; and gave them pulse (vegetables).
   17- As for these four children, God gave them knowledge and skill in all learning and wisdom, and Daniel had understanding in all visions and dreams.

So they remained faithful and were rewarded. God miraculously gave them knowledge and wisdom in the same way He miraculously made them look better physically than the other kids.

It wasn't because they ate vegetables only. Vegetables don't visually improve anyone that much in 10 days. They had no way of looking at blood cholesterol levels or anything else that 10 days on a vegan diet improves. Their more excellent health was based on a visual examination.

Moving on, this was a 3-year test and now they stood before the king himself.

> *18- Now at the end of the days* (3 years) *that King had said he should bring them in, then the prince of the eunuchs brought them before Nebuchadnezzar.*
>   *19- And the King communed with them; and among them all was found none like* <u>*Daniel, Hananiah, Mishael, and Azariah*</u>*; therefore stood they before the king*

The boys got their names back. I underlined it because I want you to notice they are using their Hebrew names again. It's three years later, and they've gotten their way to continue serving the God of Israel. No name change.

> *20- And in all* <u>*matters of wisdom and understanding*</u>*, that the king enquired of them, he found them* <u>*ten times better*</u> *than all the magicians and astrologers that were in his realm.*

We end with Daniel having wisdom and understanding 10 times greater than any of the king's current staff. Again, God miraculously gets involved. One does not get 10 times smarter than everyone else from eating vegetables for 10 days. Happy ending but still not vegan.

Another reason I don't go for the "Daniel is vegan" response is later on in:

Daniel chapter 10 verses 2 & 3

2- In those days I Daniel was morning three full weeks.
    3- I ate no pleasant bread, neither came flesh (Basar = animal flesh) *nor wine in my mouth, neither did I anoint myself at all, till three whole weeks were fulfilled.*

By this time of chapter 10, Daniel says that he did not eat any animal flesh for three weeks. Obviously, that implies that prior, he was eating animal flesh. So Daniel's veggie eating in chapter 1 was for a specific purpose and a specific time. By chapter 10, Daniel is a high-ranking official in the king's service, and he can access kosher meat if he chooses. Daniel was in a position where he could eat meat, and he obviously did.

CHAPTER 43: PSALMS 51 –TRUE REPENTANCE

King David is busted

Oh geez, here I go again. I need to shoot down another vegan favorite. The 51st chapter of Psalms has a verse that sounds vegan positive. That's only half true.

Psalms chapter 51 verse 16
For thou desires not sacrifice; else I would give it; Thou delights not in burnt offerings.

This verse looks as if God is displeased with animal sacrifices. But, 3 verses later, God can be pleased with animal sacrifices.

19- Then shalt thou be pleased with the sacrifices of righteousness, with burnt offering and whole burnt offering: then shall they offer bullocks upon thine altar.

Well, that sure sounds confusing. But it doesn't have to be. If we read the entire 51st chapter (and parts of the 50th chapter), vegans can prove God never needed sacrifices.

5Ws

Chapter 51 is the prayer/poetry of (assumably) King David. He is feeling guilty for the horrible stuff he did involving a married girl. David is usually a stand-up kinda guy, but he messed up big time when he does the dirty deed with a hottie named Bathsheba. It went down like this. Bathsheba is married to a guy named Uriah, a soldier in King David's army. While Uriah is away at war, David sees Bathsheba on her rooftop taking a bath. Nice name coincidence there. She is taking a bath, and her name is _Bath_sheba. I wonder, if she was taking a shower, would her name be "_Shower_sheba"? Haha, I just get worse.

King David sends for her, they party, and he knocks her up. To hide this adulterous affair, David arranges for her hubby Uriah to come back home. His plan is for Uriah to get with Bathsheba, making it appear she is having Uriah's baby. Smooth-move Dave.

Well, that didn't work because this Uriah guy is a real boy scout. He considered it a dishonor to his fellow soldiers currently in battle if he was to take pleasure with his wife…so he didn't.

This puts David in a big mess. He sends Uriah back to the front lines of battle with sealed instruction papers to give to the army captain. The instructions were, get Uriah to the front lines, back everyone out, leaving Uriah to fight alone. Eventually, Uriah gets killed. You can read this in 2nd Samuel, chapters 11 and 12. David has become both an adulterer and a murderer.

Busted and disgusted

About a year goes by, and God sends a prophet named Nathan to remind David of how evil his sin was. David comes to his senses and breaks down in absolute shame. This Psalm is his prayer of repentance:

Psalm chapter 51 verse 1
Have mercy upon me, oh God, according to thy love and kindness: according unto the multitude of thy tender mercies blot out my transgressions.

David knows he did wrong, and he's a broken man because of it. Notice tho, he isn't pushing the blame off on something else; he owns up to his sin. He asks God for mercy, admitting his immoral behavior, and trusting in God's love and kindness. What is David not doing? He is not offering an animal sacrifice to cover his sin.

David's state of true repentance allows him to make an animal sacrifice, but that didn't even come to mind. He knows God can forgive sin without bloodshed.

2- Wash me thoroughly from mine iniquity, and cleanse me from my sin.

3- for I acknowledged my transgressions and my sin is ever before me

In other parts of this book, I discuss God's acceptance of animal sacrifices if done with a true heart of repentance. Many people were making sacrifice, but not with genuine repentance. That is not what David is doing. He only asks for God to forgive him, and he has every reason to believe God will. Many others did too. You can see it if we briefly skip to the book of Micah.

Micah chapter 7 verse 18
Who is a God like unto thee, that pardoneth iniquity, and passeth by the transgression of the remnant of his heritage? <u>he retaineth not his anger for ever, because he delighteth in mercy</u>.

God is in the forgiveness business. He <u>delights in mercy</u>. There are many verses showing God forgives without animal blood. Let's return to the book of Psalms, chapter 51 and pick up in verse 14 as David goes on:

14- Deliver me from bloodguiltiness (murder), O God, thou God of my salvation: and my tongue shall sing aloud of thy righteousness

Here King David is admitting to being a murderer and asking God to forgive him.

16 - For thou desires not sacrifice; else I would give it; Thou delights not in burnt offerings.

I got two takeaways from this verse. David admits to being a murderer. Earlier, he admitted he was an adulterer. These sins are punishable by death. There is no law on animal sacrifice for the sins of premeditated murder or adultery. I could read the first half of verse 16, as David saying, "*Hey God, I didn't give you any sacrifice because I know you didn't authorize a sacrifice for murder or adultery sins.*"

Do you notice the difference in meaning? David is not claiming God does not want sacrifices; he is saying there exists no authorized sacrifices for murder and adultery. Still, if there was, David could sacrifice 1000 bulls if needed.

That is the possible pushback from verse 16. You can counter this with the second half of the verse. David knows God takes no pleasure in animal sacrifice.

16- Thou delightest not in burnt offering.

Are we sure God does not want animal sacrifice? How do we claim this? Pop back to chapter 50 and see what God himself said:

Psalm chapter 50 verse 8
I will not reprove thee for thy sacrifices or thy burnt offerings, to have been continually before me.
     9- I have no need of a young bull from your stall or of goats from your pens
     10- For every animal of the forest is mine, the cattle on 1000 hills
     11- I know every bird in the mountains and the cattle in the fields are mine
     12- If I were hungry I would not tell you for the world is mine and all that is in it.
     13- Do I eat the flesh of bulls or drink the blood of goats?

God is being sarcastic here. Can you imagine him saying that in a Jewish accent like Jackie Mason? Yep, I'm that old.

God establishes He has no need for any sacrifices. Think about it, what are they giving to God (sacrificing) that is not God's property already? God says He owns all the cattle on every hill. God is sarcastically saying, *do you really think I'm eating and drinking the stuff you offer me?* The answer is obviously no; God doesn't eat or drink the sacrificed items. We're not offering anything He doesn't already own. The idea a "god" needs anything from people is a pagan concept, a human idea. These people expect the pagan gods needed to eat, and the pagan gods required blood. The real God is saying *no, I don't need any of this stuff. I don't eat it, and I certainly don't drink the blood of goats. I am only allowing sacrifices for your ease of mind.* The people got self-righteous and felt they were doing God a favor. As if! God requires nothing from us.

Let's get back to **Psalm chapter 51**

     17 - The sacrifice of God are a broken spirit; a broken and contrite heart, O God, thou wilt not despise

And that is precisely what King David is offering, a broken heart. He knows God recognizes the sincerity.

On to the reason this verse is pro-sacrifice.

     18- Do good in thy good pleasure unto Zion: build thou the walls of Jerusalem.
     19- Then shalt thou be pleased with the sacrifices of righteousness, with burnt offering and whole burnt offering: then shall they offer bullocks upon thine altar.

And there you have it. Until verse 19, we had a decent argument against animal sacrifices. I'm sure that's why a lot of Christian vegans use it. But 19 comes in and puts the kibosh on it.

Having said that, chapters 50 and 51 combined hold tremendous evidence that God allowed but never wanted sacrifice.

King David committed capital sins of murder and adultery; he deserved the death penalty. But God forgave him *without animal sacrifice*, because God loves.

There was a time God recognized animal sacrifice under specific conditions. First, the person had to be sincerely regretful for their sin. Otherwise, their animal sacrifice was worthless and called blood-guiltiness. Blood-guiltiness is equivalent to murder.

CHAPTER 44: PROVERBS 12:10 – BE KIND TO ANIMALS

R ighteous people don't abuse animals.

Proverbs chapter 12 verse 10
A righteous man regardeth the life of his beast: but the tender mercies (compassion) *of the wicked are cruel.*

This verse is a vegan powerhouse. The obvious vegan take-away is humans are to have consideration for the needs of animals. A second take-away attacks the idea of humane killing.

5Ws

King Solomon is credited with writing this. That's a good thing. Christians recognize Solomon for being the wisest man ever. I want to show how Sol got that wisdom.

1st Kings chapter 3 verse 5
The LORD appeared to Solomon in a dream by night, and God said, "Ask what I shall give you."

Crazy, huh? God himself is acting like a genie from a magic lamp saying, "*I'll give you whatever you want.*" For me, that would be a 1966 Batmobile, but luckily for Israel, Solomon requested something altruistic. Check this out:

1st Kings chapter 3 verse 9

(Solomon talking to God) *Give therefore thy servant* (himself) *an understanding heart to judge thy people, that I may discern between good and bad*

That's fancy talk; Sol asks for wisdom to distinguish between good and evil. He wants to rule over God's people in *the correct way*. Yep, our political leaders could learn a lot from this story. Also, we have a wise king showing us how he uses his dominion.

And in verse 12, we see God delivering on the request:

12- Behold, I (God) *have done according to thy words: lo, I have given thee* (Solomon) *a wise and an understanding heart; so that there was none like thee before thee, neither after thee shall any arise like unto thee*

God makes Solomon the wisest man there ever was or will be. God also gave him an understanding heart. This leaves us with a new and improved King Solomon. Look at what this "God-Powered" wise man tells us regarding animals.

Proverbs chapter 12 verse 10

A righteous man regardeth (has consideration for, cares) *the life of his beast* (bhemah = cattle, livestock)*: but the tender mercies* (kindest acts) *of the wicked* (rasha = wicked, criminal) *are cruel.*

This is not some radical vegan activist sneaking this line into the Bible. God blessed Solomon to be the wisest man in the Bible, and Solomon says a righteous person will care for animals. Simple. Isn't being a righteous person what a Christian should strive to be? So, Christians should care for animals. Righteous people don't abuse animals. Vegan Win!

Tender Mercies

I've had great use with the *tender mercies* line (verse 10) when I get Christians in favor of "Humane Killing." First off, humans can not humanely kill someone that does not want to be killed. But, *in the minds of the wicked*, they genuinely consider they are offering *tender mercy* (kindness) to the animal when the death is as painless as possible. They see their cruelty (offering a painless death) as merciful. Get it? But that's not mercy. No matter how painless, they are ignoring the animal does not want or need to die at all! The creature's death is only because of a selfish lust for animal flesh. Needless death does not come from an understanding heart. Try to point that out to the carnist.

Humane

Killing healthy animals for taste pleasure is sinful and has nothing to do with humane killing. In our culture, merciful killing (humane) is real, but only employed as a last resort when the needs of the animal are put first. Imagine elderly animals with some unrelenting pain thing to relieve suffering.

Another of my nit-picky warnings

The non-vegan undertone of this verse is animals are property and can be exploited for labor. These instructions of kindness came when the culture understood an ox was used to plow the fields. They rode horses and camels for transportation. The people reading this verse are told working animals (beasts) are not to be maltreated. Not vegan, but in that era, it's a move in a positive direction.

If we apply this principle today, with the invention of tractors and access to technology never seen in Bible days, we have eliminated any biblical application for using animals as "beasts of burden".

These verses can take another application for us. Animals are used in circuses, rodeos, and other forms of entertainment for human pleasure. If you meet any Christians working in these industries, you can use these verses to challenge them. In order for animals to do tricks, they must be trained. This training involves starvation, water deprivation, and/or threat of physical pain (whips) to force animals into unnatural behaviors. Tricks are totally unnecessary and often painful to the animal. None of that shows kindness or concern for the good of the animal. These tricks have one purpose, to make a profit for the human that enslaves them.

253

CHAPTER 45:
PROVERBS 23:20 –
MEAT COMA

Don't hang out with drunk, fat friends.

A proverb is a saying, a catch-phrase illustrating a truth or maybe shares some common sense advice. The Bible has an entire book of them. Can you guess what it's called? Proverbs. Duh. The 23rd chapter has a proverb which appears vegan as it warns against hanging out with meat-eaters. Have a peek:

Proverbs chapter 23 verse 20
Do not join those who drink too much (gluttonous) *wine or gorge themselves on meat* (Basar = Flesh),
21- For drunkards and gluttons become poor, and drowsiness clothes them in rags.

On the surface, these verses criticize individuals who consume meat. That sounds very vegan, but the context does no such thing. It doesn't condemn the consumption of meat, only the <u>overindulgence of eating meat</u>. Let's opening this up with verse 20.

Do not join those who drink <u>too much</u> wine or <u>gorge them selves on meat</u>,

Please notice the words I underlined.
Gorge*: eat a large amount greedily; fill oneself with food.*
It doesn't say to avoid people who eat meat, but those who <u>gorge</u>

themselves on too much meat. Only those who eat and drink too much are targeted. A casual eating of meat is not a problem in this verse.

21- For drunkards and gluttons become poor, and drowsiness clothes them in rags.

The reason for this warning is a person will become poor and lazy. It's just a common sense urging that gluttonous behaviors are harmful to health and wealth. Sorry vegans, this verse is not about animal welfare. If it did, it would say something like: *do not hang out with people who eat meat because it's animal abuse and animal abuse is an evil sin.* No, this verse only shows concern for human wellbeing.

What's the vegan angle?

I suggest we connect how these verses link eating meat and being gluttonous. The verse specifically condemns those who gorge themselves on meat and wine. This shows eating meat is a danger equal to, and right alongside, alcoholism. Why? Because meat-eating is as addicting as alcohol. Both can cause a person to be poor and lazy. Christians often preach against alcohol, but this shows they should avoid both equally. That is our vegan attack.

One more vegan use for ya.

Verse 20 says, *Do not join those who drink too much wine or gorge them selves on meat* (Basar = Flesh)
This verse explicitly says *Meat.* Why? Because there is no concern for overeating fruits and veggies. The Bible connects gluttony with consuming animal flesh and booze only. I see no place where the Bible considers overeating fruits or veggies as gluttony.
The carnist Christian you are speaking to will agree being a drunk is sinful. Having the Bible connect the negatives of drunkenness and eating meat works for our vegan activism.
For extra credit, do a Bible search for all the listings connecting lust, gluttony drunkenness, and meat eating.

CHAPTER 46:
HOSEA 8:13 – GO BACK
TO SLAVERY

Eat your way back to slavery

Hosea chapter 8 verse 13

*As for my sacrificial gifts, They sacrifice the flesh and eat it,
But the LORD has taken no delight in them. Now He will
remember their iniquity, And punish them for their sins; They will
return* (God will send them back) *to Egypt.*

This verse sounds as if God is threatening to send Israel back into
Egyptian captivity (slavery) as punishment for eating animal flesh?

I wish a verse like that existed, but nope, not this verse. God wasn't
upset with them for making animal sacrifices. He was upset with their
disobedience and their continuous worship of false gods. It is their lack of
repentance that brought on the threat to return them to Egyptian slavery.

5Ws

Hosea is a profit. He's a good guy. He lived in the northern kingdom of
Israel during the rule of a corrupt king. The people of Israel aren't much
better than their lousy king. They keep screwing up by sacrificing to other
gods and worshiping pagan idols. God sends Hosea to remind them of their
evil. Hosea tells them they're not keeping the commandments. They
worship false gods, and if they don't change, they will end up in slavery
again.

Israel was eating the meat of the sacrifices, thus "joining" themselves to the pagan gods. Israel was half right in doing sacrifices, but still totally wrong. Their sacrifices are properly done, but empty of meaning. God knows the emptiness, and his punishment is letting them become slaves again to Egypt.

On the surface, this appears to be an anti-meat eating verse, but it's really not.

CHAPTER 47: MATTHEW 6:9 – THE LORD'S PRAYER

Thy vegan kingdom come.

Every Christian has memorized the Lord's prayer. Heck, it's so common atheists can recite it. This massive familiarity is very useful for vegan advocacy.

There are two pieces of vegan gold in this prayer, and I absolutely love using them both.

This prayer is in the New Testament books of Luke, in chapter 11 and in Matthew, chapter 6. I will start with Matthew's telling of the prayer.

Matthew chapter 6 verse 9
After this manner therefore pray ye: <u>Our Father which art in heaven</u>, Hallowed be thy name.

We start off with Jesus teaching the disciples how to pray. We learn God is in Heaven and in the next verse, Heaven is separate from earth.

10- <u>Thy kingdom come</u>. Thy will be done in earth, <u>as it is in heaven</u>.

This is the first punch in the nose to a carnist Christian. When a meat-eater prays this prayer, he is asking God to bring the kingdom of heaven to earth. That is huge! Why? Because we learned earlier that the kingdom (see Isaiah chapter 11) will be 100% vegan.

There is no death in heaven and there is no death in the future kingdom. When there is no death, there are no cheeseburgers, or bacon, or any animal products. Don't you just love it! Carnist Christians are praying for the end of meat-eating every time they recite the Lord's prayer. These goofballs don't even know it! Hah!

11- Give us this day our <u>daily bread</u> (artos: bread, a loaf).

Oh, this just keeps getting better for vegan outreach. Jesus is teaching the apostles to pray for their daily need for food. Jesus specifically tells them to ask for bread, not salami, not corned beef, not pastrami or any kind of meat, but bread.

12- And forgive us our debts, as we forgive our debtors.

I know this is called "The Lord's Prayer" but right here, in verse 12, it speaks of forgiveness for sins. OK, cool, but Jesus has no sins to be forgiven. This is not the Lord's (Jesus) Prayer, but an example of prayer for the disciples. In actuality, this is more of a "Sinners Prayer". Bible geek time over, back to vegan outreach in verse 13:

And lead us not into temptation, but deliver us from evil: <u>For thine is the kingdom, and the power, and the glory,</u> for ever. Amen.

Look at who the kingdom belongs to. Who has the power in the kingdom? Look at who gets all the glory. The kingdom, the power and the glory are for God. You cannot sneak human supremacy or human dominion into the kingdom in any way. God is not handing over dominion to the people. Humans cannot corrupt the gift of dominion and turn it into domination. Nope, the kingdom is God's and eating animals isn't in the future for Christians.

CHAPTER 48: MATTHEW 6:26 – MORE THAN BIRDS

Humans are worth more than birds, so Christians can torture them

The argument presented to vegan activists is this: there are 3 places in the New Testament where Jesus says humans are worth more than birds. Somehow, that allows Christians to ignore their suffering so they can eat their bodies. We are going to look at those verses and learn how to deal with the claim. Let's first look at:

Matthew chapter 6 verse 26
Behold the fowls of the air: for they sow not, neither do they reap, nor gather into barns; yet your heavenly Father feedeth them. <u>Are ye not much better than they?</u>

5Ws

Jesus is speaking to the disciples who are in a bad way. They are concerned where they will get their next meal, where they will stay, and they are in constant fear for their lives.

Jesus is telling them to just chill out, God has got their backs. He uses birds (fowl) as an example of how God has the entire world under His care. This verse is about emotional comfort during times of fear and worry. If a meat-eater uses this verse to set up a ranking structure of humans over birds, they are missing the point.

Two-thirds of the verse

Jesus saying humans are better is only *the end* of the verse. The opening ⅔ of the verse shows Jesus using animals to represent God's immense love for humanity. The verse says God's love for animals (fowl/birds) is so strong that he feeds and cares for each of their needs. God's love for the birds must be tremendous for this comparison to make sense. It would be silly if Jesus was comparing humans to something of low value. Like…a pencil. Try it out; imagine if Jesus said, *"Are you not much better than pencils"?*

Zero-sum game

I try to convince the carnist Christians that God does not put humans and animals in competition. Often, Christians selfishly view life as an "us versus them" (humans vs. animals) kind of situation. They mistakenly assume, if animals are given any small degree of importance, then humans get less importance. This is a selfish human concept coupled with selfish human fears. God does not make His love a "zero-sum" game where one species gains are the other species' loss. God is not limited to only "100 units" of love, and if animals get 20 units, that leaves humans only 80 units. God's love is limitless, and He can give 100 units of love to all His creations equally. God's love is endless, and He has plenty to share, birds included. Humans lose nothing if God cares for animals.

Let's look at it from a "money" angle as reported in:

Matthew chapter 10 verse

29- *Are not two sparrows sold for <u>a farthing</u> (a few pennies)? and one of them shall not fall on the ground without your Father.*

30- But the very <u>hairs of your head</u> are all numbered.

31- Fear ye not therefore, ye are of more value than many sparrows

I say the people hearing these words understood this in an insulting way. God's love goes beyond money, but here is a comparison being made in human terms of financial value. Humans put a value of a few pennies on sparrows, but God knows when every single sparrow falls to the ground. Imagine how they felt being told God cares for something they treat as disposable property. God is being nice, I would have said it differently:

"You idiots torment and kill over 50 billion chickens a year, and God sees each one you kill. He knows you lock them in tiny cages, you cut off their toes and beaks, you pump their bodies full of harmful chemicals till the day you hang them upside-down and cut their throats, all for your gluttonous taste pleasure. You treat them as cheap replaceable objects yet God knows each one of those chicks you abuse just as he knows the numbers of hairs on your head."

Did saying it like that make more sense? Too harsh? Nahhhhhh.

A year later, Jesus uses a similar illustration:

Luke chapter 12 verses 6 & 7
6- Are not five sparrows sold for two farthings, and not one of them is forgotten before God?

When Jesus quotes the monetary value of <u>*two farthings*</u> (a few cents), he uses the value humans put on the birds. To humans, sparrows are only pennies, but to God, they are never forgotten and cared for in every facet of their lives. Do you notice the contrast? This is not setting up human superiority, but shaming them in their low view of animals (birds). But what if it is human superiority? So what! These verses show that *even if* humans are above animals, God still has love and concern for their care. Being made in His image, so should Christians.

Moving on, in verse:

7- But even the very hairs of your head are all numbered. Fear not therefore: <u>ye are of more value than many sparrows.</u>

When Jesus says humans are worth more <u>*than many sparrows,*</u> it's not intended to show humans are better. I mean really, today, a sparrow's financial value is $1 at the most. I could multiply $1 by many sparrows; oh heck, let's multiply it by 100 sparrows. I end up with $100 bucks. Does the carnist Christian realize if he goes with humans are worth more than "many sparrows," then humans are worth maybe a hundred bucks? Haha! I love this argument.

What I've noticed is God cares immensely for the animals, and people don't. I continuously point this out to the carnist. God values things differently, and so should we.

I think of **Matthew chapter 18 verse 12**
If any man has a hundred sheep, and one of them has gone astray, does he not leave the ninety-nine on the mountains and go and search for the one that is straying?

In this story, Jesus presents a lesson on value that is dramatically different from the people. He is saying a good shepherd leaves 99 safe sheep to go save a lost one. But a bad shepherd wouldn't risk losing the 99 just to save one because the financial value of the 99 is so much greater. Humans put *a monetary value* on animals to determine their worth, but Jesus puts a spiritual value on every living creature. Jesus offers equal love, be it 1 or 99. This is another time that animal welfare is discussed to show human value.

God is whipped

Come to think about it, animals might have a better arrangement than humans. Re-read this verse from the Sermon on the Mount:

Matthew chapter 6 verse 26
Behold the fowls of the air; for they sow not, neither do they reap,
nor gather into barns; yet your heavenly father feedeth them. Are
you not much better than they are?

Jesus says the animals don't plant seeds (sow) but still God feeds them. The animals don't tend to their gardens (reap), but God feeds them. They don't build barns, but God provides housing for them. They don't have to cook, clean or do anything; God does it for them. It seems the animals have God wrapped around their little finger! Humans work for food and a place to stay. So who's winning in this deal, huh? Ya, I'm a goof.

CHAPTER 49: MATTHEW 7 – JUDGE NOT

Jesus says not to judge, then teaches us how to judge.

I bet every activist had a Christian say, *"Jesus tells us not to judge."* Those Christians should read the rest of the chapter. Further in, Jesus instructs *how to judge* correctly, not with hypocrisy but with love.

This can be very supportive of vegan advocacy, and I use it often. I'll share an aggressive way to approach this verse but also tell you not to be aggressive because, well, it's not nice.

The idea of not judging comes from the seventh chapter of Matthew.

Matthew chapter 7 verse 1-5
1- Judge not, that ye be not judged.

If this chapter had only this one verse, I could understand why Christians say we can't judge. But Jesus wasn't done talking:

2- for with <u>what judgment ye judge, ye shall be judged</u> and with what measure the mete (use) *it shall be measured to you again.*

Did you catch that? The very next verse gives us the rules on how we will be judged. It says, if you judge someone, be prepared to be judged by the same measure.

Well, Duh! I'm a vegan, so yeah, sure. Come, judge me and my meat-eating; I'm good with that because I don't eat meat!

There is also a dispensational problem for the carnist Christian. If a

"Saved by Grace" Christian holds to this, *don't judge or you will be judged* idea, they are living under the Old Testament Law of conditional blessings. Christians, saved by Grace, will never be judged. Their judgment hangs with Christ on the cross. It's over. This verse is a works-oriented message of legalism. Legalism does not apply to the Christian church today.

This gets even better for vegans:

3- And why beholdest thou the moat (small pieces of wood) *that is in thy brother's eye but considerest not the beam that is in thine own eye?*

Ok, mote is a weird word. A mote is a tiny speck of wood or sawdust.

4- Or how will thou say to thy brother, let me pull the mote out of thine eye: and behold, a beam is in thine own eye?

It's not that activists can't judge; it's saying don't judge hypocritically. Don't call attention to the speck of sawdust in someone's eye while you got a massive 2X4 in your eye. Don't call someone out on their sin if you're doing the same sin yourself.

Read what I underlined in the next verse. It caught me in an activist way.

5-Thou hypocrite first cast out the beam (2 x 4) *out of thine own eye: and then shalt thou see clearly to cast out the mote* (sawdust) *out of thy brother's eye.*

We're back to that 2 x 4 in your eye. Did these people have no goggles? Verse 5 is permission to judge, but don't be hypocritical. We are instructed to first get the 2X4 out of our own eye. Then, we can see clearly to get the wood chip out of our brother's eye. But did you pick up what I heard? Let me lay it out. You are a vegan. You've got that meat-eating and animal abusing 2 x 4 out of your eye. Now, you are ideally equipped and approved by Jesus to help them get the meat-eating 2 x 4 out of their eye! These verses used to stop judging are actually a call to vegan activism. Can you dig it?

A different view

Let's consider the application of these verses using alcoholism as an example. Let's say you are an alcoholic who has quit drinking for...oh, I dunno; let's say, you've been sober for 5 years. You've beaten the sin of alcoholism; you've got control over it. This puts you in a perfect place to help someone with an alcohol problem. As an ex-drinker, you qualify to make a well-informed judgment of their activities. Verse 5 gives you biblical permission to advise others on beating alcoholism.

Can you see how that works for vegan activism? Vegans beat the addiction to animal flesh, so we have biblical approval to aid others.

Side note: similar approach of judging in Luke chapter 6 if you want extra credit stars.

So you can judge, but don't run off being judgmental and rude. Let this verse be a reminder:

2nd Timothy chapter 2 verses 24 & 25
24- And the servant of the Lord must not strive (quarrelsome), *but be gentle unto all men, apt to teach, patient,*
   25- In meekness instructing those that oppose themselves; if God may grant them repentance to the acknowledging of the truth

For me, this verse is a reminder to be nice. And if they're rude, still be nice. Be patient, have a goal to educate. You may have pointed out their sin in proper fashion, but no one likes to have their sin brought to their attention. They might get hurt or defensive; they might get rude but don't take it personally. It's human nature to go on the defensive when criticized. Always strive to be nice. I need to remind myself of this often. It seems the older I get, the more frustrated I become, which leads to obnoxious advocacy. Not good.

Ask which judgement verse

When Christians quote from the Bible, ask, "to which verse are you referring"? The vast majority of the time, they won't be able to tell you where or know its full context. This is not a stab at them. I'm guilty too. Luckily, we live in the age of cell phones. I keep a Bible app on my phone to show the carnist the entire text of the verse they quote. You don't even have to be shy about it. You can reply, *"I heard that verse on judging and I got a note of it on my phone. Maybe you can help me with your understanding because I see it differently"*. Then, bust out your phone and continue on with your discussion and show its true context.

How to judge

The same Jesus that said "judge not" teaches us how to judge. So let's start with proof of judging:

John chapter 7 verse 24:
Judge not according to the appearance, but judge righteous judgment.

Time for another stupid story. I'll use me as an example. Since the 1970s, I've had long hair. If you're not old enough to remember the 70s, the perception was, long-haired guys are on drugs. I've been straight edge (drug and alcohol-free lifestyle) my entire life. But the judgment was, and still is, I am a druggie. One day, when I was in an alley with two short-haired friends, they (not me) were smoking pot. Unexpectedly, the police rolled up, cuffed me, and pushed my face down on the hood of their squad car, and searched my pockets. My short-haired friends had to answer random questions, no cuffs, no searches of pockets, just questions. See what happened? That was judging by appearance. Oh, and I've learned that having long hair violates my white privilege perks.

However, Jesus approves righteous judgment. If a Christian's food is sourced from beastiality, animal abuse, or for gluttonous pleasure, telling them it is wrong, is giving righteous (truthful) judgement. We've got approval.

Activists may need examples showing permission and instructions for judging.

1st Corinthians chapter 5, starting in verses 9 and up to **13-** "Purge the evil person from among you."

We are to determine (judge) who is evil within the church and kick them out if necessary.

Romans chapter 12 verse 9 says:
Let love be without dissimulation. Abhor (hate) *that which is evil; cleave* (connect) *to that which is good.*

How can we know what evil to hate if we can't judge something as evil? We can't cleave to something good if we can't judge it as good.

One more:

James chapter 5 verses 19 & 20:
19- Brethren, if any of you do err (wander or stray) *from the truth, and one convert him;*
    20- Let him know (judge) *that he which converteth the sinner from the error of his way shall save a soul from death, and shall hide a multitude of sins.*

We are commanded to *let them know* (judge) if a brother wanders from the truth. This is God-given approval to make a judgment, such as telling them to stop abusing animals.

So to my Christian vegan activists, you got the OK to judge other believers on their immoral food choices, but I suggest being careful. Don't judge to make yourself feel superior or better; you are there for the animals first.

So what if I do?

I have had fun with this response too. When challenged on being judgmental, I reply, *so what?* As a vegan activist, I have no power to enforce anything. I tell the carnist; I am not God or the boss of you. I am not judging your soul or your salvation. I can not put you in jail or control your food purchases. I am just some random guy making an observation of a Christian choosing violence when compassionate choices are available. You can ignore my judgements if you like. I have no power in your life, so what are you so upset about?

Proverbs 25:15
And a soft tongue (not aggressive words) *breaketh the bone*

Sometimes, a soft tongue is needed to break a person. Be nice and lift the people that have fallen. Don't behave like me at this lunch.

Pastor: I don't want to go to lunch with you; it feels like you're always judging me, haha.

Steve: Nope, only making observations based on what you teach about compassion and kindness.

Pastor: You forget Jesus ate fish.

Steve: I'm not having lunch with Jesus in the first century. I'm here with you, and unlike anyone in Jesus' day, you have cruelty free options. Every place we go, you choose animal abuse.

Pastor: See, there you go, judging me.

Steve: No, I'm observing your habit. Every meal you get is made from animal abuse. You make a choice that contradicts your teachings from the pulpit.

Pastor: I never taught not to eat meat.

Steve: You teach beastiality is evil, then pay people to forcefully do sexual acts on animals. You teach mercy but do not extend that to animals except your pet dog.

Pastor: That's judging.

Steve: No, that's an observation of your hypocrisy and sin. If you taught it's ok to shove an electric dildo in a bull's butthole while holding its penis, I wouldn't be able to criticize. Or, if you taught it's ok to shoot a dog in the head with a bolt gun, I wouldn't be able to correct you when you pay people to do it to cows for gluttonous eating pleasures.

Pastor: I never spoke about dogs like that.

Steve: Your lunch purchase shows it's ok to hurt cows, chickens, and pigs but not dogs? I'm confused.

Pastor: You are twisting my words as usual.

Steve: I'm only observing your actions. You preach on kindness and mercy but arbitrarily drew the line at dogs.

Pastor: Why do you have to be like that?

Steve: Like what, honest?

Ok, I was in a mood. What can I say? Everyplace we went together I could get a vegan option, but he got cruelty. I was aggressive because we had gentle conversations many times before. I turned the other cheek so many times I ran out of cheeks. I was done. Bottom line, it's not judging when you bring truth to their attention. Christians purchasing items created from dead animals are taking part in animal abuse. It's not judgmental or hate to make them acknowledge that.

CHAPTER 50:
MATTHEW 12 – BETTER
THAN SHEEP

Pull the wool over your eyes

If accused of pulling the wool over someone's eyes, you have deceived them. That's part of what the Pharisees had done in this chapter of Matthew. They convinced Israel the Sabbath is a strict set of rules made for man to follow. With a reference to sheep, Jesus brings their deception to everyone's attention.

Matthew chapter 12 verse 12
How much then is a _man better than a sheep_? Wherefore it is lawful to do well on the sabbath days.

Christians will quote verse 12 to prove humans are better than animals. Reading only verse 12, I see how they reach such an understanding. This verse is not Jesus establishing a hierarchy between humans and animals. His reply is an attack on the corrupt religious leaders (Pharisees) of the time. These leaders are trying to trap Jesus into breaking a religious law. Sneaky jerks!

5Ws

Jesus has people who love him, others who aren't sure about him, and the Pharisees, well, they hate Jesus and want him dead. What they're trying to do in Matthew chapter 12 is trick Jesus into breaking the Sabbath law of not working one day a week.

Keeping the Sabbath is one of the 10 Commandments (the written law). But the Pharisees (the Jewish leaders of the time) also followed the *oral law*. There were many extra rules in the oral law about not working on the Sabbath. For example, healing a sick person is considered "work." Hence, the Pharisees believed healing on the Sabbath was a big no-no. Jesus was having no part of that. We have to step back into verse 10 to get an immediate context.

The Entrapment

10- And, behold, there was a man which had his hand withered (Withered: dry and shriveled from age or disease). *And they (Pharisees) asked him* (Jesus), *saying, Is it lawful to heal on the sabbath days? So that they might accuse him.*

Did you notice the entrapment process begins when they said, *so that they might accuse him?* The **NIV** translates that line as: *Looking for a reason to bring charges against Jesus.*

Will Jesus heal this man in need, thus breaking the oral law? I say the Pharisees (the corrupt religious leaders who hated Jesus) created this "set-up" knowing Jesus would heal the bad hand man. The purpose was to put Jesus on the spot in front of his followers. Jesus' reply has absolutely nothing to do with establishing human supremacy. Let's continue with the entrapment.

11- And he (Jesus) *said unto them, What man shall there be among you, that shall have one sheep, and if it fall into a pit on the sabbath day, will he not lay hold on it, and lift it out* (work)?

Ask yourself, why use a strange analogy with a sheep stuck in a pit? Why is Jesus comparing a sheep in need to a human in need? Check it out.

12- How much more valuable is a person than a sheep! Wherefore it is lawful to do well (do good) *on the sabbath days.*

Jesus knew the Pharisees put a financial value on their sheep. With such high value, they wouldn't challenge "working" on the Sabbath to rescue their sheep. This comparison made it obvious the Pharisees cared more for their possessions (the sheep) than for a poor human with the (withered) bad hand. Jesus proclaims helping a sheep, or a man, is equal reason to show love and mercy. Jesus puts a spiritual value on the sheep while the religious leaders' only concern is financial. Remember earlier with the bird comparison? Same kind of thing.

It's fine if the comparison shows humans are better, but it isn't very significant. This comparison elevates the view of animals closer to the value of humans.

13- Then saith he to the man, Stretch forth thine hand. And he stretched it forth; and it was restored whole, like as the other.

The Pharisees had corrupted the Sabbath so much that doing a work involving their money (saving a sheep) is an acceptable reason to break the Sabbath. But healing someone (showing love or mercy) is unacceptable! How messed up is that? Jesus is not establishing a hierarchy of human over animal. He is shaming the religious leaders for the lack of love. We see this same corruption in organized religion today. When "religion" doesn't allow doing good deeds, we've got some serious problems. Jesus is pointing out animals are worth breaking their idea of the Sabbath and so are humans.

Their efforts to entrap Jesus backfired. Jesus ended up showing everybody the Pharisees cared only for their personal wealth. Look at what he said.

Mark chapter 2 verse 27
And he said unto them, The Sabbath was made for man, and not man for the Sabbath:

Jesus knew the law because...well, he wrote it! He showed the Pharisees were using the regulations for financial gain, but Jesus brought it back to what the Sabbath should be about: rest, love, and mercy. This disturbed the Pharisees, as proven by their response.

14 -Then the Pharisees went out, and held a council against him, how they might destroy him

Notice, they didn't respond as if Jesus's words proved human supremacy over sheep. No need. They already felt superior. This was shocking because Jesus is putting animals on a level very close to human value.

Jesus *"working"* (good deed) during the Sabbath is the issue. After he does his healing thing, the Pharisees come up with a plan for killing him. Are you seeing this chapter's meaning? This corrupt religious group is trying to keep a hold on their place of power over the people. Jesus threatens their position with a sheep story the people can relate to and understand. It's not meant to establish the value of humans over animals.

Supremacy tho...

If the meat-eating Christian wants to claim human supremacy here, don't let it bother you. Superior or not, this verse does not permit killing animals because they might have a lesser value. Just the contrary. Jesus says people can break one of the 10 commandments to save a sheep, making sheep (animals) of tremendous value. Additionally, activists can suggest Jesus put the healing of a human in a similar category of need as an animal (sheep) in trouble. How equalizing is that! The point is, animals do have value. That value was determined by God when he created them. An animal's value is not determined by how much humans enjoy the way they taste, but based on God's intention for his creation.

Before we leave this sheep story, we have another animal stuck in a well. **Luke chapter 14, verse 5.**

Then he asked them, "If one of you has a child or an ox that falls into a well on the Sabbath day, will you not immediately pull it out?"

The Sabbath is a big deal to the Jews. Again, Jesus is giving permission to break the Sabbath to save a human or an ox. Are you catching that? "If" humans are above animals, it does not matter in this verse. A human child or an ox equally deserves help, even if it requires breaking the sabbath law. In this chapter, we see a level of equality for humans and animals. Also, there were a lot of open wells in those days. Clumsy kids and farm animals, beware!

CHAPTER 51: MATTHEW 14 – MULTIPLYING THE LOAVES

Feeding the multitudes

There are two separate occasions that Jesus miraculously multiplied loaves of bread and fish...or did he?

On the first reported occasion, he fed a group of 5000. On the second occasion, he provided for a group of 4000. We are going to study those verses and compare them between each of the Gospel reports. If you are observant, you might find something...fishy. Hahaha, I just get worse.

5Ws

To set this up for ya, the disciples bring news to Jesus that John the Baptist had his head cut off. Harsh times! Jesus goes on a boat to get away from it all. He returns to a large group of people waiting for him. It happened in the middle of nowhere. People were getting hungry and UberEats was not a thing yet, so they had no food.

Let's start with:

Breaking bread

In this story, the breaking of the bread mentioned is a literal breaking or tearing of bread into pieces. Eating bread with someone had additional meaning in their culture. It was a way of connecting with others. Let's say you and I share a hot, gooey vegan cinnamon roll. It was one roll, and we each ate of it. We ingest that sweet cinnamon goodness, and it becomes our bodies through digestion. That single roll unites us. Isn't that sweet? Hahaha, cinnamon rolls are sweet, get it? But ya, our bodies are now, in part, made of the same substance. Culture and custom say we are bodily joined. I think this custom still carries on today when we asked someone to join us for dinner.

Feeding the 5000

Mathew chapter 14 verse 17
And they say unto him, we have here but five loaves, and two fishes.

My first issue is with the word *we*. It gives the false impression the disciples carried fish and bread with them. Not true and as you read on, this chapter will give evidence the disciples were veggie heads. We learn in the Gospel of John, chapter 6:9, they collected the fish from a kid in the crowd. More on this later.

18- He (Jesus) *said, Bring them hither to me.*
19- And he commanded the multitude to sit down on the grass, and took the five loaves, and the two fishes, and looking up to the heaven, he blessed, and break, and gave the loaves to his disciples, and the disciples to the multitude.

Just bread

I underlined the word break. Think about it, you can break bread, but you don't *break a fish*. It just doesn't work that way. The next non-fishy thing in verse 19 is Jesus giving only the loaves back to the disciples. "*and gave the loaves to his disciples.*" Although the disciples gave him bread and (allegedly) fish, it didn't say he gave the fish back to the disciples (verse 19) to disperse amongst the multitudes of people. It only mentions the loaves of bread being distributed.

Now let's look at another view of the same story in **Mark chapter 6 verse 36:**

Send them away, that they may go into the country round about, and into the villages, and buy themselves bread: for they have nothing to eat.

In verse 36, they're telling Jesus the people have nothing to eat, so let's send them to get bread. Fish was not even on their mind.

37- He (Jesus) *answered and said unto them, Give ye them to eat. and they* (the apostles) *say unto him, Shall we go and buy 200 pennyworth of bread, and give them to eat?*

In verse 37, they say we have 200 pennyworth. I don't know what value a "pennyworth" is, so let's assume they had $200. Whatever the amount, they spoke only of buying bread, not fish. Think what that implies. These dudes used to be fishermen, and they didn't offer to go fishing. Their idea of food is bread and bread alone. More evidence they were all veg-heads. Cool, huh?

Moving on:

38- *He saith unto them, how many loaves have ye? Go and see. And when they knew, they say, Five, and two fishes*

In verse 38, and Jesus asks, "*How many loaves of bread do you have*"? Jesus did not ask how many fish, only bread. We can see, this wasn't about fish.

So his disciples gather up food from the people. They tell him they have five loaves of bread and a couple of fish. Jesus has been focused on bread, bread, and more bread. It is only because *the people* brought fish, that fish is introduced to this story.

God always worked with people where they culturally are, with intent to move them in the direction He wants them to go. God does this repeatedly throughout the Bible with the Jews. I suggest Jesus is doing the same. He's taking what they got and working with it.

We are still in the gospel of **Mark chapter 6:**

39- *And he commanded them to make all sit down by companies upon the green grass*
    40- *And they sat down in ranks, by 100's, and by '50s.*
    41- *And when he had taken the five loaves and the two fishes, he looked up to the heaven, and blessed, and break the loaves, and gave them to his disciples to set before them; and two fishes divided he among them all.*

In verse 41, we have Jesus breaking loaves of bread and giving this bread to the disciples to share among the people. Only after he multiplied the bread does the verse mention, he divided the fish. It could be implied Jesus gave his disciples the fish and not the multitudes. Regardless, if Jesus is creating dead fish, no suffering is involved.

Side note: When scribes (assistants) wrote this stuff, they weren't doing it on the spot, at the moment this was going down. The writers recorded these versions many years after. Some of them were not even there. These scribes were not eyewitnesses. They were writing what they knew of only from oral traditions they heard. I mention that because it sounds like the fish part was added. It was always about bread, bread, and more bread, and then, suddenly—Pow!—"*and the fish.*" I mean, come on now, who talks like that?

When I read it, that fish part seems forced into the story. It's saying, "I fed them so much bread we have left over baskets full of this bread. Oh ya, and fish":

> **42-** *And they did or eat, and were filled.*
> **43-** *And they took up 12 baskets full of the fragments, and of the fishes.*
> **44-** *And they that did eat of the loaves were about 5000 men.*

Verse 44 says, *"They did eat of the loaves were about 5000"*. Loaves again? Where's the fish? Here, in verse 44, we are back to acknowledging only the bread.

Fresh fish

Consider the situation. If you were traveling far away from food sources, would you bring a fish? They didn't have coolers in those days. Fish will quickly spoil, but bread lasts for days.

I say the fish part was added and I'm not alone with my no fish position. Several of the early church fathers echo my fish-less sentiments. Most pastors recognize and accept these, but many Christians are unfamiliar with.

Against the heathen, Arnobius
Demonstratio Evangelica, Eusebius
Against heresies, Irenaeus

These books, written by big-time church leaders of their time (the first, second and third centuries), also write of this story. All three guys report loaves only. *Never* a mention of fish.

Back to the Bible and every Christian's irrefutable source, Jesus. The nail in the coffin for *any presence of fish* is when Jesus retells the story in Matthew 16. Jesus does not mention fish either; check it out:

Matthew chapter 16 verse 9
Do you not yet understand, neither remember that five loaves of the 5000 and how many baskets you took up?

> *10- Neither the seven loaves of the 4000 and how many baskets you took up?*

And again in Mark chapter 8 verse 19
When I brake the five loaves among five thousand, how many baskets full of fragments took ye up? They say unto him, Twelve.

> *20- And when the seven among four thousand, how many baskets full of fragments took ye up? And they said, Seven.*

Here we have Jesus recalling the story with no mention of fish, only

bread. See? I'm not so crazy to say the fish was added later.
Now, compare the story as recorded in the Gospel of John.

John chapter 6 verse 5
When Jesus lifted up his eyes, he saw a great company come unto him, he saith unto Phillip, whence shall <u>we buy bread</u>, that these may eat?

More bread confirmations:

6- And this he (Jesus) *said to prove* (test) *him: for he himself knew what he would do.*
7- Philip answered him, <u>200 pennyworth of bread</u> is not sufficient for them, that every one of them may take a little.

Again, nobody is talking of fish, ugh! I can make the point about there being only bread just so many times before it gets monotonous.

8- One of his disciples Andrew, Simon and Peter's brother, saith unto him,
9- There is a lad here, which hath five barley loaves, and two small fishes: but what are they among so many?

In verse number 9, we learn how fish get into the story. A kid in the crowd brought two. Do you know what this means? We can find two vegan wins from this. First, Jesus and his entourage don't travel with the fish. This is more evidence (not proof) that JC and the boys were veg-heads. The second vegan win, in a gathering of 5000 people, they can only get two fish. That confirms how rarely people eat animal products.

10- And Jesus said make the men and sit down. Now there was much grass in the place. So the men sat down, in number about 5000.
11- And Jesus <u>took the loaves</u>; and when he had given thanks, he distributed to the disciples, and the disciples to them that were set down; and <u>likewise of the fishes</u> as much as they would.

When I read verse 11, I notice an uncomfortable sounding addition *"likewise of the fishes."* Again, read it to yourself out loud; it doesn't flow. Especially out of sync by the time we get to verse 13. They gathered the leftover food and filled 12 baskets, but it says the baskets were filled with fragments of...are you ready...<u>loaves of bread</u>. No mention of fish at all.

12- And when they were filled, he said unto his disciples, gather up the fragments that remain, that nothing be lost.
13- Therefore they gather them together, and filled 12

baskets with the fragments of the five barley loaves, which remained over and above onto them that had eaten.

AGAIN! So this makes me question, were fish ever there? Let's look at this story one more time.

Luke chapter 9 verse 16
Then he took the five loaves and the two fishes, and looking up to heaven, he blessed them, and break, and gave to the disciples to set before the multitude.
        17- And they did eat, and were all filled, and there was taken up fragments that remained 12 baskets.

Regarding Luke

There are a couple of things regarding the book of Luke. Although Luke is most likely the author, there are scholars who question that. Regardless, Luke was not an eyewitness to this event (Luke 1:1-3). He is telling the story as it was told to him. Luke's gospel came many years after these miraculous events. Luke only interviewed the people who saw this event and hung out with Jesus. Luke was not one of the 12 disciples, nor did Luke ever meet Jesus in person.

Let me ask the Christians reading a question. Is this the first time you've realized Luke was not one of the 12? My experience is, the average Christian brought up in the church never heard that. That blows my mind.

Finishing up in verse 17, notice I underlined the word fragment. I looked it up in Greek, and the word is Klasma: *a broken piece.* Now the King James Version of the Bible uses the word fragment, but I looked at several other versions, and they use the word "pieces." When I think of pieces, I only think of leftover bread in those 12 baskets. In an age with no refrigeration to preserve them, would the disciples collect uneaten fish pieces to eat later? The USDA guidelines recommend never to leave fish out over two hours. Imagine the bacteria growth by the next day? It's reasons like that, I keep thinking it's all about the bread. If they saved the rotting fish, we may have to credit Jesus for unreported healings of botulism.

Why is bread such a big deal?

To help understand why bread, not fish, is so important, I want to look at John chapter 6.

John chapter 6 verse 35:
And Jesus said unto them, I am the bread of life: he that comes to me shall never hunger; and he that believe it on me shall never thirst.

Why is bread such a huge deal in the Bible? Bread is one of the essential foods of the time. Rarely did people eat meat. I'm not claiming that because they were vegan, but because they were poor. These people couldn't afford meat, so they needed bread to survive. After these multiplying miracles, when Jesus said he was the *bread*, he is saying he is essential for life. But not just physical life, but also for eternal life. He is letting them know he is the Messiah.

Anytime we hear fish introduced into the story, we can see Jesus bring the focus on the bread only. Jesus is making the claim he is the Messiah. He is the bread of life. He is not a dead animal but a living Savior.

Feeding 4000

We have a different but similar event. This time we have a gathering of 4000 people. This is in the Gospels of Mark and Matthew.

Mark chapter 8 I will start you at verse:

4- And his disciples answered him, From whence can a man <u>satisfy these men with bread</u> (artos= bread, loaf) *here in the wilderness?*

This report starts when Jesus was presented with the need to feed 4000 people. The disciples asked about bread, not fish.

5- And he (Jesus) *asked them, how <u>many loaves</u>* (artos= bread, loaf) *have you? And they said seven.*

6- And he commanded the people to sit down on the ground and he <u>took the seven loaves,</u> and gave thanks, and break, and gave to his disciples to set before them; and they did set them before the people.

Yet again, Jesus' response was only about bread; no fish is mentioned. So he blessed the bread, broke the bread. It goes on to say the disciples distributed the bread. The scene is, people are sitting and eating bread, got it? It would take a considerable amount of time for 12 guys to distribute bread to 4000 people. I'm sure they picked up additional volunteers to pass out the food. But by the time they gave bread to the last thousand people, I'm sure the first 3000 people were done eating. It's logical to assume these people ate their fill since they later collected 7 baskets full of leftover bread (verse 8). Then, outta nowhere, we get this crazy verse:

7- And they had a few small fishes, and he blessed and commanded to set them also before them.

Good grief, it sure seems as if they put verse 7 in after the fact. It's one of those *"oh yeah, and there were fish"* type of verses. The addition of fish makes no sense. Picture this: Jesus, already multiplied the bread. Jesus already blessed the bread. Jesus already gave the bread to the disciples to distribute among the 4000 people. The disciples already fed the 4000 people with bread and then (this sounds so silly) and then, after they were fed, Jesus repeats this with fish??? For what reason? Like, was the fish dessert or something?

I hope you see why I say this fish thing was added. Perhaps a well-meaning scribe wanted to establish Jesus as a more relatable miracle worker to a city of fishermen.

But what if?

Sometimes, activists can make a significant win by agreeing. So, let's consider, what if Jesus multiplied fish? Jesus used his miraculous abilities to multiply fish that are already dead. One person ate the original dead fish, and the other 4999 people ate fish that were miraculously created. No death involved. Our compassionate God fed the hungry by creating food without suffering. Not something you and I can do today, is it? Do you remember that God easily created coats in Genesis without animals suffering?

Personally, I don't go for this "what if" scenario. I'm still holding onto the disciples, only distributing bread. There was no mention of fish multiplication.

Okay, I think we got this.

I claim writers that were not present at the event possibly forced into the text the addition of fish. When told to gather the leftovers, Jesus speaks only of bread. If there were fish, Jesus didn't care enough to even mention them. His goal is to feed people bread. Then, connect that to himself, being the bread of life.

If you go deeper into the study, you'll hear talk of the five loaves representing the five books of the Torah for 5000 people. Maybe the 12 baskets representing the 12 tribes of Israel, or maybe the 12 disciples. Nothing we need for vegan outreach, so I'm going to shut up and have a slice of toast.

CHAPTER 52:
MATTHEW 17 – MONEY-
MOUTHED FISHY

Is Jesus giving permission to go fishing?

Peter was called away from fishing to become a fisher of men. But now, Jesus tells Peter to go fishing! So what's up with that?

Matthew chapter 17 verse 27
Go to the lake and throw out your line. Take the first fish you catch; open its mouth and you will find a four drachma coin. Take it and give it to them for my tax and yours.

5Ws

To understand this situation, we have to pop back to verse 24. The Jewish leaders tax the Jewish people. This was not a Roman tax. It was a way of supporting the Jewish temple (Exodus chapter 30).

The problem starts with Peter (AKA Simon or Simon-Peter) getting questioned.

24- After Jesus and his disciples arrived in Capernaum, the (tax) *collectors of the two-drachma* (money/Sheckle) *temple tax came to Peter and asked, "Doesn't your teacher* (Jesus) *pay the temple tax?"*

Peter opens his big mouth and says,

25 -Yes, he does.

When we look at the rest of verse 25, we discover Peter didn't know, or he was in fear and lied.

When Peter came into the house, Jesus was the first to speak.

Did you notice Jesus was the first to speak? Jesus already knew the conversation Peter had with the tax collectors. That's some creepy mind-reading stuff, huh? Let's get the rest of verse **25.**

"What do you think, Simon (Peter)*?" he asked. "From whom do the kings of the earth collect duty and taxes—from their own children or from others?"*

Jesus is asking, *"Do kings collect money from their children?"* Of course not. But how does that apply to Jesus? Jesus is saying he is exempt from paying the Jewish temple tax because he is the son of God, making *this his temple.* Collecting funds from himself just so he could give it to himself does not apply. That is a very serious claim on his part. To substantiate that claim, he does a miracle in verse 27.

But, going back to verse 25, Peter messed up when he told the tax collectors Jesus pays the tax. Jesus didn't want to create a scandal, so watch how Jesus shrewdly handles it.

27- But so that we may <u>not cause offense</u> (like a tax scandal)*, go to the lake and throw out your line. Take the first fish you catch; open its mouth and you will find a four-drachma* (Greek currency/money) *coin. Take it and give it to them for my tax and yours.*

Showing off

Peter backed Jesus into a corner when he said (lied) Jesus paid the tax. Not wanting to create a scandal, Jesus decides to pay the tax, but in a way, connecting him to the temple. That is why he commands this kooky way to pay.

First, know this: he is Jesus. Jesus could have pulled money out of his hat (if Jesus had a hat) and paid the tax privately. Instead, he told Peter to go to the sea of Galilee for a reason. Everyone could observe what Peter did. Now the miracles begin. Peter was to cast a single fishing line into the ocean. Of all the fish in the ocean, Peter will catch one that has money in its mouth. Peter will then take that money and publicly give it to the tax collectors. Do you recognize the showmanship of this? This would be Jesus saying, *"OK, fine, I'll pay your tax and I'll do it in a way that demonstrates my sovereignty and power over all."*

When we first read of this money-mouthed fish, it sounds like a stupid Las Vegas magic trick. But, when you know the situation, you'll see this as Jesus' way of publicly displaying his power while still satisfying the Jewish tax collectors. Clever, huh?

Jesus is starting the connection that he is the "new temple." This is not permission to continue fishing.

Let's discuss this miracle fish.

This was not a random fish. I'm not a fish expert, but I'm sure a random fish would be busy trying to get this coin out of its mouth and not looking to bite on Peter's hook. So I say that Jesus created this specific fish, this particular coin, and this entire unique situation to prove he is God.

Some Christians have argued against this "miracle fish" viewpoint I offer because it has no scripture to support it. I agree, but also, there's no scripture to deny it or support Peter actually did this! You see, Jesus said to go to the sea and catch the money fish. But did you read what happened in verse 28? Of course not. There is no verse 28! We never get confirmation Peter actually caught the fish with a coin. We don't know the end, so my guess is as good as anyone.

Also, as I mentioned in earlier chapters, I have no idea why Christians are so willing to accept Jesus can raise people from the dead, heal the blind and cure leprosy, but somehow, creating a fish with a coin is a stretch. There is no stretch if you accept the miracles of Jesus.

Don't worry about the tiny details...yet

There is a hint in this on how to advocate for vegan issues. Jesus was saying he is the temple, so there's no reason he should give/get money to support himself. Jesus was in full right to be tax exempt. But, so he doesn't offend, he pays the tax. Jesus is right, but he gives the tax collectors a win, knowing it allows him the freedom to go about his ministry. Jesus doesn't need to be encumbered with a little deal of unpaid taxes. Lose a battle, win the war kind of thing.

This is why I sometimes allow speciesism from the meat-eating Christian. Like Jesus, I don't want to get bogged down over a principle that takes care of itself when I focus on the central message of compassion, mercy, and love. Getting thrown off track by fighting speciesism eats up valuable time. But, if we can convince the carnist love is the ultimate trip, then anti-speciesism will follow.

CHAPTER 53: MATTHEW 23:37 – MOTHER HEN

Matthew chapter 23 verse 37

Oh Jerusalem that kills your profits and stones them that are sent onto her! How often I would've gathered the children together even as a hen gathers her chickens under her wings and you would not!

God and Jesus state chickens can offer love, be protective and desire safety. Why do carnist Christians take that away?

5Ws

Jesus is upset while speaking about the hypocrisy of the Pharisees. He changes his tune a bit when discussing his desire to care for Jerusalem. To express this care, Jesus chooses a mother hen, a chicken, to illustrate his love and protection. For our vegan advocacy, that rocks! Nowadays, to represent a protective mother, we'd say "Don't mess with Mama-bear," or maybe describe a lioness protecting her cubs. But a chicken? No way, not in today's culture. However, back then, Jesus' example was 100% solid and recognized by the people listening as accurate. Although, I'm sure Jerusalem preferred he called 1000 warrior angels to zap the bad guys with cosmic lightning bolts, they understood this chicken illustration.

Sadly, in our culture, things have drastically changed for chickens. Chickens are considered dumb, weak, and not worthy of much protection at all. The truth is, chickens can love, think, feel, hurt, cry and, according to Jesus, embrace and protect their babies. Are the carnist Christians acting morally when they deny chickens the behaviors Jesus boasts about?

Psalm chapter 91 verse 4
He shall cover thee with his feathers, and under his wings shalt thou trust: his truth shall be thy shield and buckler.

In this Psalm, God's example of what His love and protection looks like is a bird. Outstanding! Both God and Jesus choose birds as a symbol of protection based on how strongly they love their offspring. This is a great vegan win. This passage is good for proof-text God made chickens (fowl, birds, animals) with emotional capacities to love. So much love they are the choice of example used.

Christians and chickens

This part may be more for the carnist Christian than the activist. I'd like you, the meat-eating Christian, to consider the treatment of chickens today. Current federal farm laws offer little to no protection for chickens. Animal agriculture laws will allow farmers (many of whom are Christian) to treat chickens in almost any way they choose. With profit as their goal, Farmers cut off toes, and beaks of live baby chicks with no painkillers. Pain relief drugs cost time and money, so forget that. Kept indoors in tiny cages, never to see the light of day. They genetically breed chickens in ways to make them grow so fast they suffer heart attacks. They do not give chickens medical care when ill, cheaper to let them die. Billions (yes; I said billions) of baby male chicks are suffocated in plastic bags or ground up in giant blender-like machines while fully conscious. All this suffering happens every day. Why,? Money and gluttony. If you eat eggs, you pay for this torment with every egg purchase you make. Does any of this sound like a Christian thing to do?

More than protective

This verse tells us that God made chickens to be highly protective. He also made them smart enough to teach each other things. They have their own language, they recognize and snuggle with their chicks, and if they are pets, snuggle with their "owners". They can learn tricks, dream and communicate with baby chicks even before they hatch. Does subverting these instinctual needs sound like a Christian thing to do?

Eggs

When God made chickens, He made them to produce about one egg a month. Today, humans messed with their genetics, causing them to produce an egg a day. Can you imagine the suffering? If you're a female reading this, think about what this means. Imagine being forced (through chemicals and breeding) into having your period every single day of your life.

The torment doesn't end there. When egg production drops, they force chickens into a time of starvation. This starvation process will cause them to produce more eggs. By this time, their bodies are weak from lack of proper food and worn out from overproduction of eggs. They try to their best abilities to protect their babies, but heartless humans use their "Dominion" to take those eggs. Why? To satisfy the lust of eggs for breakfast. Does any of that sound like a Christian thing to do? Is this continuing on in God's Image?

Am I too harsh? Naaahhhhh.

CHAPTER 54:
MARK 5 & LUKE 8 –
GERASENE DEMONIAC

Does Jesus hate pigs?

The Bible has a story called The Gerasene Demoniac. It's about Jesus meeting a guy filled with a bunch of demons. The demons leave the man and possess a herd of 2000 pigs that were peacefully grazing nearby. The pigs go crazy as if they are on a bad acid trip and drown themselves. Jesus gets the credit for saving a guy, but also the blame for killing the swine.

Carnists use this story to declare one human being means more to God than thousands of animals. Other times, used to support vivisection with the claim its approval to kill thousands of animals if it will save a human.

This story is told in three of the Gospels. My experience is most Christians believe this to be a true event. However, there are many believers that claim this to only be a *political allegory,* a myth or tale to present a hidden criticism of Rome during the Roman-Jewish war in the first century. Vegan activist don't have to deal with the few Christians who believe this to be a political or military story because no animals actually die. I will focus only on refuting the standard idea that Jesus killed 2000 pigs.

Jesus and the pigs

This demon pig story is in the Gospels of Mark, Matthew, and Luke. I will start us in:

Luke chapter 8 verse 27
And when he went forth to land, there met him out of the city a certain man, which had devils long time, and ware no clothes, neither abode in any house, but in the tombs.

The Gospel of Mark agrees with Luke. There was one guy, but in the gospel of Matthew chapter 8 it says;

28- And when he was come to the other side into the country of the Gergesenes, there met him two possessed with devils,

How many demon-dudes are there? Eh, for our vegan outreach, it doesn't matter, just like it didn't matter to Mark and Matthew that the guy was naked. I guess they didn't notice or only Luke noticed because he's a perv!
Alright, back to the story as recorded in the book of Mark chapter 5:

7- And (the demon guy) *cried with a loud voice, and said, What have I to do with thee, Jesus, thou Son of the most high God? I adjure thee by God, that thou torment me not.*

We have some awesome Jesus stuff going on here. I believe this to be the first time the Bible states Jesus is God, and it's through the mouth of demons. How cool is that?

8- For he (Jesus) *said unto him, Come out of the man, thou unclean spirit.*

This part of the story leads to controversy regarding demon possession. The claim is Jesus does not have total power over demons because in verse 8, Jesus told them to *come out,* but they didn't. Not immediately. In verse 9, the demons stayed in the guy long enough to barter a deal on where to go.
This is the important part for our vegan defense. Jesus only instructed them to come out of the man. Jesus didn't say to enter the pigs.

9- And he (Jesus) *asked him* (demon-guy), *What is thy name? And he answered, saying, My name is legion: for we are many.*

Legion

In that era and location, the word "Legion" is a particular Roman term. The people immediately understand legion as a military word for an army. Each Legion is about 6000 (some say 6800+ but you get the idea) soldiers. The name implies there were over 6000 demons in this one particular guy.

10- And he (demon) *besought* (begged, asked) *him much that he would not send them away out of the country.*

Luke chapter 8 reports they said:

31- And they (the demons) *besought him* (Jesus) *that he would not command them to go out into the abyss* (the abyss is often understood as Hell)

Did your vegan ears catch that? Jesus said get out, that's it. The demons understood that command to leave the man and go into the country or hell. Either option has nothing to imply Jesus wanted the demons to go into pigs or any living creature.

Back to the gospel of Mark where the pigs enter the story:

11- Now there was there nigh unto the mountains a great herd of swine feeding.
12- And all the devils besought (asked/begged) *him, saying, Send us into the swine, that we may enter into them.*

So whether a military allegory or an actual event happening, it makes no difference in our vegan defense. The devils asked (besought) to be sent into the pigs. This piggy possession was the demon's idea, not Jesus'. As they saw it, Jesus was there for 2 possible actions: to send them away to another country or send them back to Hell. The demons requested the pigs; it was their idea.

13- And forthwith Jesus gave them leave. And the unclean spirits went out, and entered into the swine: and the herd ran violently down a steep place into the sea, (they were about two thousand;) and were choked (drowned) *in the sea.*

The demons go into the pigs. Jesus didn't order it; he just *gave them leave*, which ended his involvement with the pigs.

Bible study side note: The line in verse 13 claiming 2000 pigs is in parentheses. When we see ( ) it usually means the translator inserted it long after. An actual number may not have been given, but most Christians I speak with quote the number 2000 as if it's fact. I just go with it.

Man over pig

Carnists argue this sets a precedent that one human life is worth more than a couple thousand animals. I don't think Scripture will allow us to accept that. None of the verses imply Jesus was going to kill the demons. If Jesus wanted the demons dead, he could have done a "Thanos Snap" of his fingers and Poof! Demons all gone. Jesus did not have to send the demons into pigs, then make the pigs go berserk and drown themselves. All Jesus did was to allow them to go. It was the demons that made the ask to enter the pigs, and it was the demons that killed the pigs, not Jesus.

It doesn't contradict scripture to say Jesus allowing the demons to enter the pigs may have been his end goal. Demons would have no way to do anything while trapped inside pigs to cause harm to any people. The piggies future in a Gentile land is slaughter.

Why the swine suicide?

Maybe, when the demons got control over the pigs, it drove them crazy like the man. Look back to verse 5.

> *Constantly, night and day, he* (demon guy) *was in the mountains, and in the tombs, crying, and <u>cutting</u> himself with stones.*

The demon-man was harming himself, cutting himself, and such. He wasn't doing that for giggles; the demons were tormenting him, forcing him to hurt himself. These demons are now tormenting the pigs and eventually killing the pigs.

Or, maybe the demons understood the command of Jesus to mean they were to go back to Hell (abyss) and suffer eternal torment. A quick pig suicide would be better than eternity in the abyss.

Either way, don't let the meat-eater blame the pig death on Jesus; this was done by the demons, if it was done at all.

Yep, I'm one of those allegory guys. Could you tell?

CHAPTER 55: MARK 7:19 – ALL FOOD CLEAN

ave we been eating dirty foods?

H In Mark chapter 7, Jesus is alleged to have made all foods clean. By "Clean", it means ritually clean, as in Kosher or permissible under the law. This is going down when select food items were off limits for religious reasons. This alleged statement put an end to eating only kosher foods and allowing all meat, even pigs, to be eaten. Carnist Christians use this story to defend their meat-eating.

Once you know the **5Ws**, you'll see this is not about all food becoming clean, but two other issues. First, Jesus teaches acceptance by God is determined by the inner motivations (what is in one's heart) instead of external activities, such as the foods they eat. The second, Jesus criticizes man-made religious laws becoming of more importance than God's laws. Jesus will use bread (not meat) to point this out to the Pharisees and his confused disciples. To get us plugged in, I will start with the story as reported by Peter's assistant, Mark.

Mark chapter 7 verse 1:
Then came together unto him the <u>Pharisees</u> (Pharisees: the separated ones)*, and certain of the scribes, which came from Jerusalem.*

Let's talk about the Pharisees again. Today we might know them as the Orthodox Rabbis or Orthodox Jews. The Pharisees had 2 sources for their laws, The Written Torah and The Oral Torah. Most Christians will know the Written Torah as the first 5 books of the Bible. The Oral Torah are the laws, statutes and interpretations that are not from the first 5 books. Most Christians will have no idea of this difference, making our vegan advocacy harder.

The Pharisees were sticklers for the "Oral" Torah (Law). They considered this Oral Torah a fence built around the Written Torah to protect people from getting too close to breaking the Written Torah Laws. For example, the Written Torah teaches not to work on the Sabbath. The Oral Torah is a set of rules describing all the things they determined to be work. The Pharisees were a nit-picky bunch with rules like the Shulchan Aruch. It required you to put on your right shoe first, but not tie it. Put on your left shoe, tie it, only then can you go back and tie the right shoe. If you didn't follow the rules, they were out to get you. So ya, very strict, got it?

Jesus stood only for the Written Torah and was often against the Oral Law. Why is that a problem? The Pharisees' political and religious systems, along with their income, were being threatened by Jesus doing this. So quite often, they were out to get him.

2- And when they saw some of his disciples eat bread with defiled, that is to say, with unwashen, hands, they found fault.

Eating with dirty hands

The activity upsetting the Pharisees is the disciples are eating bread with ceremonially unclean hands. Please notice that animal flesh is not part of this conversation.

Regarding the need for washing. The Pharisees were not concerned with germs, dirt under the fingernails, or filth on the disciples' hands. By *"unwashen,"* they were complaining the guys did not go through the required religious cleansing rituals before eating. The tradition known as Mayim Rishonim (first waters), or netilat Yadayim (handwashing), is required in any meal that includes bread. This was only about eating while being ceremonially unclean. Another thing, these hand-washings are u*nnecessary when eating only meat.*

3- For the Pharisees, and all the Jews, except they wash their hands oft, eat not, holding the tradition of the elders.

The tradition of the elders is the Oral Law. To Jesus, the Oral Law is good, but often dangerous because these traditions of men (religious leaders) are becoming more urgent than serving God.

4- And when they come from the market, except they wash, they eat not. And many other things there be, which they have received to hold, as the washing of cups, and pots, brasen vessels, and of tables.

Jesus and his merry men aren't doing any of the expected "Man-Made" rituals or traditions.

5- Then the Pharisees and scribes asked him (Jesus)*, Why walk not thy disciples according to the <u>tradition of the elders</u>, but <u>eat bread</u> with unwashen hands?*

This complaint is, the disciples were not going through the religious rituals required by the elders (not God) to make eating *bread* permissible. Here in verse five, we have added vegan confirmation that the food in question is <u>bread</u>. They still are not talking about animal flesh/meat.

6- He (Jesus) *answered and said unto them, Well hath Esaias prophesied of you <u>hypocrites</u>, as it is written, This people <u>honoureth me with their lips, but their heart is far from me.</u>*

Jesus calls the Pharisees hypocrites. Even though they're doing the religious rituals (hand washings), their hearts are just not in the right place (*far from me*) when they do it. We went over that a lot in the Old Testament, remember? They were doing the rituals just for show.

7- Howbeit in vain do they worship me, teaching for doctrines the commandments of men.

Their worship is nothing more than worthless human rules done in public (vain) to make themselves look holy. They are just doing the traditions of men and ignoring the genuine desires of God.

8- For <u>laying aside the commandment of God</u> (God's written Torah law)*, <u>ye hold the tradition of men,</u>* (man-made oral Torah law) *as the washing of pots and cups: and many other such like things ye do.*
9- And he said unto them, Full well ye reject the commandment of God, that ye may keep your own tradition.

They're putting more value on man-made traditions (washing cups and hands) and ignoring the written laws of God.
We see this same story in Matthew chapter 15. Jesus emphasizes Oral Law = bad, Written Law = good.
Back to Mark chapter 7:

13- <u>Making the word of God of none effect through your tradition</u>, which ye have delivered: and many such like things do ye.

Jesus is criticizing their man-made traditions (Oral Torah laws) that are nullifying God's word. This verse by verse breakdown is not intended to sneak in a Bible study. You'll need this background for vegan defense. Please take note, we are halfway through the story, and still no mention of meat. In no way is this about declaring meat clean. Let's keep looking.

> *15- There is <u>nothing from outside</u> a man, that entering into him <u>can defile him</u>: but the things which come out of him, those are they that defile the man.*

Jesus says that people are not defiled by the food going into their bodies. That would mean the bread they are going to eat, whether it be ceremonially clean or unclean. It doesn't mess up their standing before God. God judges a man's heart, only that can defile him.

> *16- If any man have ears to hear, let him hear.*

This saying cracks me up. It's not as if Jesus is talking to an audience of earless people. When the Bible says *hear*, it usually means more than just listening. It means accepting and taking action on what was just heard.

> *17- And when he was entered into the house from the people, his disciples asked him concerning the parable.*

The Oral Law of the Pharisees heavily influenced the disciples. After all, they were still practicing Jews. Hearing this from Jesus left them confused. When Jesus and the boys are in a house away from everyone else, JC explains.

> *18- And he (Jesus) saith unto them, Are ye so without understanding also? Do ye not perceive, that <u>whatsoever thing</u> from without entereth into the man, it <u>cannot defile him</u>;*
> *19- Because it entereth not into his heart, but into the belly, and goeth out into the draught, purging all <u>meats</u>.*
> *(Thus He declared all foods clean.)*

I love reading verses 18 and 19 as if it happened today. It would be like Jesus saying, "What are you guys stupid? Don't you get it? Whatever you eat is just going in your belly and later pooped out."

Meat

Now we got that sticky problem with the King James Version using the word <u>meats</u> in verse 19. Other literal translations, such as the New American Standard Bible, the English Standard Version, and the New English translation. They don't have the word meat at all.

They end the verse with *"purging all."* That's it, just *eliminating all, purging all*, or *being expelled*. (Yes, that means poop)

Have a look at a few:

English Standard Version: *since it enters not his heart but his stomach, and is expelled* (pooped)? *(Thus he declared all foods clean.)*

New International Version: *For it doesn't go into their heart but into their stomach, and then out (pooped) of the body.* (In saying this, Jesus declared all foods clean.)

New American Standard Bible: *because it does not go into his heart, but into his stomach, and is eliminated* (and again, pooped)? *(Thus He declared all foods clean.)*

Now look again at:

King James Version: *Because it entereth not into his heart, but into the belly, and goeth out* (pooped) *into the draught, purging all meats?*

See? Lots of pooping going no but no mention of meat except in the King James Version.

The KJV translators take it upon themselves to add the word *meat*. I have no idea why meat is added when the only food spoken of in this chapter is bread. Over and over again, bread! But, to their credit, the KJV doesn't add a line as the others do. Check it out:

All foods are clean

Now on to that last line:

(Thus He declared all foods clean.)

When the Bible has a sentence in parentheses ( ), you are reading a supplementary note added for clarification by the translators. *"Declaring all foods clean"* was not in the early Greek manuscripts of Mark. So, ya, it's a real mess, but Jesus never did say that. Translators added it long after.

Peter helps confirm

Suppose the carnist Christian wants proof Jesus *never declared all foods permissible* to eat. Sure, we can offer that. We need to check in with Peter when, years after this, he had a vision about eating animals.

Acts chapter 10 verse 14
But Peter said, Not so, Lord; for I have never eaten any thing that is common or unclean.

This vision in Acts happened several years after Jesus died, and Peter was still keeping the kosher laws. Why is that a big deal? Peter was there when Jesus was putting the smack-down on the Pharisees about these hand washing rituals. If Jesus said all foods were permissible, Peter would have heard it, and Acts 10:14 would make no sense. We have more in the Book of Acts.

Acts chapter 15 verse 29:
That ye abstain from meats offered to idols, and from blood, and
from things strangled, and from fornication: from which if ye keep
yourselves, ye shall do well. Fare ye well

Notice the apostles are still observing the Old Testament kosher diet
restrictions. Again, years after Jesus "allegedly" declared all foods clean.

Jesus did not cancel the kosher food laws. *Jesus was a practicing Jew*
and still kept the written Torah, kosher food laws. Christians forget that.
The New Testament (think of it as Jesus' last will and testament) didn't
kick in until after Jesus died. The Old Testament laws still stand until after
Jesus dies.

Considering these situations in the book of Acts, Jesus being a
practicing Jew and that sentence in parentheses gives serious doubt Jesus
ever said all foods are clean.

Before I close, let's consider this event from the Gospel of Matthew,
chapter 15. It's pretty much the same; the Pharisees were ticked-off over
hand washing. Absent is any translators notes in parentheses ( ) about
making all food clean.

Read the entire chapter if you like. I'll just grab the verses showing
this situation can not be approval for meat-eating:

Matthew chapter 15 verse 11
11- It's not what goes into the mouth that defiles a man, but what
comes out of the mouth, this defiles a man

And more in verse:

19- For out of the heart proceed evil thoughts, murders,
adulteries, fornications, thefts, false witness, blasphemies:
*   20- These are the things which defile a man: but to eat with*
unwashen hands defileth not a man

These verses make the same point mentioned by Mark. People are not
defiled when they eat without the traditional hand cleaning rituals. No
mention of declaring all foods clean.

What if?

Suppose this was making all meat clean. Wouldn't scripture report having
a celebration? After 1200 years of restrictions, the Jews finally get to eat
pigs and shellfish. Wouldn't there be at least one feast recorded that
mentions pork? Nope, there is nothing of the sort in the New Testament.
I'll tell ya why; they understood this was another attack on man-made
religious rituals. Reread the story in Matthew, and you'll see the report goes
on about defilement, not permission to eat all foods. Jesus did not declare

all foods clean. What makes a person "clean" is in their heart.

If a Christian uses this story to defend meat-eating, you can always press back. Ask them, "what is in your heart when you continuously choose food created from the torture of God's creation when your survival does not require it?"

CHAPTER 56:
MARK 11 – JESUS RIDES
A DONKEY

The Triumphal Entry

The last week in the life of Jesus starts on Palm Sunday with him riding a baby donkey. This brings the argument, if Jesus can ride a donkey, then people can ride horses. My quick reply; the next time you're traveling into Jerusalem and the townspeople are praising you as their new Messiah, and you are fulfilling a 500-year-old prophecy on your way to being crucified, then yeah, sure, hop on your horsey.

Jesus is living a situation of "Special Privilege". Special Privilege is *a concession granted to an individual or group, to the exclusion of others.* Jesus is fulfilling a onetime prophecy that excludes all others and no one else in history can lay claim to duplicate. He is not setting a precedent to follow with horses.

5Ws

Each of the four Gospels record the story known as The Triumphal Entry. The people of Jerusalem are excited about Jesus. They expect him to be their new king, Messiah, or a warrior general to lead them in revolt against Rome. That didn't go as they expected. By the end of the week, they flip-flopped and wanted Jesus crucified. Geez, people are fickle.

There are many layers of symbolism going on in the story. Let's look at some of these layers and see why it's Special Privilege, not permission to ride.

Mark chapter 11 verse 2

Go your way into the village over against you: and as soon as ye be entered into it, ye shall find a colt tied, <u>whereon never man sat;</u> loose him, and bring him.

Jesus is giving his boys some instructions on where to find a donkey he can ride. Here we have an absolute miracle. No, not that Jesus knew where a donkey was tied. But he plans to ride a donkey that has <u>never been sat on</u>. Why is that a big deal? Let's discuss.

Breaking a horse

All horse abusers—uh, I mean, horseback riders—know they have to *break a horse* before they can ride it. Horses have a "spirit". Not a ghost or soul kind of spirit, but a set of behaviors, instincts, needs and desires, given to horses by God. Breaking a horse is stifling God's design and removes their independent "spirit". The training often involves food and water depravation, threats of violence (whipping), and force such as putting uncomfortable and often painful reins (metal control straps) in their mouths. Breaking may continue up to 90 days until the horsey no longer tries to buck people off, run away or kick you in the face for trying to climb on it.

Just knowing trainers have to break its spirit to allow people on its back should tell them riding is wrong. Obviously, not an activity that the animal wants. Don't Christians ever think of that? If a horse has a spirit, an instinct, then God put it there. Who are we to destroy that God given spirt and exploit them? For a proud, powerful animal like a horse to be locked in a stall, unable to express its natural behaviors is traumatizing and cruel.

Back to our story

> ***Verse 3-*** *And if any man* (like the donkey owner) *say unto you, Why do ye this? say ye that the Lord hath need of him; and straightway he will send him hither.*
> ***4-*** *And they went their way, and found the colt tied by the door without in a place where two ways met; and they loose him.*
> ***5-*** *And certain of them that stood there said unto them, What do ye, loosing the colt?*
> ***6-*** *And they said unto them even as Jesus had commanded: and they* (the donkey owner) *let them go.*

We see confirmation the disciples didn't steal the donkey. The owner was good with this.

But what's the deal with the Donkey?

This donkey ride had a prophetic meaning connected to it. It was the fulfillment of a prophecy made 500 years earlier.

Zechariah chapter 9 verse 9
Rejoice greatly, Daughter Zion! Shout, Daughter Jerusalem! See, your king comes to you, righteous and victorious, lowly and riding on a donkey, on a colt, the foal of a donkey.

In his earthly ministry, Jesus fulfilled hundreds (over 300) of Old Testament prophecies; This donkey deal is one of many.

7- And they brought the colt to Jesus, and cast their garments on him; and he sat upon him.

When the guys put their coats (*cast their garments on him*) on the back of the colt, it offered some comfort. Not a vegan thing, but still, trying to twist this as approval to saddle horses still won't hold.

8- And many spread their garments in the way: and others cut down branches off the trees, and strawed them in the way.

The people put more coats and tree branches on the ground in front of the donkey as it walked.

9- And they that went before, and they that followed, cried, saying, Hosanna; Blessed is he that cometh in the name of the Lord:

Back to the burro

I've got more reasons Jesus asked for a young donkey. Young = inexperienced. This donkey had no experience in large public crowds. The donkey allowed people to put their coats on him as he walked into a crowded city, yet didn't get spooked. This same donkey stepped on people's coats as they laid them, along with palm branches, in front of him. We can't forget the whole Palm Sunday scene. A young donkey, untrained and unbroken, would flip out. We are seeing proof of who Jesus is. Do not confuse this as a joyful horseback ride. A horseback rider will recognize the placing of a colorful coat in front of a horse that has never been around anything like this, would get a rider thrown. I've said it before, this is a fulfillment of prophecy and Jesus proving his sovereign power. This is not permission to ride horses.

If you're asking why the coats, scripture addresses this in the Old Testament book of 2nd Kings, but it's really dull. So I'll save you the yawn and tell you this coat thing shows respect for royalty. These people are accepting Jesus as their king.

Ok, I just can't end without dealing with:

My horse loves to be ridden

No, the horse has been brainwashed, and that's not love.

A "Broke" horse has similarities to a person with "Stockholm Syndrome". Stockholm syndrome is a mental condition in which kidnap victims or hostages develop a psychological, sometimes "loving" bond with their captors during their captivity.

Once a horse is broken in, it realizes its "owner" will give it access to the area outside of its corral. The horse will be able to run and do behaviors horses yearn for. The horse has been re-programmed to connect humans as a source of satisfaction for those instinctual desires that humans deprived them of when bred into captivity, and made them property. A wild horse, with its spirit intact, would never run up to a human and say, "*Hey, please climb on me and cause injury to my spine and skeletal structure. I really do want a painful metal bit in my mouth. Please ignore my needs, I'd rather follow your every whim*".

To the carnists reading, if you have a horse you truly love, you can build an equal, if not better, loving relationship by staying off its back. God made animals for companionship. That companionship pleasure can be achieved without exploitation. Try long walks with the horse, grooming the horse, eating carrots or other treats with the horse. Sing to the horse. I have even seen people play fetch with horses. None of those activities requires breaking their God-given spirit. Today, riding is a selfish human pleasure.

CHAPTER 57:
LUKE 5:6 – FISHERS OF
MEN

F ollow me, and I will make you fishers of men.

Carnist Christians have used the following verse to support their selfish desire to go fishing. The claim is, if Jesus helped Peter catch a multitude of fish, then fishing is good.

Luke chapter 5 verse 6
When they had done so, they caught such a large number of fish that their nets began to break

There are three reports of this event. In Matthew chapter 4, Mark chapter 1, and Luke chapter 5. Why are 3 reports a problem? Because Matthew and Mark agree, but Luke tells a different story. Ugh! Confusing, I know.

Bible stories can conflict. When that happens, I look to get the general meaning and don't sweat the little details. This story gives an overall view of how Jesus called his disciples. The contradictory points don't interfere with the general meaning, so no big deal there. However, the many contradictions make me question the accuracy of the part about the fish and that matters to us compassionate vegans. As we look into this, please remember that Simon is also Peter, one dude, two names. More confusion, I know.

Let's start with Liar—*uh*, I mean Luke.

The Big Catch

Luke is reporting Jesus gave instructions on how to catch a bunch of fish. They listened and caught so many they needed more boats for all the fish. That is quite a story, but we know how fishermen tell stories.

> **Luke chapter 5 verse 2:**
> *And he saw two ships standing by the lake: but the fishermen were gone out of them, and were <u>washing their nets.</u>*
> *3- And he (Jesus) entered into one of the ships, which was Simon's (Peter), and prayed (asked) him that he would thrust out a little from the land. And he sat down, and taught the people out of the ship.*

A crowd of people is gathering to hear Jesus speak. Jesus sees a couple of boats and gets an idea. He asks Simon Peter to let him preach from his ship.

> *4- Now when he (Jesus) had left (finished) speaking, he said unto Simon, Launch out into the deep, and let down your nets for a draught (Agra = hunting, a catch).*

Jesus finished his sermon. Then, with no hint of why, he tells Simon to go out and start fishing. Huh?

> *5- And Simon (Peter), answering said unto him, Master, we have toiled all the night, and have taken nothing: nevertheless at thy word I will let down the net.*

Simon Peter whines about not catching anything earlier, but he'll do it because Jesus asked.

> *6- And when they had this done, they inclosed (caught) a <u>great multitude of fishes</u> (ichthus= fish): and <u>their net brake.</u>*
> *7- And they <u>beckoned unto their partners</u>, which were in the other ship, that they should come and help them. And they came, and filled both the ships, so that <u>they began to sink.</u>*

We are left with nets breaking and two sinking boats full of fish. Wow, that's quite a story.

> *8- When Simon Peter saw it, he fell down at Jesus' knees, saying, Depart from me; for I am a sinful man, O Lord.*
> *9- For he was astonished, and all that were with him, at the draught of the fishes which they had taken:*

Simon then falls to his knees in amazement and admits he is sinful. More on that sinful part later.

10- And so was also James, and John, the sons of Zebedee, which were partners with Simon. And Jesus said unto Simon, Fear not; from henceforth thou shalt catch men.
    11- And when they had brought their ships to land, they forsook all, and followed him.

Now Jesus calls them to become his disciples and make them "Fishers of Men." Ok, but what are we told from the other gospels:
In **chapter 4, Matthew** tells the story in a different way:

18- And Jesus, walking by the sea of Galilee, saw two brethren, Simon, called Peter, and Andrew his brother, casting a net into the sea: for they were fishers.

Difference #1: Jesus was walking, not preaching.
Difference #2: Simon was casting nets into the sea, but in Luke, they were not in their boats. Instead, they were on shore washing their nets.
Difference #3: Jesus does not get on any boat to preach.

19- And he saith unto them, Follow me, and I will make you fishers of men.
    20- And they straightway (immediately) left their nets, and followed him.

Pay attention to the word "straightaway." Jesus says he called them immediately to leave their jobs as fishers to become fishers of men.

21- And going on from thence, he saw other two brethren, James the son of Zebedee, and John his brother, in a ship with Zebedee their father, mending their nets; and he called them.
    22- And they immediately left the ship and their father, and followed him.

Same story here; they *immediately* followed Jesus. No filling up nets with multitudes of fish. No filling of boats to the point of sinking. If Luke was telling the truth, these are pretty big miracles for Matthew to leave out, Dontcha think?
    Let's see what Mark says:

Mark chapter 1 verse 16
Now as he walked by the sea of Galilee, he saw Simon (Peter), and Andrew his brother casting a net into the sea: for they were fishers.

> *17- And Jesus said unto them, Come ye after me, and I will make you to become fishers of men.*

Same in Matthew's report. All Jesus did was walk and talk. No multitudes of fish in bursting nets. No sinking of boats. There was no preaching from the boat. No help from other boats to save them from sinking.

> *18- And straightway* (immediately), *they forsook* (abandoned) *their nets, and followed him.*
> *19- And when he had gone a little further thence, he saw James the son of Zebedee, and John, his brother, who also were in the ship mending their nets.*
> *20- And straightway* (immediately) *he called them: and they left their father Zebedee in the ship with the hired servants, and went after him.*

You might notice that each time I have underlined the word straightway or immediately. Whatever did happen, happened fast. There was no time for Jesus to get on a boat. No time for this big catch. No contact with another boat to help them pull in a multitude of fish.

So one of these reports has the story wrong.

Let's consider the account written by Luke. I know I've talked about this before, but an important fact is that *Luke wasn't there.* Luke only reported what he was told by others. Luke never even met Jesus. If I had to question one of these reports' accuracy, Luke is the loser.

Are the others any better?

Matthew was one of the 12, so he most likely got the story from Andrew, Peter, James, or John, since they hung out and partied together. Mark worked for Peter (Simon), so he presumably got the story directly from Peter (Simon).

I am just teasing when I imply Luke was lying. I don't think it was intentional. He got his information and reported it the way he received it. Maybe it was a story blown out of proportion by well-meaning townspeople by the time Luke got it. Think about it, if you were a fisherman, which story would be more impressive to you?

Ask what book?

Suppose a carnist Christian challenges you by saying Jesus made them catch a multitude of fish. In that case, I suggest asking them from which book they got the information. If it was Matthew or Mark, they wouldn't find it. But, if they use the book of Luke, well, now you can discuss the multitude of fish thing might not have happened.

CHAPTER 58:
LUKE 10:8 – EAT
WHATEVER

But what if they offered a cheeseburger?

Here in chapter 10, Jesus told 70 guys to eat whatever is offered. But what if they offered a cheeseburger? First off, Jews wouldn't have cheeseburgers, but yes, Jesus was allowing them to eat meat if offered. But this allowance was only for a group of 70 people and not meant for future generations to follow. It becomes more evident by the time we get to verse 19.

5Ws

In verse 1, we have Jesus sending an advance group of 70 people to check out places he plans to preach.

1- After these things <u>the Lord appointed other seventy</u> also, and <u>sent them</u> two and two before his face into every city and place, whither he himself would come.

He was not sending these people on a pleasure vacation. There is going to be danger, and he warns them.

3- I send you forth as lambs among wolves.

That means expect threats from the townspeople. They are against you and will be out to get ya.

In verses 4&5 he gave them some specific instructions:

4- Carry neither purse, or bag, or shoes.
    5- And into whatsoever house ye enter, first say, Peace be to this house.

They were instructed to find a place to stay. So with only the clothes they were wearing and no money for a hotel, they had to rely totally on God providing all their needs. Being sent to an inhospitable town, with no way to provide for yourself, is a test of commitment. This is not about permission to eat meat.

The rich townspeople were not on *team Jesus*. Chances are the 70 guys ended up staying with very poor people who believed in their mission. What did poor people eat? Well, it sure wasn't steak. The poor ate vegetables most of the time because that's what they could afford. Chances are, it was pretty crappy food, too.

Luke chapter 10 verse 8
And into whatsoever city you enter, and they receive you, <u>eat such things as are set before you</u>:

When Jesus said, eat what they give, he was simply saying to be courteous and have some freaking manners. Don't complain if it's slop because slop might be all this poor family can afford.

Another thought is they would stay with others that believed as they do. One such group of Jewish Christians was known as Ebionites. There is evidence the Ebionites (Ebionites means "the Poor") were vegetarian, therefore, they wouldn't have meat to offer.

But whatever they served, just be grateful. If it was meat, then yeah, fine, but this is not Jesus approving unrestricted meat consumption. Remember what I said earlier. Food made from compassion should always be the Christian's choice over food from violence *when a choice* is an option. Unfortunately, these 70 guys had no choice.

That should be enough to deal with a carnist if they use that verse. But, to get a good understanding of how unique this situation is, let's look at what else the 70 were instructed to do.

In verse 9, they were told to heal the sick. Then, in verse 19, they were given the power to trample on serpents and scorpions. Basically, venom would not hurt them.

19- Behold, I give unto you power to tread on serpents and scorpions, and over all the power of the enemy: and nothing shall by any means hurt you.

This verse, along with **Mark 16:18,** would also have us handling venomous reptiles if we took it for our usage today.

They shall take up serpents; and if they drink any deadly thing, it shall not hurt them; they shall lay hands on the sick, and they shall recover.

If a carnist Christian says Jesus gave us permission to eat whatever is put before us, ask him to consider the entire situation back then and reconsider if it applies to their situation now. Did today's meat-eating Christian get these orders? Did today's meat-eating Christian get sent into a city full of people that would hurt them? Are today's meat-eating Christians able to heal sick people with their magical healing powers? Were they able to get bitten by a venomous rattlesnake and live?

This was a particular and unique circumstance for a specific group of 70 people at a specific time. I would not argue that meat was a possibility, but using this verse would be a pretty lazy argument in favor of eating meat today.

CHAPTER 59:
LUKE 11:11 – FISH OR SERPENT

B read, stone, fish, or snake
Luke chapter 11 verse 11

If a son shall ask bread of any of you that is a father, will he give him a stone? Or if he ask a fish, will he for a fish give him a serpent?

This verse is from a classic speech called The Sermon on the Mount. Since Jesus talks about giving someone an egg or a fish, I thought I'd play with this one.

Some carnist Christians use this verse to argue that offering children an egg or fish is permissible. You will learn in upcoming chapters, just because something is lawful does not mean it's good. But let's work this one over.

5Ws

5- And he said onto <u>them</u> (the people listening to Jesus), *which of you shall have a friend, and shall go onto him at midnight, and say unto him friend, lend me <u>three loaves</u>*

6- for a friend of mine in his journey has come to me, and <u>I have nothing</u> to set before him?

The first word I underline is the word <u>them</u>. We need to ask, who was listening and needed to understand this teaching? This was happening in primarily, a fishing community. It's a good chance they were fishermen.

We are going to get good vegan stuff here. Verse 5 starts with a story, not an actual event. A story about a pesky friend who receives an unexpected, late night visitor. He's got no snacks to offer his unexpected visitor, so he goes to his sleeping neighbor's house and says, "hey, wake up and give me food" He specifically asked for 3 loaves of bread (artos = bread, a loaf). When Jesus starts this story, he does not mention fish or any animal flesh...yet.

7- And he (sleeping neighbor) *from within shall answer and say trouble me not, the door is now shut, and my children are with me in bed, I cannot rise and give thee.*

8- I say unto you, though he will not rise and give him, because he is his friend, yet because of his importunity (persistence, complaining) *he will rise and give him as many as you needeth*

Now we're getting to the heart of this parable (a parable is a narrative used to explain a moral or spiritual lesson). This sleepy neighbor guy doesn't want to get out of bed and help the pesky neighbor by giving him three loaves of bread. So Pesky neighbor keeps banging on the door, saying, "give me some food." So the sleepy neighbor guy is like, "*Fine, whatever man, here is your bread. Just go away, my kids are sleeping. It's late.*"

Sleepy neighbor guy gives in to pesky neighbor requests, but it's not because he is a good person; it was only because pesky neighbor was a nuisance.

Now Jesus is going to show how God will care for us in a fatherly kind of way. God gives not because we're being a pest, but because He loves us.

9- And I say unto you, Ask, and it shall be given to you; seek, and you shall find; knock, and it shall be opened unto you

10- For everyone that asketh receiveth; and he that seeketh findeth; and to him that knocketh it shall be opened

11- If a son shall ask bread of any of you that is a father, will he give him a stone? Or if he ask a fish, will he for a fish give him a serpent?

12- Or if he shall ask an egg, will he offer him a scorpion?

When we get to verse 11, we see that Jesus first makes his point using bread. Then, he connects it to the people listening, the fisherman. Jesus isn't saying God would give them a fish or a serpent or an egg or a scorpion; he's asking *which of you, that are fathers,* would do that.

He's giving them stories with fish they can connect with because they were fishermen. These verses aren't given to approve or disapprove of fishing or eating eggs. It's like this, if Jesus was speaking to a bunch of computer geeks, he probably would've said, *"If your child asked you for an iPad would you give him a Palm Pilot"?* Got it?

This next vegan defense is not one of my favorites but in verse 13 Jesus says,

13- if ye then, being evil (human nature being evil), *know how to give good gifts unto your children, how much more shall your heavenly father give the Holy Spirit to them and ask him?*

I don't think Jesus is telling everyone they are evil but saying people can still give good gifts to their kids, even if they have an evil nature. The "good gifts" that "evil" people give are in the previous verse, fish and eggs. Products that come from animal abuse and are full of cholesterol. Jesus started off saying the neighbor is looking for three loaves of bread. He ended by saying those who are evil will do what they consider good. Like, offer products of animal abuse as food to children. That's a bit tough to get across, but an interesting thought to keep in your back pocket.

Some stories suck

When Jesus tells parables, he is using the customs of the people to whom he speaks. It is so they can learn. Using a cultural custom in a parable is not a stamp of approval to do the actions in the parable. If everything Jesus spoke of in a parable is "Jesus approved", then what will the Christians do with what Jesus said about slavery in Matthew 18? These were just relatable examples Jesus picked and never meant as a thumbs-up for evil behaviors.

This fish/egg/serpent story is for a comparison. God isn't a grumpy neighbor who won't give you bread. Jesus is telling them, just ask God for something. He will give to you because He loves you, not because you're a pest banging on His door.

CHAPTER 60:
LUKE 22:7 – PASSOVER

Jesus must have eaten lamb at Passover.

Many Christians argue Jesus taking part in a Passover meal at The Last Supper proves Jesus ate animals. Don't stress, we can win this one, but we've got some schooling to do.

The Last Supper, Passover or Not?

The famous "The Last Supper" is in Matthew chapter 26, Mark chapter 14, and Luke chapter 22. They imply this last supper party is the Passover meal that requires a sacrificed Lamb. However, this gets messy for Christians because **John chapter 19:14** claims Jesus died before Passover formally began. If so, this could not be a Passover meal. This has been an issue within the church for a while. It's not something I can solve now, even if I devoted 10 chapters to the subject. I'll give some basics, but it doesn't matter what side of the controversy you stand on to defend the vegan viewpoint.

5Ws

Let's deal with what the Passover is, who it was for, why it's a tradition, and so on.

Just in case you haven't seen Charlton Heston as Moses in The 10 Commandments (am I showing my age?), here is how the story goes. The people of Israel are slaves under an evil Pharaoh in Egypt. God sends Moses to convince Pharaoh to let his people go. Moses invokes 10 strange plagues. If you think the plagues were strange, it's because you are not Israel living around 1400 BC. You see, the people believed in many false gods. Each plague was a direct attack on their false gods, thus proving the God of Moses is the real deal.

Moving on, 9 plagues skipped the people of Israel, affecting only Pharaoh's communities. Strangely, the last of the plagues will kill the firstborn child in every house, including Israel's kids.

To bypass this "death plague," Israel was instructed to sacrifice a lamb and drain its blood. Then, take that blood and wipe it on the doorposts of their home so the *Angel of Death* (cool name that) would "Passover" their house, only killing Egyptian kids. Nasty, huh?

I never understood why, only the last of these 10 plagues required Israel to do this bloody ritual. It's confusing because God skipped over Israel for the other plagues (see Exodus chapter 9). Still, without these bloody doorposts, the 10th plague would affect Israel's children too. The Jewish faith has a lot of symbolism. I'm sure if I looked more into it, I'd find a solid answer. But, it's not relevant to the vegan message, so I will not go much further on this. I just like to kvetch when scripture bothers me.

Moving on, this plague on the firstborn was the final straw for Pharaoh. He let the people of Israel go. God does not want Israel to forget where they came from. He gives rules on re-creating this bloody Passover night every year for remembrance. I just want to say I'm with you atheists on this. I think this whole situation is pretty messed up, but carnist Christians have no problem with it, so on with the story.

Rules

This annual Passover commemoration permits eating meat, but it's not a requirement. Not all Jews practiced the Passover in the same ways. There were Jewish groups such as the Ebionites and Essenes (Nazoraeans and the Ossaeans) that had their rules, of which some were vegetarianism. Each of these groups were big into ritual purity. They kept close adherence to the Jewish laws but denied animal sacrifice. Some of the Essenes rejected slavery, which was also a common practice of the time. As you can see, just as Christians today hold different views on issues, so did the Jews regarding Passover.

Prepare us for the Passover.

Verse 7 is not an order to kill.

> *Then came the day of unleavened bread, when the Passover must be killed.*
> *8- And he* (Jesus) *sent Peter and John, saying, go prepare us the Passover, that we may eat*

Many people automatically assume when Jesus said *"prepare us for the Passover"*, he was talking of preparation for the animal sacrifice. Not so. Verse 7 gives us, the readers, the day as a reference.

Passover preparations

Many people were poor and could not afford to kill a lamb. Those people could use vegetable substitutes such as a beet. Broiled beets are halakhically (legally) acceptable to use as a replacement.

Preparing for the Passover involves many rituals. Killing a lamb is only one part of the preparations. For example, leavened bread represents sin in our lives. The entire house must be clean from any leavened bread. Even a tiny crumb of regular bread in your home will nullify the ritual. Why? Symbolism. Sometimes big sins (like an entire slice of bread) are easy to find in our lives, but a little tiny crumb-sized sin can remain hidden. That's the symbolic reason for the removal of every tiny little crumb. There are many ceremonial cleanings and preparations for the Passover that do not involve the sacrifice of animals.

When Peter and John prepared the upper room for a Passover, they were only cleaning it. Or maybe they were getting the required 4 cups of wine. Or perhaps they were bringing the bitter herbs. Maybe they were preparing the unleavened bread. Don't let Christians read animal sacrifice into everything to support their meat-eating blood lust.

So what did JC eat? Nothing!

Now, back to the Last Supper.

Jesus and his guys are about to eat the last meal they have together. They will crucify Jesus the next day. There are verses in Luke telling us what Jesus actually ate.

Luke chapter 22 verse 15
And he said unto them, With desire I have desired to eat this Passover with you before I suffer

16- For I say unto you, I will not any more eat thereof, until it be fulfilled in the kingdom of God

17- And he took the cup, and gave thanks, and said, Take this and divide it among yourselves

18- For I say unto you, I will not drink of the fruit of the vine, until the kingdom of God shall come.

19- And he took bread, and gave thanks (blessing), and break it, and gave unto them saying, this is my body which is given for you: this do in remembrance of me.

Look at the repeated underlining I did to highlight the foods that were present. The scripture only mentions bread and wine. There is no mention of any lamb.

You ask, "What if the lamb was there but left out of the story"? Verse 16 to the vegan rescue. Even if the lamb was served, Jesus chose not to eat any of it. Instead, he gave it to the disciples. Jesus drank nothing. Jesus was a Nazoraean, they believed in abstinence from alcohol (and believed to be vegetarian). So, by choice, Jesus did not eat the bread or the lamb if lamb was available. This should squelch their claim that Jesus ate meat.

But, if the carnist holds to lamb being present, ask, "if Jesus served a sacrificial lamb, why in verse 19 did he give them bread and not a piece of lamb?"

This (bread*) is my body which is given for you.*

He didn't say this dead lamb represents my body.

I have additional confirmation no meat was there. Years later, in 1st Corinthians chapter 11, when the apostle Paul practices the "Last Supper", he speaks only of bread and wine. If eating lamb was the custom, it stopped by the time of Paul.

If they stick to the belief there had to be a Passover sacrifice, activists can come back with yet another reply. Ask, "where did the disciples get money for a lamb? Weren't the disciples dirt broke and having to borrow a room from a generous person (possibly Mark's mother) to do this last supper"? Only the well-to-do could afford a perfect, unblemished lamb.

Jesus had to eat the Passover.

Another carnist argument is, Jesus would have eaten the Passover lamb (see Exodus 12) at least once a year while growing up. I have two replies to consider. First, there are things Jesus did not do that were required. For example, he skipped paying the temple tax as in Matthew chapter 17. Jesus was the temple and the son of God, so he considered himself to be exempt.

Matthew chapter 17 verse 26:
Jesus said to him, "Then the sons are exempt."

This shows Jesus could have considered himself exempt from partaking in the Passover ritual. Also, there are alternatives to a lamb in Passover celebrations. Jewish law allowed the poor to use alternate offerings if need (Leviticus 12:8).

Jesus' earthly parents were so poor they had to use doves in their offerings (Luke 2:24). But there were those so very poor they couldn't even afford pigeons, so beets, carrots and yams were substituted. Jesus may have done only beet offerings or such growing up.

My "use all the rules," argument

Suppose today's meat-eater won't let go of using the Passover as their current justification to eat animals. If they do, let them, but it's only fair to use *every rule of Passover*. Here is where they lose any ground to stand on.

First, according to the Talmud (Jewish civil and ceremonial laws), since the destruction of the Temple, Jews have no way to fulfill the requirements that go along with eating meat. Also, alternatives are approved options. Eating animals is a choice, not an obligation. Nevertheless, let's peek at the rules.

Exodus chapter 12 verse 3
Speak ye unto all the congregation of Israel, saying in the 10th day of this month they shall take to them every man a lamb, according to the house of their fathers, a lamb for an house

In verse 3, God is speaking to Moses and Aaron, telling them to give this information to the congregation of Israel, no one else. So if a meat-eating Christian claims God said he (or she) can eat lamb for Passover, you can ask, "are you a Jew keeping the Old Testament law of Moses"? If you live according to the Law, you are not a Christian. Christians live under "Grace." By keeping the Law, you have actually "Fallen from Grace." Yep, the Bible teaches there is only one way to fall from Grace, and that happens when a person tries to save themselves by keeping the law:

Galatians chapter 5 verse 4
Whosoever of you are justified by the Law (keeping the Law as a means of salvation); *ye are fallen from grace.*

A big meat-eater fail is for a "Grace Believer" (Christian) to use the Passover as permission to eat animals today.

My next underline was the day of the month. Remember, this allowance to eat lamb was once a year on a specific day. Is the meat-eating Christian only eating meat once a year? Only on the 10th day of the month of Nisan (March or April)? If they're going to use the Passover allowance to eat meat, again I say, they have got to follow the Passover rules. I just agree with them and say sure, eat meat once a year and the 364 other days go vegan. This one is "iffy" but we can use it.

Verse 5
Your lamb shall be without blemish, a male of the first year: he shall take it out from the sheep, or from the goats:
    6- And ye shall keep it up until the 14th day of the same month and the whole assembly of the congregation of Israel shall kill it in the evening.

If the carnist wants to continue with his Passover allowance to eat animals, ask him, "is there any blemish on your lamb"? Then ask "Are you sure it was a male only a year old"? Then ask "Are you going to kill it with the rest of the Jews you hang out with"? Again, meat-eater fail, especially if he gets his meat from a factory farm which automatically makes it not permissible or possibly (treif) un-kosher.

Verse 7

*And they shall take the blood, and strike it on the two side posts
and on the upper door post of the houses. Where in they shall eat
it*

Come on now, we know they didn't rub their steak dinner on the door
before they ate it.

I'm sure you can see where I'm going with this "use all the rules"
argument. The carnist Christian cannot use the Passover verses to defend
his meat-eating and still be a Christian. These laws were given to a specific
group of people (Israel) at a certain time in history, for a specific purpose
while living under the Law! If you are a Christian, that purpose was *never
meant for you*. If you choose to live under the Law, you are rejecting God's
Grace through Jesus.

The Bottom Line: Compassion is how a Christian determines food,
not ancient Jewish rituals.

Verse 8

*And they shall eat the flesh in that night, roast with fire, and
unleavened bread and the bitter herbs they shall eat it.*

I'm sure the carnist Christian is not killing the lamb themselves and
eating it on the same day with bitter herbs (like horseradish) as a side dish.
Reading the 12th chapter of Exodus will show many more requirements,
which no Christian today is required to keep. People today eat meat for
pleasure. The Jews did Passover for remembrance of hard times, not
pleasure. I am sure you can see the Passover from back then has no support
for eating animals today.

Any approval to eat animals is upsetting, but through these very
limiting rules, God is moving Israel towards an end goal of eliminating
animal sacrifice completely. That will come through in the teachings of the
later prophets, such as Jeremiah and Isaiah.

Trust me, this is good for vegan activism. Sounds contradictory, I
know, but it gets worked out in this ongoing story of God's redemption for
his people and the gradual abolishment of the sacrificial system.

CHAPTER 61: LUKE 24:42 – JESUS ATE FISH

Jesus ate fish, so shut up, you stinking vegans

Luke chapter 24 verse 42:
And they gave him a piece of broiled fish, and of a honeycomb.
43- And he took it, and did eat before them.

Carnist Christian: "Take that vegan. Jesus ate fish, so we can too."
I'd say Ya, well, Jesus was a kosher Jew. So if you only eat what he did, there goes your pepperoni pizza!

That's me being a jerk with my reply, but these verses were not meant to lay down a formula for what we are to eat today. For a vegan understanding, we need to look into the entire situation.

5Ws

Jesus had just been crucified. The apostles worried the Jewish leaders would come get them next.

John chapter 20 verse 19
When the doors were shut where the disciples were assembled for fear of the Jews.

They were afraid and hiding in a locked room. Then, outta nowhere, Jesus appeared.

Luke chapter 24
36- And as they thus spake, Jesus himself stood in the midst of them.
     37- But they were terrified and affrighted, and supposed that they had seen a spirit

The disciples, thinking they were seeing a non-physical spirit, freaked out. They had no PKE Meter to confirm ghost activity (no? Ghostbusters? Anyone? Ahhh, forget it). Jesus knew they doubted he was real.

39- Behold my hands and my feet, that it is I myself: handle me, and see; for a spirit hath not flesh and bones, as ye see me have

So he was like, "Dudes, why are you so frightened? It's really me, your pal. Check out my hands and feet, see the wounds from the crucifixion?"
     The apostles didn't know Jesus was going to raise from the dead, much less in a natural body. Jesus even said they could touch him to verify he was real, but they were still afraid. Jesus wants them to understand he is flesh and blood. The touching didn't get the message across. In a continued effort to prove himself with a physical body, Jesus asked the guys for something to eat. Why? he knew their belief that a ghost could not eat real food.

41- And while they yet believed not for joy, and wondered, he said unto them, Have ye here any meat (brósimos)?
     42- And they gave him a piece of a broiled fish, and of an honeycomb

Once again, we need to sidetrack and deal with the King James Bible erroneously translating the Greek word *brósimos to* the word "meat."
     Brósimos means "food, eatable, suitable for food."
     Jesus didn't say, "Have ye any meat?" he asked, "Have ye anything to eat?" Jesus was asking for *any food.* But, unfortunately, the KJV's poor translation has today's carnist thinking Jesus specifically asked for animal flesh. Wrong!
     Have the carnist look at the NIV, ESV, NASB, HCSB, or many other legit translations. They translated the sentence *"Do you have anything here to eat?"*

But why ask for food at all?

Jesus is not eating because he is hungry. This is the same Jesus who went 40 days and 40 nights in the wilderness (Matthew chapter 4) with no food. Jesus has a new and glorified body that will never die. He can rise from the dead, walk through walls and ascend into heaven, yet Christians think he *needed to eat a fish.* Heck no, Jesus was not hungry. The disciples believed a ghost couldn't eat, so Jesus was working with that belief by saying, *give me something to eat* as proof he was not a spirit.

Did Jesus eat the honey and fish?

To prove he is real, Jesus ate whatever was available in that locked room. It could have been a PB&J sandwich and he still would have gotten the same point across. In verse 42, they handed Jesus 2 things to eat: fish and honeycomb. But in 43, he only took *it*, not them.

And he took it, and did eat before them.

We can argue Jesus only took "it," one item, the honey. I don't find this to be a solid reply, but usable to at least cast doubt Jesus ate animal flesh. But we have to deal with neither fish nor honey being vegan. I'd like you to consider the possibility eating honey can be humane...back then.

Ethical Honey?

Now we have a couple of problems with the honey part. First, we'll look at what I said about honey possibly being humane. Then, I'll deal with possible additions to the text as the honeycomb part doesn't even exist in most Bible translations now.

The honey

Bees lived in the caves and trees throughout Palestine during the first century. The method in which honey was collected didn't involve any of the intense farming practices we know today. Instead, a piece of wood or a bowl would be laid underneath a natural beehive. Whatever dripped out onto these pieces of wood, people took for themselves. The bees were never touched, manipulated, or harassed in any way. Admittedly, the insects were exploited, but no physical harm was being done. So was it vegan? No. Was it humane? Eh, pretty much so for that place and time.

No honeycomb at all

Now let's take a peek at why some Bible translations include the honeycomb and other versions do not. I don't want to spend time on this and apparently, neither did other church leaders because so they wrote little on the subject. The meaning of this story is not what Jesus ate, but that he could eat.

Early church fathers didn't seem to care if it was honey, fish, or even a pizza when they told the story. They were all about Jesus being bodily resurrected. Offering to eat food, along with being able to be touched, was his proof. A spirit or ghost could not do this.

Dinner plate

Let's consider verse 43 from another perspective. If someone told you they had a steak dinner, would you think there was *only steak on the plate*? Typically, they'd have mashed potatoes and maybe some corn on the side. It's kind of like that when they offered fish and honeycomb. Simply because the apostle only reported a fish doesn't necessarily mean there were no side items.

43- And he took it, and did eat before them.

When verse 43 says, *he took it and did eat before them.* The "*It*" could have been the dinner plate full of food, of which Jesus only ate part of. But heck, if Jesus only ate the side of mashed potatoes, that would do the job of proving him as physical. The writers didn't think it mattered to be detailed about each piece of food offered or eaten, so they just said he took it.

Another look

Jesus is considered the moral baseline of what to do. So if Jesus ate fish back then, people can today. I'm going to drop a couple of verses to combat the idea that everything Jesus did applied for all time. Let's look in Luke where Jesus healed the man with leprosy.

Luke chapter 5 verse 14
Then Jesus ordered him, tell no man: but go, and shew thyself to the priest, and offer thy cleansing (make a sacrifice), *according as Moses commanded*

Jesus is telling someone to go and make sacrifices. Obviously, Christians today don't make animal sacrifices. The lesson is, just because Jesus commanded something doesn't mean we are to do it. Let's take one more into consideration.

Matthew chapter 23 verse 1-3
Then Jesus speak to the multitude, and to his disciples
    2- Saying, the scribes and the Pharisees sit in Moses' seat:
    3- All therefore whatsoever they bid you do observe, that observe and do

The scribes and the Pharisees are considered the new Moses. Moses taught the law, so the scribes and Pharisees are the law teachers. Jesus is telling his followers to *comply with* the Jewish laws. That meant kosher laws, purity laws, dozens of baptisms, and so much more. None of which is required today. Again, I say, we are not to do all Jesus did. Jesus said many things meant only for those Jews living under the law. Much of which can not be applied to Christians today. Knowing where to "rightly divide" (2 Timothy 2:15) the word of truth is very important.

Bible Geek side note: When I read the book of Matthew in its original Hebrew, not Greek, I get a much better understanding of this verse. Jesus is actually saying *do what Moses commanded in the Written Torah* and *ignore what is in the Oral Torah.* But that is for another study. Either way, both translations work for our vegan advocacy.

That was then, and this is now.

With the scarcity of food available, I can't imagine Jesus, the Apostles, Moses, or any Bible dudes being full-on vegan. But that was then, and this is now. What people ate to survive back then does not determine our food now. Many people were poor; they didn't own any land to grow their own foods. Sometimes, sustaining themselves by eating fish (the oceans were free and open to all) was necessary to survive. Today, in the 21st-century, fruits and vegetables are available from around the world. We have a choice. People then did not.

Eat as JC did

If someone claims they can eat fish because Jesus did, they would also be *required to do it the way Jesus did.* That included keeping the kosher laws because Jesus was a Jew.

In the Torah, there are 613 laws, and over 100 of them are about minimizing animal suffering. Compassion for animals is a strong value in Judaism. None of those rules are being followed by today's fishing industries. If Jesus was walking the earth now, he'd refuse the piece of factory-farmed fish being offered as cruelty violates Jewish dietary regulations. Heck, step it back. The apostles wouldn't even have had factory farmed fish to offer in the first place.

Also, we have no report Jesus ate any animal flesh other than maybe, just maybe, a single fish. No cows, no chickens, and being a jew, no pigs. So if the carnist wants to eat like Jesus…No bacon!

Jesus was not a vegetarian

As much as I believe he was, I honestly can't use the Bible to prove Jesus was a vegetarian. There is plenty of evidence in the Non-Conical (unauthorized) books.

But, Christians only accept the 66 books currently in the Old and New Testaments. If we activists quote non-canonical books to prove a veggie Jesus, they will label us as cult members. It will probably hinder any valuable ground we could have gained for veganism. So, I try to use only the books accepted by fundamentalist Christians. Those non-canonical books are not bad. I love them! I gain so much insight into the culture the Bible leaves out. But, when talking with 21st century Christian, I meet them where they are at with their mindset, be it wrong or right. Besides, I've given enough ammunition to deal with the fish story without reaching into the non-canonical scriptures.

Jesus in the wilderness.

Earlier, I mentioned Matthew chapter 4 when Jesus was fasting. "Fasting" is when you give up food for a religious reason. I can grab an additional vegan tidbit from this to show how Jesus never desired to eat animals, and we can thank Satan for this one.

Mark chapter 1 verse 13
And he was there in the wilderness forty days, tempted of Satan; and was with the wild beasts; and the angels ministered unto him.

Mark reports Jesus was with angels and animals during this fasting time. Got that? Ok, moving on.

Matthew chapter 4
2- And when he had fasted forty days and forty nights, he was afterward an hungred.
    3- And when the tempter (Satan) *came to him, he said, If thou be the Son of God, command that these <u>stones be made bread</u>.*

And again in:

Luke chapter 4 verse 3
And the devil said unto him, If thou be the Son of God, command this stone that <u>it be made bread.</u>

We see Jesus at what could be his hungriest time ever and he was surrounded by animals. The vegan grab we have is Satan didn't say, *"Go eat the animals."* Instead, Satan tempted Jesus with the food he knew Jesus preferred: bread. Thank you, Mr. Devil, for that vegan win.

CHAPTER 62:
JOHN 2:15 – CLEANSING
THE TEMPLE

Table turning for Animal Liberation. I wish.

John chapter 2 verse 15
And when he had made a scourge of small cords, he drove them all out of the temple, and the sheep, and the oxen; and poured out the changers' money, and <u>overthrew the tables</u>;

This story is often quoted as the only place Jesus ever got mad. Three of the four gospels tell of Jesus turning over tables in an act of anger when seeing the temple turned into a market. His table-turning action released many animals intended for sacrifice. It is called *The Cleansing of the Temple*. Many vegan Christian activists will use this story, saying Jesus released the animals in an act of animal liberation. Sounds good but sorry, I don't buy it. Animals do get released, but this event is much more. It deals with unscrupulous religious leaders profiting off the sacrificial system, and Jesus ending that system by his death and resurrection. The story has a little vegan ammunition, but there's just way too much involved to make it solely an act of animal liberation.

5Ws

I will use the 1st "Cleansing of the Temple" as presented in the Gospel of John. Yep, I said 1st as there might be 2 cleansing stories…or maybe not. It might be the same story, but offered at different times. In John, the 1st cleansing is at the beginning of Jesus' ministry. The 2nd cleansing happens

3 years later, as described in the Gospels of Matthew, Mark, and Luke. Christians have a problem with this, it steps on the inerrancy of the scriptures. Not a vegan activist thing you'll need to know, so don't make a big deal of it.

At the Passover festival

At the Passover festival, thousands of people gathered to offer their sacrifice, making the temple a giant nasty slaughterhouse. Local people had it easy. They could bring their own perfect, unblemished animals and their own money. Many people traveled from long distances, making it difficult to bring a perfect animal with them. Rather than travel with an animal, they could buy one from a local temple vendor (*those that sold*). If their foreign money wasn't accepted, people known as Money Changers converted what they had into an allowed currency.

Thieves in the temple

Travel created opportunity for vendors, money changers, and priests to team up and rip off good people. Let me give an example so you can wrap your brain around the scam. Let's say there is a dude named Benjamin taking part in the Passover. Benjamin is a decent guy and follows the religious rules. Benjamin traveled hundreds of miles to take part in this Passover and brought his own lamb. The lamb is supposed to be perfect for sacrifice. During Ben's hundred-mile journey, the lamb got a scratch, making it imperfect. Or, maybe it is perfect, but the priests might lie and say "oh look, a tiny little scratch on the bottom of the left leg. It's no good, so you got to buy one of our pre-approved lambs". Benjamin is now forced to buy a perfect animal from the local salespeople (*those that sold*) at whatever exorbitant price they make. The mark-up is ridiculous, Benjamin gets ripped off.

The vendors and the priest were working together. They were taking advantage of sincere people like Benjamin, who just wanted to serve God. There were other ways they were being thieves and robbers, but I trust you get the idea.

Also, more on this in a bit, but keep in mind, the temple was supposed to be a place all nations could gather to pray. Now, it has become a tremendous source of money for corrupt priests through ritual animal slaughter. Imagine the world's biggest butcher shop run by the mob.

John chapter 2 verse 13.
And the Jews' Passover was at hand, and Jesus went up to Jerusalem,

If you are introducing the cleansing story into your vegan conversation, be prepared for verse 13 to bite you. Jesus is going to the Passover. Christians might deflect from the cleansing story to say Jesus was going to do the Passover sacrifice of a lamb. I give defense for this in another chapter, but why go there if you don't need.

14- And found in the temple <u>those that sold</u> oxen and sheep and doves, and the <u>changers of money</u> (bankers) *sitting:*

In verse 14, we read the initial focus of what Jesus found upsetting. It was <u>the people who sold</u> the animals, and those who <u>changed money.</u> We could replace the animals with bread or incense, and it wouldn't make a difference to the meaning of verse 14. Jesus took action after seeing this.

15- And when he had made a scourge (whip) *of small cords, <u>he drove them all out</u> of the temple, and the sheep, and the oxen; and poured out the changers' money, and overthrew the tables;*

A small whip, really? We've got hundreds of crooks and Jesus takes them on with a small whip he made on the spot? This is some serious Indiana Jones kind of crap going on. Notice my underline: *<u>he drove them all out</u> of the temple, <u>and</u> the sheep, and the oxen.*

Jesus did not "liberate" animals alone, he drove out the people too. The animals benefited from this cleansing, but this was not done for their sake alone. Also, the carnist could push back saying Jesus used a whip on the innocent creatures. Not good.

16- And said unto them that sold doves, Take these things hence (away); *make not <u>my Father's house</u> a house of <u>merchandise</u>* (emporiou: a place of traffic, a market, market-house).

I want you to pay attention to why Jesus complained and how he expressed it. Also, ask to who is Jesus speaking? The people (Jews) hearing Jesus say *"my father's house"* freaked. Why? Because in saying God was his father, Jesus is making himself equal to God. The Jews picked up on that right away. I will get back to that.

I have another concern in using this cleansing as an animal liberation story. Activists lose ground because Jesus doesn't say, "don't make my father's house a place of slaughter." Instead, Jesus says not to make his father's house a <u>place of merchandise</u>. In this verse, the word for merchandise is ***Emporiou***: *a place of traffic, mart, market, market-house.* We are reading of an attack on the selling of any goods, be it animals, incense, or TV sets, if they had TVs. You get the idea.

17- And his disciples remembered that it was written, Zeal for Your house will consume me (Psalm 69).
    18- Then answered the Jews and said unto him, What <u>sign</u> shewest thou unto us, seeing that thou doest these things?

Remember what I said in verse 16 about Jesus claiming to be equal with God? Here in verse 18, we read the Jews confirming this claim of equality is precisely what they perceived. When they say to Jesus, *"show us a sign"* or in the fancy King James version, *shewest thou unto us,* they expected to see a miracle. They knew the Messiah, or God's Son, will do miracles. There is no clue from their reaction that animal liberation was an issue. They don't even comment on the animals being freed. The requesting of a sign (miracle) shows they knew the cleansing of the temple was about Jesus being equal to God.

19- Jesus answered and said unto them, <u>Destroy this temple</u>, and in three days I will raise it up.

In verse 19, the *"Temple"* Jesus speaks of is himself. He is saying, if you kill me, I will come back in 3 days. His resurrection is the *sign* he will show them. You see, no one knew Jesus was the new temple. His temple remark is another reason it's hard for me to accept this as an act of animal liberation. Jesus has an opportunity to say, *"Hey, you got the prophets teaching that God did not want animal sacrifices, and here you are 400 years later still doing them, and worst of all, in God's house,"* but he doesn't. Jesus focuses on who he is, *the temple*. Any issue of the animals gets pushed into the background. So much so, no one comments on the released animals.

20- Then said the Jews, Forty and six years was this temple in building, and wilt thou rear it up in three days?
21- But he (Jesus) *spake of the temple of his body.*

Jesus is saying, destroy my body on the cross, and in three days I will raise from the dead. Think, Good Friday thru Easter, got it?

We've got the basics of the event as recorded in the gospel of John. Jesus was cleansing the temple of wicked men that cheated the sincere worshipers and proving he is God's son. OK, but we still have other accounts to consider.

Possible 2nd Cleansing

Another reason I avoid claiming animal liberation. In Luke, Mark and Matthew, we see no mention of animals in the possible second cleansing, only doves. Which is interesting because the poor typically offered doves. This could imply Jesus was showing concern for the poor. As the poorest of the poor, they could not afford any animal. Other non-living things are allowed as offerings and sacrifices.

However, this is another opportunity for Jesus to speak out against animal sacrifice, but the focus is only on the sellers being robbers and thieves.

Before I end, let's have one more verse that leads me away from the animal liberation view.

Mark chapter 11 verse 18
And the scribes and chief priests heard it, and sought how they might destroy him:

The religious leaders started making plans to assassinate Jesus because of what he had just done. A priest doesn't plan to kill a person liberating animals. The chief priests looked at Jesus' action as the beginning of the end of their sacrificial system. That system made the priests extremely rich and powerful. They wanted Jesus stopped and dead. Animals did benefit, but that is not the reason for the cleansing. Or maybe it's only a part of many.

Violent thieves?

There is another view on this that I really like. I have some success with it, but rarely used. It assumes reading both "cleansings" as only one. Again, I have no issue with that, just go with what your target carnist believes. Be it one or two makes no difference to your activism.
Let's reread and compare **John chapter 2 verse 16:**

And said unto them that sold doves, Take these things hence: make not my Father's house <u>a house of merchandise</u>

Now we compare. When Matthew 21:13, Mark11:17 and Luke19:46 tell the story, they use a different phrase than John. They add "house of prayer" and say "den of thieves".
For example:

Mark chapter 11 verse 17
And he taught, saying unto them, Is it not written, My house shall be called of all nations the <u>house of prayer</u>? But ye have made it a <u>den of thieves</u>.

New differences

My fathers house is now a *house of prayer*.
A *house or merchandise* is now a *den of thieves*.
Jesus said this in Greek. The Geek word used for thieves is "Léstés". Léstés: a thief who plunders and pillages–an unscrupulous marauder, exploiting the vulnerable without <u>hesitating to use violence</u>.
I underlined the last part of the definition for a reason. The word *léstés* implies the use of violence. When I think of a thief, I think of someone who sneaks into a place, steals something in leaves. I don't think of a violent murder. Now ask, why did Jesus use such a word? Because the

verse is a call back to Jeremiah, and the Hebrew word is much more violent than our current understanding of the word thief.

Jeremiah chapter 7 verse 11
Is this house, which is called by my name, become a den of robbers (parits) *in your eyes?*

In Hebrew, the word used for robber or thief is ***Parits: violent one.***

When Jeremiah said it, the Hebrew implies something different from just a sneaky common thief. It implies crooks who are not just robbers and thieves, but violent murderers. One who sheds blood.

Do you see the differences in how Mark quotes Jesus compared to John?

We've got a house of prayer, den of murderous thieves, house of merchandise. Quite the differences.

Ending sacrifice

According to Mark's Gospel, Jesus sees this temple should be a house of prayer. Sadly, it has been corrupted into a house of *parits: bloodshed, murder.* The temple has degenerated into a place of sacrifice.

Something I like is this supports the idea of killing animals is murder. That's a win for veganism. So reading this story with all the gospel accounts in mind, and knowing the call back to the book of Jeremiah, you can kind of argue this was about ending violence and sacrifice. It's hard to get there but a slight win if you want to use it. Now, I really do like this, but the rest of the story, in all accounts, still has Jesus paying no attention to the animals. Let's look.

After the table turning

In **Matthew chapter 21 verses 12-17**, only doves are mentioned. After the tables are flipped, Jesus goes on to heal the blind. No further talk of animals.

In **Mark chapter 11 verses 15-19**, only doves are mentioned and Jesus goes on to stop any further merchandise (Greek: skeuos) being brought in. The word used for merchandise is *skeuos: a vessel, implement, goods.* This refers to products. No further talk of animals.

Lastly, in **Luke chapter 19 verses 45 - 48**, there is no table turning and no mention of any animals at all. Jesus went on to preach while the priests planned on killing him.

So, even with the understanding of a violent act involved with the term thief or robber, the verses that follow add no support for this action being done solely to save animals.

Wrap up

Even though animals were set free, I don't think that's the message for our vegan outreach. It could be argued when Jesus made a callback to Jeremiah, he was calling the people that were selling animals murderers, but that's a hard, hard direction to go in. It's much easier for our activism to show Jesus turned the tables to announce the entire system, including sacrifices, is under judgment from God. This synagogue, its rituals and sacrifices, will be destroyed and eventually, Jesus is the new temple.

CHAPTER 63: JOHN 21 – RE-COMMISSIONING OF PETER

Peter gets a second chance

John chapter 21 is used to suggest Jesus was OK with fishing. When you understand the context, you see this about Jesus reconnecting with Peter after his sin of denial and disobedience. The example used was fish but it could've been french fries, and it wouldn't make any difference in the meaning.

5Ws

Jesus is making another appearance after his resurrection. Simon Peter and six other disciples are at the waterfront. I want you to pay attention to what Simon Peter says, starting in verse 3:

> **John chapter 21**
> *I go fishing.* They (the other disciples) *say onto him, we also go with thee. They went forth, and entered into the ship immediately, and that night they caught nothing.*

Before his crucifixion, Jesus told them (Matthew chapter 4, Mark chapter 1) he would make them *fishers of men*. They responded to his call by leaving their fishing business and immediately followed him. Why is this important?

Disobeyed

Peter says in verse 3, *"I'm gonna go back to fishing."* Why is that bad? Because Peter was instructed to continue preaching the gospel, not return to fishing. To make matters worse, the rest of the gang followed Peter back to a life of fishing.

I would cut them a little slack. Things were happening so fast and the guys weren't sure what was going on. But still, they weren't doing as assigned. Peter's return to fishing showed he no longer had faith in Jesus. The other disciples must have lost their faith too, because they followed Pete.

I also underlined they didn't catch a thing after an entire night of fishing. I say Jesus was at work during that moment, too. He can command the fish to fill the nets, and he can command the opposite. This also impressed upon them fishing was not the right thing to do.

Relish

In verse number 4, morning comes, and they're still out in the boat, but Jesus is on the shore.

> *4- But when the morning was come, Jesus stood on the shore: but the disciples knew not that it was Jesus.*

No one knows why, but they didn't recognize Jesus. Maybe because they fished at night and the sun had yet to come up, making it hard to see. Then we get into verse 5.

> *5- Then Jesus said unto them, Children, have you any meat* (prosphagion / Relish)*? They answered him, No.*

The KJV once again gives another poor translation leading to believe Jesus asked for actual fish (meat). The Greek word used in this verse is *Prosphagion, a relish eaten with bread / a dried Mediterranean seaweed.* That's not animal flesh. Go ahead and check your Greek Interlinear. Jesus really asked if they had any relish, such as this seaweed stuff.

Imagine the scene. Jesus is shoreline, standing by a fire. On the fire, Jesus supplied bread, and whatever this relish stuff is. So Jesus already has food to feed them. Jesus did not bring fish to eat, remember that.

Hey kids

A common question among fishermen would be, *"Hey dudes, catch anything"?* But that's not the way Jesus asked. Jesus called them "children." Ya, that's not the way adults talk to each other. One does not call grown men *"children"* in that culture, it's insulting. The sarcasm will become more obvious.

6- And he (Jesus) *said unto them, Cast the net on the right side of the ship, and ye shall find. They cast therefore, and now they were not able to draw it for the multitude of fishes* (ichthus).

The Greek word for fish is *ichthus*. We will jump back and forth between this relish (prosphagion) stuff and actual (ichthus) fish. It gets confusing, but it works out for a vegan win in the end.

Busted

The scene so far: Peter is out in his boat and notices a person (Jesus) but does not recognize him. Jesus is on the shore telling them to throw the net on a specific side of the boat. Sound familiar? Remember the story in Luke chapter 5 with the nets being full? Jesus does this again so they can make the connection to who he is. Finally, in verse 7, John figures out it's Jesus, and he tells Peter:

7- Therefore that disciple whom Jesus loved saith unto Peter, it is the Lord. Now when Simon Peter heard it was the Lord, he girt his fisher's coat onto him (for he was naked) and did cast himself into the sea.

No skinny-dipping

Peter "girts" himself, which means he puts on clothes because Peter fishes naked. I guess that's what they did in those days, fish naked. Man, I'd worry about the hook! But there's an interesting point why they added the naked part. Sometimes being naked in the Bible means having your sin being spiritually exposed. It doesn't always equal physical nudity, tho it can. But this time, it's like when Adam covered himself, for he was naked and ashamed (Genesis chapter 3). What Peter is going through is shame. His sin of not having continued faith is exposed. Peter knows he backslid into fishing when he was supposed to be out preaching the gospel. He's doing the very thing that Jesus called him away from doing. This was about shame on that occasion. Don't think so? People don't put on their coats (girts) to jump in the water. He could have just skinny-dipped, but nope, he put his coat on to swim. So again, I say it was about shame. Now back to our story.

The other disciples followed, dragging the fish with them.

Verse 9
As soon as they were come to land, they saw a fire of coals there, and fish (opsarion = a relish or other fish related food) *laid thereon, and bread.*

10- Jesus saith unto them, Bring of the fish which ye have caught.

Inviting someone to share a meal is intimate. It unites people. Here we have Jesus ready to join them in a breakfast meal of relish and bread. I repeat, Jesus brought bread and relish. Next, in verse 10, Jesus invites them to add <u>what they caught </u>to the breakfast fire. There is meaning within this invite to add their food. Jesus is allowing them to reestablish a relationship with him even while in their backslidden condition.

This whole thing is a reconnection between Peter and Jesus. If you remember, before the crucifixion, Peter denied Jesus <u>three times</u>:

Matthew 26 verse 34
Jesus said to him, verily I say into thee, That this night, before the cock crow, <u>thou shalt deny me thrice</u>

Waiting…waiting…OK, I was waiting for the giggling at the word *"cock"* to stop. But in this passage, Peter declared he would die for Jesus. Not long after his crucifixion, Peter denied him <u>three times</u>. Remember this denial because it is of key importance in upcoming verses. Watch as Jesus asks Peter something <u>three times</u>. Are you getting the symbolism of this yet?

11- Simon Peter went up and drew the net to the land full of great fishes (ichthus), *150 and three, and for all there were so many, yet was not the lead broken.*

OK, this cracked me up; somebody actually counted 153 fish. Like, why is it even necessary for us to know this number? Haha.

12- Jesus saith onto them, come and dine. And none of the disciples dared ask him, who art thou? Knowing it was the Lord

In verse 12, I don't get the impression much conversation is happening. They knew they had done wrong, and we're probably feeling pretty bad. They had instructions to wait for the Lord in Galilee. But they returned to their old fishing jobs. This wasn't God's will for them; they were stone-cold busted for disobeying.

13- Jesus then cometh, and taketh bread and giveth them and fish (opsarion: little or cooked fish) *likewise.*

At the end of verse 13, it says Jesus gave them fish. This time, the word is *opsarion*: little or cooked fish. Prior, Jesus only had bread and *prosphagion*: relish to offer. This gives evidence Jesus did not bring fish (verse 9), but the disciples added the fish.

Coming up in verse 15, we see more of why Jesus is doing this fish stuff. So whether a relish or an actual fish, it doesn't matter when we hear the line of questioning Jesus is about to give Peter.

They are done eating and sitting by the fish, nets, and fire. Nothing else is mentioned, and Jesus starts asking Peter questions.

15- So when they have dined, Jesus says to Simon Peter, Simon, son of Jonas, lovest tho me more than these? Peter said unto him, Yea Lord, thou knows that I love thee. Jesus said unto him, Feed my lambs

  16- He saith unto him the second time, Simon son of Jonas, Lovest thou me? He say that to him yea Lord, thou knowest that I love thee, Jesus said unto him, Feed my sheep

  17- Jesus saith unto him a third time, Simon, son of Jonas. Loves thou me? Peter was grieved because he said unto him the third time, lovest thou me? And he said unto him, Lord, thou knowest all things; thou knowest that I love thee. Jesus saith unto him, Feed my sheep.

Jesus told Peter (Simon) three times that you'll feed my sheep if you love me. In other words, share the gospel (feed) with the people (sheep) I left in your care. So what was Peter doing? Well, he wasn't going out and feeding (caring) the sheep (people) as instructed. Instead, he went back to fishing. Jesus is sarcastically making a point.

If you'll notice, in verse 15, I underlined where Jesus said *do you love me more than these*. I don't think I ever heard a single sermon confirming what "*these* things" are that Jesus is referring. I say "these" weren't the other disciples because disciples aren't "things." Besides, they were doing the same sin Peter was doing in their backsliding. When JC said "these things", he was referring to what I noted earlier; it was the nets, the fire, and the fish. Jesus is saying do you love me more than your work as a fisherman. Do you love me more than your nets, your boats, your possessions? Do you love me more than your former life, and are you finally willing to give up your past profession once and for all to follow me?

Ahhh, I bet you're getting it now.

Pete or Simon?

Another reason I claim Jesus is being a little sarcastic is his use of Peter's old name, *Simon*. Let's get you up to speed on this name game stuff. His original name in Hebrew was Simon. But in:

John chapter 1 verse 42
And he brought him to Jesus. And when Jesus beheld him, he said, Thou art Simon the son of Jona: thou shalt be called Peter (Cephas) *which is by interpretation, a stone.*

Earlier, Jesus changed Simon's name to Peter to signify that Peter is a new man. Some translations say the name *Cephas,* which is Aramaic, while *Peter* is Greek. Both names mean rock, but you don't need to know this. But now, when we look in verses 15 through 17, Jesus is going back to calling him Simon. That was his name from his "sinner" days. Because Peter has fallen so far away, Jesus is sarcastically calling him by his old "sinner" name. As if he's become the old person he was before he left all to follow Jesus.

Wrap up

Asking Peter three times, Jesus is making sure Peter is committed to Jesus more than his earlier promise.

When dealing with a fisherman, Jesus used relatable things to explain what he wanted. It was a way to reconnect with their purpose in his ministry. This isn't approval for fishing, or I'd think Jesus would have started out with fish, not relish and bread. Jesus used their stuff to reconnect, showing his forgiveness, and point out their sin.

CHAPTER 64:
ACT 10:12 – PETER'S VISION

Peter's kill and eat vision

Today's Christian thinks this vision is an approval to kill and eat animals, but Peter saw it differently.

Acts Chapter 10
12- Wherein were all manner of fourfooted beasts of the earth, and wild beasts, and creeping things, and fowls of the air
  13- and there came a voice to him, rise, Peter; kill, and eat

Before I go further, let me just say: EEEKKKKKK! Verse 13 sounds like something out of a horror movie. In verse 16, this *kill and eat* thing was repeated three times. Kill-kill-kill, eat-eat-eat. Freak me out big time if I didn't learn the entire context, and you know what? Chances are, meat-eating Christians don't recognize the context either. I can't blame them. Separated from the rest of the chapter, those verses imply eating animals is a direct command from God. So let's get into it.

5Ws

The "Who" in this story is Peter, a practicing Jew. The "When" is Peter's cultural background, a time of segregation between Jew and Gentile. The "Why" is Peter's religious views at the time of this vision.

To most Christians, the book of Acts has the start of the Christian church in chapter 2. If you noticed, I wrote the word *most*. I am not in that group. Those educated on this subject consider me a Mid-Acts Dispensationalist. I try to avoid going there, but it's relevant for understanding this passage.

A "Mid-Acts" dispensationalist believes the church started with the Apostle Paul somewhere around the middle of the book of Acts. Like, right around chapter 10, when Peter gets this gross vision.

It's not the New Testament yet.

"Hey Steve, why is this important"? Glad you asked. Until this time, the apostles continued teaching the Old Testament Law of Moses.

Old Testement = Law, New Testement = Grace

A widespread misunderstanding among Christians today is the Law of Moses ended with the book of Malachi. Then, assuming the New Testament is in chronological order, salvation under Grace begins with the Gospel of Matthew.

I don't see it that way. My view is, until the book of Acts reaches chapter 10, the apostles are in a transitionary time. Leaving the old laws of conditional blessing and moving to God's unmerited Grace. This change was not taught instantly. In Acts chapter 10, the apostles were not yet teaching forgiveness via Grace; they were still teaching that salvation is through The Law, through Israel.

Knowing the timing of this split is significant to comprehend Peter's reply to this animal vision. This will put you miles ahead of what most Christians will understand.

First, let's look at the other verses for the rest of the context. I will come back to this separation of Law and Grace.

Acts chapter 10 verses 1-8
In a town called Caesarea lived a gentile (non-Jew) *guy named Cornelius. He is not a Jew, but he generously gave and prayed to God* (verse 2)*, so he's on Team God. Cornelius got a vision* (verse 3) *from God telling him to send a couple of his guys (gentile) to the city of Joppa to bring Peter* (Jew) *back to his house in Caesarea* (verse 5).

As I continue verse by verse, remember that Peter is a Jew, Cornelius is a Gentile, and they have restrictions on being together. And now on to Peter.

Chapter 10
9- On the morrow (next day) *as they went on their journey, and drew nigh into the city, Peter went up on the housetop to pray about the sixth hour*

10- And he became very hungry, and would have eaten; but while they made ready, he fell into a trance,

11- And saw heaven opened in certain vessel descending unto him, as it had been a great sheet knit at the four corners, and let down to the earth;

Peter is on a journey and gets tired and hungry. No big deal till he falls into a trance as Cornelius did in verse 3. While in this trance, he sees something that looks like an enormous sheet being lowered from heaven. There are many kinds of animals on this bed sheet thingy. In verse 12, pay attention to what Peter noticed about the animals:

12- Wherein were all manner of four-footed beasts of the earth, and <u>wild beasts</u>, and <u>creeping things</u>, and <u>fowls</u> of the air

Throwback alert Remember what I wrote of in Genesis where God has all these categories for each group of animals? Well, He still does, and <u>creeping things</u> remain a specific category of animal, separate from <u>birds</u> and <u>beasts</u>.

13- And there came a voice to him, rise, Peter; kill, and eat
14- But Peter said, Not so, Lord, for I have never eaten anything that is common or unclean

Common or unclean means NOT kosher or approved under Jewish dietary laws (Leviticus 11:11, Deuteronomy 14:3). Do you understand why I brought up that Mid-Acts Dispensational stuff earlier? Dig the timing on this situation. Several years after Jesus died on the cross, Peter, one of the chief apostles, is still eating kosher! Peter says *<u>I have never eaten anything common or unclean</u>*. Peter is still keeping the Old Testament kosher diet during the New Testament era!

This refusal to eat unclean food is 10 years after the death, burial, and resurrection of Jesus. Peter was still not grasping salvation under Grace alone through Jesus Christ. This is huge, and very few churches teach this.

This verse and so many more like it are why I am a Mid-Acts dispensationalist. For the sake of our vegan advocacy, it will make more sense when we read further.

15- And a voice spake unto him again saying the <u>second time</u>, What God hath cleansed, that call not thou common.

So for the second time, the voice was trying to get Peter to understand the vision's meaning.

Call nothing impure that God has made clean. Are you catching that meaning? Animals may be the object God is using to make the point, but soon, Peter will understand the separation of Jews and Gentiles is ended. You'll get more of that next.

16- This was done thrice, and the vessel was received up again into heaven.

17- Now while <u>Peter doubted in himself what this vision which he had seen should mean,</u> behold, the men which were sent from <u>Cornelius</u> (a gentile) had made inquiry for Simon's house, and stood before the gate

Note what I underlined in verse 17. Today's meat-eating Christian may think verse 13 with its *Kill and Eat* means we now have full permission from God to kill and eat any animals. But Peter didn't get that meaning at all. Reread verse 17, <u>Peter himself doubted</u> the meaning.

19- While Peter thought on the vision, <u>the Spirit said</u> unto him, behold three men seek thee.

20- <u>Arise therefore</u> and get thee down, and go with them, <u>doubting nothing</u> for I have sent them.

Another common mistake is thinking Peter's vision ended when the sheet went back up into heaven. Look at what I underlined in verse 20. Peter was still in *vision-mode* after the sheet was lifted back to heaven.

The rest of this vision is instruction to go with gentiles. The Spirit was saying, "Hey Pete, snap out of it (arise therefore) and go with the 3 Gentile dudes at the door, I know they are Gentiles but chill (doubting nothing) 'cuz I sent them, so it's cool". Why would the spirit say not to doubt? Well, Peter was questioning if he could do something unclean. Going with the 3 "unclean" Gentile guys at the door would be wrong. Remember, Peter was still keeping the Law, and Jews could not hang out with Gentiles. Peter hadn't put it together yet. Think of it this way. "New Testament" Peter was still living in "Old Testament" Law.

So they stayed the night, and by the time we hit verse 25, they get to Cornelius' house and it goes like this:

25- And as Peter was coming, Cornelius met him, fell down at his feet and worshipped him.

26- But Peter raised him up saying, stand up; I myself also am a man.

27- And as he talked with him, he went in and found many that were come together

So Peter is being a good guy. He tells the Gentile people he is nothing special. Just because he partied with Jesus, he is not worthy of worship, so stop that craziness. Then he goes into the house and sees more people. Here is what ties it up in a nice vegan package, proving this isn't about eating animals.

28- And he (Peter) said to them, Ye know how <u>it is an unlawful</u>

thing for a man that is a Jew to keep company or come unto one of another nation (this Cornelius guy was in a Jewish "No-Fly Zone"); _but God hath shewed me that I should not call any **man** (anthrópos) common or unclean_

And again in verse:

34- Then Peter opened his mouth, and said, Of a truth I perceive that God is no respecter of persons:
   35- But in every nation he that feareth (reverential awe) _him, and worketh righteousness, is accepted with him._

BOOM! That gives us our vegan win for this vision. Peter finally understands the meaning. Peter himself tells everyone the vision's message is God makes everyone equal, and Gentiles are as "clean" as Jews.

Another vegan BOOM is in that sentence. Did you catch it? Peter says man, not animals. Read it again, Peter says man, not animals. There is no way in heck Peter understood this vision as permission to eat animals. The Greek word he used is _anthrópos: a man, human, mankind._ That's added confirmation this animal vision meant equality for all humans, Jew and Gentile.

Did you notice Peter didn't _kill and eat_ anything after the vision? What does that tell ya? It's crazy that 2000 years after this happened, today's meat-eaters will interpret this vision to support meat consumption, while Peter, the guy who actually had the vision, interprets the meaning differently.

God confirms

Later on in verses 45 & 46:

45- And they of the circumcision (Jews) _which believed were astonished, as many as came with Peter, because that on the Gentiles also was poured out the gift of the Holy Ghost._
   46- For they heard them speak with tongues, and magnify God.

We observe God's endorsement for Peter's _non-food_ understanding when God poured the gifts of the Holy Spirit on the Gentiles.

Retelling the vision

Now we know what Peter's vision in Acts chapter 10 is about. But, if you get a Christian wanting more proof, I got it for you. Later on, Pete goes back to see the guys:

Acts chapter 11

1- And the apostles and brethren that were in Judaea heard that the Gentiles had also received the word of God.

2- And when Peter was come up to Jerusalem, they that were of the circumcision (the Jews) *contended with him,*

3- Saying, Thou wentest in to men uncircumcised (gentiles)*, and didst eat with them.*

When Peter got back to the Jewish Christians, they were upset. They heard gossip that Peter ate with Gentiles, which is a big no-no for Old Testament Law keeping Jews. They didn't know God told Peter all people were equal in this vision. So they challenged him about it.

Starting in verse 5, Peter tells them the vision situation.

I was in the city of Joppa praying: and in a trance I saw a vision, A certain vessel descend, as it had been a great sheet, let down from heaven by four corners; and it came even to me:

6- Upon the which when I had fastened mine eyes, I considered, and saw fourfooted beasts of the earth, and wild beasts, and creeping things, and fowls of the air.

Peter is retelling the vision.

7- And I heard a voice saying unto me, Arise, Peter; slay and eat.

8- But I said, Not so, Lord: for nothing common or unclean hath at any time entered into my mouth

9- But the voice answered me again from heaven, What God hath cleansed, that call not thou common.

10- And this was done three times: and all were drawn up again into heaven.

11- And, behold, immediately there were three men already come unto the house where I was, sent from Caesarea unto me.

No mistaking here, Peter is telling of the animal vision, so let's skip to verse 18 when we see how they, the gossipy Jews, understood the vision:

When they (Jews) *heard these things, they held their peace, and glorified God, saying, Then hath God also to the Gentiles granted repentance unto life.*

See? They didn't say, let's kill a pig and eat! They saw this vision exactly as Peter did. This is God allowing repentance to the Gentile people. As a result, the apostles can go to the entire world preaching the gospel of Jesus Christ. No more need to segregate.

Transitory times

Acts chapter 10 is a transitional time. Everyone, including Peter, is just beginning to understand the "Mystery" of Grace the apostle Paul got directly from Jesus (research the mystery in Romans 1.1, Ephesians 3:9, Romans 16:25, Ephesians 3:3).

Paul is not one of the 12 apostles. He is unique in his ministry. The things Paul taught (Grace) had major differences from what the 12 apostles were still preaching (Law). This is Peter's kick in the butt to move out of the Law and fully into Grace. Paul confirms this change in Romans.

Romans chapter 3 verse
29- Is he the God of the Jews only? Is he not also of the Gentiles? Yes, of the Gentiles also:

Also, look at any verses that talk of the apostles and food. It was always kosher until Paul introduces the mystery program years after the death of Jesus.

Sorry Atheist, I'm sure this dispensational stuff is boring, but I am sure many Christians are flipping out. I just handed them dispensational keys to understanding many of their Bible difficulties. Or they are getting really mad at me.

My Christian vegans reading this can agree or disagree with me on the dispensational part, but I trust I showed how to discuss this verse in your activism.

CHAPTER 65:
ROMANS 1:32 – YUM,
BACON!

Knee-Jerk Reaction

Something disturbing happens just about every night I do public vegan outreach. While playing videos of animals suffering in slaughterhouses, I'll get a meat-eating Christian laugh, and say, "*Yum, bacon*"!

Strange, but carnists see video of a living animal covered in its own feces and somehow their brain tells them to say, "Yum Bacon." These same carnists are grossed out should they find a hair on their dinner plate. The cognitive disconnect is strong, even in Christians.

When someone shouts such a cold-hearted comment, what we are getting is a "Knee-Jerk" reaction. An unthinking, emotional response on a subject in which a person is highly sensitive. Their insensitive joke is their way of dealing with the judgement they experience in that moment. Christians admit animal abuse is a sin and vegan activists make the Christian aware they caused this abuse. Their brain scrambles, looking to relieve this hypocrisy. They will say anything, even "Yum bacon" rather than admit they are sinning. Well, this happens a lot. I wanted a verse to deal with this heartless reaction and I found something useable in the first chapter of Romans.

Romans chapter 1 verse 28:
And just as they did not see fit to acknowledge God any longer, God gave them over to a depraved mind, to do those things which are not proper

In this verse, the apostle Paul talks of God being fed up with heartless people, so God gave them over to their depraved minds. These communities did terrible things. The Holman Christian Standard Bible calls those things "morally wrong". The New International Version says "what ought not to be done." Sure sounds like it applies to meat-eaters because they admit animal abuse is morally wrong but still do what ought not be done.

What is depraved?

In verses 29–31, the apostle Paul lists those wrongful, depraved things as having no love, inventing evil things, and being unmerciful. That is exactly what happens at a slaughterhouse. There is no love when creatures capable of love are denied a single minute of affection their entire lives. There is no mercy when profit determines their suffering. They invent evil things such as machines to burn off chicken's beaks and toes. What is happening is morally wrong and ought not to be done.

Paul further describes these "Yum bacon" Christians in verse 32.

They know the judgment of God, that if they commit such things they are worthy of death, they not only do the same, but have pleasure in them that do them.

Sadly, these Christians will comment "Yum" while viewing a video of an animal suffering. And they will receive pleasure as they eat products made from these evil activities. Crazy, huh? Christians taking pleasure from evil actions and call them good, humane or natural.

Woe unto them that call animal abuse humane

I also see these verses and remember:

Isaiah chapter 5 verse 20
Woe unto them that call evil good, and good evil; that put darkness for light, and light for darkness; that put bitter for sweet, and sweet for bitter!

Today's carnist Christians call evil good, or in this case, humane. To get this across, present the following:
Animals are forcefully bred into existence, only to be killed.
Animals have body parts cut off for human financial needs. No pain killers are given as it would cut into the profits.
Animals are deprived of the natural behaviors God gave them.
Animals are caged their entire lives. Some never see the sun or touch the ground.
Animals are fed unnatural foods to make them grow painfully fast.
Animals are forced into transport trucks with electric shockers.

Animals are forced into slaughter houses.
Animals are forced into gas chambers.
Animals are killed by getting their throats cut.

Christians call this humane. They might want to accept they are victims of brain-washing as their defense. Because if not, they are doing these evils on purpose, making them evil and heartless abusers of animals. Or as Isaiah said, *Woe unto them that call evil good, and good evil.*

Calling a Christian brain-washed is aggressive. My replies are aggressive because they're "Yum bacon" is aggressive. Typically done to upset the activist. I am just meeting them with the energy they start.

CHAPTER 66: ROMANS 14 – VEGANS ARE WIMPS

Vegans are weak

Didn't the Apostle Paul say people that ate veggies are weak in the faith?

Romans chapter 14 verse 2
One person has faith that he may eat all things, but he who is weak eats vegetables only.

Yep, sure looks like he did, but Paul isn't saying the *item of food* makes them weak. It's what the item of food represents. There is also a lesson on judging in this chapter, so let's dig in.

5Ws

By the 14th chapter of Romans, Jews and Gentiles are finally worshiping God together. However, they have a few differences. The apostle is straightening this out.

These new Jewish and Gentile converts were unsure of the boundaries within their newfound freedoms in Christ. Before Christ, the boundaries were in the Law of Moses. Their new liberties expanded what they could eat, what they could drink, and the sabbath day as a mandatory day for worship and more. Where they stood on these issues determined if they were "weak" or "strong".

Pagan meat or non-pagan veggies

Time to discuss why meat and veggies are in Paul's examples. They rarely used veggies in worship to pagan gods. So 99% of the time veggies are considered "clean" foods, got that? Pagan religions predominantly used animal sacrifices for their gods. The pagan followers ate most of the meat after the rituals. Many converts to this new Christianity considered meat sourced in that way as "unclean".

For sale

If there was leftover meat from these pagan rituals, it was sold afterward in the marketplace at a discounted rate. A rich person could purchase guaranteed "clean meat," but a poor person might unknowingly get this leftover "pagan meat" a little cheaper in the marketplace.

Since the meat was offered to a bogus god, new converts felt purchasing/eating this pagan meat violated moral conscience. I repeat, the new believers felt eating any sacrificed food item joins them to the pagan gods spiritually. In doing so, they would be subsidizing pagan worship. Make sure you understand this; it is essential to this situation.

Weak or Strong

A *weak Christian* was a new convert who didn't yet fully grasp how the death of Jesus Christ fulfilled the Law and made unclean foods lawful to eat.

A *strong Christian* is one that understands their liberty through Jesus Christ. They knew any foods were permissible, even pagan meals once offered to idols.

We cannot consider this Paul's condemnation of veganism, as these new "weak" converts were not vegans. They ate meat; they only refrained from meat sacrificed to pagan idols. Strong believers didn't care where their food was sourced.

Why permissible?

Paul knows pagan gods are nothing but images carved on wood or stone. It's like offering food to a chair or a brick wall. Therefore, the food itself is none the better or nothing worse. The only concern the apostle has is if someone sees a Christian eat "pagan meat," they wrongly assume they are serving or supporting these false deities by taking part in the eating. We are dealing with an issue of their newfound Christian liberty versus a matter of a new converts conscience.

Chapter 14 starts out talking about food, and then it will speak about specific days. The chapter will end with matters of what they drink. Let's go through it.

1- Him that is <u>*weak*</u> (new) *in the faith receive ye* (accept him)*, but not to doubtful disputations.*

   2- For one believeth that he may eat all things (pagan meat)*: another, who is weak, eateth herbs* (vegetables)

The apostle Paul recommends that if somebody is new to the faith and "weak," don't give him grief about it; accept him. For example, if they only want to eat foods not offered to pagan gods (veggies), don't stress about it and get all judgmental. Receive them into the group and give them time to adjust. They will come to understand their full Christian liberty and get "strong" later. We all got to start some place, right?

3- Let not him that eateth (strong believer) *despise him that eateth not* (weak believer)*: and let not him which eateth not judge him that eateth: for God received him*

   4- Who art thou that judgest another man servant? To his own master he standeth or falleth. Yea, he shall be holden up: for God is able to make him stand.

   5- One man <u>*esteemeth one day*</u> *more sacred: another estemeth every day alike. Let every man be fully persuaded in his own mind.*

In verse 5, Paul adds the worshiping on certain days to the list of differences between the weak and strong, which shows these comparisons are of Old Testament Law issues, not meat versus veggies.

   Let's not forget that numbered verses did not exist when Paul wrote this. It was one continuous thought. Their meaning is we can't judge the weak Christian because they keep old religious rituals such as eating, drinking, or days of worship. Give them time to grow.

   Paul instructs the stronger believers to let God be their judge/master (verse 4). God will deal with their wish to continue old religious rituals. Strong brothers in the faith are not to criticize or judge the weak in their slowness in growth. Let God deal with their conscience in his perfect timing.

If it was today

Eating foodstuff offered to idols is not an issue in today's Christian society, but we still differ. Weak Christians now argue whether a strong Christian can dance, listen to rock music, have tattoos, smoke a cigar, wear jewelry, or a host of other things that divide the church. So again, this isn't a *"meat"* issue. Instead, Paul uses meat to point out past religious rituals and their current relevance in the age of grace through Jesus Christ. Think about it, would the apostle Paul, a guy who bragged on his super Bible knowledge, put down eating veggies knowing that God commanded a vegan diet in the beginning? Nahhhhh.

So can vegans judge?

There is no comparison between this 1st century judging, and what vegan activists are currently doing. Vegan activists are not judging people for keeping obsolete religious rituals such as holy days or food offered to idols. Instead, vegan activists question and criticize the lack of moral consistency in carnist Christians' dietary choices. Vegans questioning Christians is very appropriate. Especially today, when so many delicious cruelty-free options are available in this 21st century. This is not the 1st century Rome; get over it ya meat-heads!

Verse 14
I know, and am persuaded by the Lord Jesus, that there is nothing <u>unclean</u> of itself.

Here the apostle Paul references the food being eaten on whether <u>clean or unclean</u>. That could also be read as kosher or not kosher. This verse does not proclaim "meat is for the strong" and "vegetables are for the weak," but whether a Christian needed to eat kosher/permissible foods. I repeat, it's not the item of food but what the food item represents. Activists need to know this as there are many more meat verses like this coming up.

Verse 15
But if thy brother be grieved with thy <u>meat</u> (broma = food of any kind)*, now walkest thou not charitably. Destroy not him with thy <u>meat</u>* (bromati = food of any kind)*, for whom Christ died.*

Here we go again with the poor translation of the Greek word "broma." The King James interpretation often translates broma to "meat." Other Bible translations, such as the New International Version, the English Standard Version, New American Standard Bible, convert *broma* to *food*. Reading those versions confirms this isn't a meat eating versus vegetable eating issue, but a kosher versus un-kosher issue. Oh, none of these translations are by done by tree-hugging hippie vegans, so don't let carnist say you have a bias.

Verse 17
For the kingdom of God is <u>not</u> meat (brósis: eating, food) *and <u>drink</u>; but righteousness, peace, and joy in the Holy Ghost.*

Note that verse 17 adds drinking. Why is that a big deal? Because it shows this chapter is about Jewish dietary laws, not a vegetarian against carnivore situation. And meat is a poor translation…again.

Verse 20
For <u>meat</u> (bromates = food of any kind) *destroy not the work of*

God.

Here we have another use of the word *meat* that does not mean animal flesh, but food of any kind. I am quoting the King James version here, but most other translations use *food*. For that reason, they cannot use verse 20 as a defense for meat-eaters.

The point is, no one can undo the work of God because of the food they eat. Idols are nonexistent beings, a figment of the people's imagination. Eating that food, veggie or meat has no effect on anyone's standing with God.

Verse 21

It is good neither to eat flesh (kreas=flesh), *nor drink wine, nor anything whereby thy brother stumbleth, or is offended, or is made weak.*

Paul says to avoid eating animal flesh if the situation pressures someone else into doing what they know is sinful. This includes drinking wine. It's like this: If you're out with a buddy who is a struggling alcoholic, then maybe it is best not to have a beer in front of him. Imagine how this principle applies at a church dinner or BBQ. If a Christian tries to convince a vegan to eat the barbecue ribs, he would cause him to stumble. The vegan knows animal abuse is a sin, so if a Christian offers a vegan some meat, they would encourage him to do a sinful thing.

In verse 21, there is another thing to note. The word used for flesh is *Kreas.* Thayer's Greek Lexicon gives us this: *Kreas (the) flesh (of a sacrificed animal).* Again, making the point, this is not about eating animal flesh, but specifically eating flesh offered to idols.

Vegans aren't weak

For additional proof that Paul doesn't think veggies make people weak, look to 1st Corinthians. We see a repeat of verse 21. Paul wasn't fighting veganism, his concern was eating any foods causing a brother to (stumble) fall into a sinful act.

1st Corinthians chapter 8 verse 13

Therefore, if what I eat causes my brother or sister to fall into sin, I will never eat meat again, so that I will not cause them to fall.

Paul was a meat eater. Much of what he says comes from a meat eating point of view. However, Romans chapter 14 verse 21, and this verse from 1st Corinthians chapter 8, can be used to fight the point of view that vegans are weak. Paul, a meat-eater himself, will give up meat if eating it would cause someone else to sin. Christians giving up something they can eat for the benefit of others is a sign of strength and love.

Was Daniel weak in faith?

To wrap this up and prove vegans don't have weak faith, let's look at a guy with very strong faith. Do you remember the story of Daniel eating plant-based? Well, since it's such a popular tale, what the heck, let's use it.

Daniel chapter 1 verse 12
Please test your servants for ten days, and let us be given some vegetables to eat and water to drink.

Daniel and his buddies refused the meat that King Nebuchadnezzar wanted them to have. They requested only veggies while training for the king's service. Such a request could have got their heads cut off. Daniel risked getting killed for refusing the king's food. That took a lot of <u>strong faith</u>. Later, Daniel faces a fiery furnace (Daniel 3) and being eaten alive in a lion's den (Daniel 6:16). Does that sound like weak faith to you? This makes it obvious that veggies and weakness aren't connected.

CHAPTER 67:
1ST CORINTHIANS 6 & 10
– IS IT LAWFUL?

All things are lawful, but some things are just awful

There are two places in 1st Corinthians implying it's lawful to eat meat. Not to worry, activists can win this one by agreeing, and then showing God says not to. Sound confusing? Ya, the Bible works like that.

1st Corinthians chapter 6 verse 12
All things are lawful onto me, but all things are not expedient: All things are lawful for me, but I will not be brought under the power of any.
  13 - Meats (bromata = food of any kind) *for the belly, and the belly for meats* (bromasin = foods of any kind)*: but God shall destroy both it and them. Now the body is not for fornication* (sex)*, but for the Lord; and the Lord for the body.*

I will repeat a lot when I discuss this *"All Things Lawful"* stuff in chapter 6 and again from chapter 10. I'll get more confusing when I step back to chapter 8, so please, bear with my Bible Hop-Scotch.

5Ws

1st Corinthians is a letter from the apostle Paul to Christians in the city of Corinth. Corinth is a rich and powerful metropolis occupied by Romans and Greeks. They had many temples to worship their Roman and Greek gods. Paul spent over a year in Corinth teaching about Jesus and making new Christian converts. Yay for Paul!

Once these Christian churches were up and running, Paul left to continue his preachy-teachy stuff in Ephesus (modern-day Turkey). While Paul is away, he gets a message saying these Corinthian churches are messing up. There were problems with sexual issues, disorderly worship, and creating divisions in the church with what foods could be eaten.

I'll skip the other disputes and focus on the food problems. It wasn't they were cooking it wrong. It was about foods, usually meat, offered to their Greek and Roman gods. So yep, here we go again.

The meat connection

The people of Corinth believed eating meat that was offered to a god, spiritually connected them to that god. This "connecting" was part of the sexual issues in the temples. You see, Corinth had temple prostitutes that were "representatives" of the various pagan gods. If the people fornicate (have sex) with those prostitutes, they were "joining" themselves with the specific god that prostitute represented. Much like joining oneself when eating food offered to pagan gods. That is why in verse 13, we read the strange pairing of eating and sex. Strange, unless your hooker is also your chef.

Here we go again

We are dealing with a similar situation to Romans chapter 14. The educated (strong) Christians believed the pagan gods were nothing but imaginary beings. Strong Christians had no problem eating the foods offered to these fictional gods.

The confusion comes from uneducated (weak) Christians seeing the educated (strong) Christians eating pagan foods. They'd assume the strong Christians were joining in the worship of pagan gods. I hope you get that because you are going to hear it a lot..

Perception differs from reality.

Paul is giving the Corinthian Christians guidelines on this leftover pagan meat. Because yes, it is lawful for them to eat the meat. But, if eating provokes someone else to assume Christians are worshipping other pagan gods, then it's wrong, get it? That's what brings us to Paul offering to be vegan...kinda.

Chapter 8 verse 13
Therefore, if meat causes my brother to offend (skandalizó= to put a snare in the way, hence to cause to stumble, to fall into sin), *I will eat no flesh while the world standeth, lest I make my brother to offend*

Dig that! The apostle Paul says it's better to never eat meat again than cause someone to stumble into sin. Are you catching what that implies? The next time you vegans go to a Christian Thanksgiving dinner, tell them you're hurt (offended) deeply by their meat eating. Then, remind them the apostle Paul recommends they stop. How totally cool is that? OK, OK, that's a bit of scripture twisting, but it sure is fun. More on this in the next chapter.

We don't have to deal with sacrifices to idols in today's church, but we can make these verses connect to 21st century veganism. Help the carnist Christian understand there will be repercussions if they choose to eat animals. Carnist Christians are selecting food products made from the torture and abuse of animals. This shows approval of animal abuse. Got that? They really can't get meat without the unnecessary death of an animal. Violence does not represent Christ. By eating meat, they are connecting to animal abuse, which is a sin. I hope you see how this can work in our vegan favor, even though it says it's "lawful" to eat meat.

Seek his own

But we're not done with the study yet. Let's get to a similar verse in **chapter 10, verses 23 & 24.**

23- All things are lawful for me, but all things are not expedient:
all things are lawful for me, but all things edify not
       24- Let no man seek his own, but every man another's wealth.

Paul says all actions are lawful, but not all actions are good. Just because Christians can do an activity does not mean Christians should. Thankfully, Paul doesn't leave us hanging. He teaches how to determine what is not good and meat definitely isn't good.

In verse 24, I underlined seek his own. Christianity is love. Christians should act with love even if it means giving up what is lawful, like eating meat. Giving up meat is best for the environment and the animals. So yes, even if animal flesh is allowed, it's self-serving or "seeking your own". As a Christian, your body has a higher purpose than seeking a brief moment of taste pleasure.

Notice how Paul closes this chapter:

1 Corinthians chapter 10 verse 31
Whether therefore you eat, or drink, or whatsoever you do, do all
to the glory of God.

See that? Eat, drink, or whatever you do, do to the glory of God. Looking at what we've learned, can anyone be eating *to the glory of God* if the food choice involves the torture, sexual molestation, and abuse of an innocent animal? Of course not. Come on, meat-eaters, you know what to do. Quit fighting compassion.

CHAPTER 68:
1ST CORINTHIANS 8:13 –
OFFEND A BROTHER

Did the Apostle Paul go vegan?

1st Corinthians chapter 8 verse 13
Therefore, if meat causes my brother to offend, <u>I will eat no flesh while the world standeth,</u> lest I make my brother to offend

What a great verse, huh? The apostle Paul says that he will go vegan forever if eating meat offends his brother! If only it were that easy.

In the previous chapter, I discussed how activists can use this verse. This time, I'll focus on how this verse works *against* our vegan outreach.

When the apostle Paul says *I will eat no flesh,* he is not rejecting meat because he opposes animal cruelty. Paul is showing how to be a (strong) example of a Christian to a new (weak) believer. Because the association of meat with idol worship is so commonplace, Paul is willing to go meatless for the rest of his life. This has everything to do with idolatry but, sadly, nothing to do with compassion for animals.

Many animal advocates use this verse, but not me. I will teach why it's a dead end, but I won't let you down. There remains a vegan-friendly chunk of truth we can harvest. So let's discuss.

5Ws

This passage is not about meat. Paul is discussing any food from questionable sources. It could be any food. It could be meat, or it could be pickles. The food item is of no issue. The focus is on *eating things once offered in sacrifice to idols.* Knowing the difference is essential before we go any further. And uh…It's also essential to know that pagan idols don't like pickles, so forget what I said about pickles :-)

Paul is acting with love and consideration for "old school" Christians who do not understand their "new school" liberty to eat questionably sourced foodstuffs. We will start back in verse 4.

> *As concerning therefore the eating of those things that are offered in sacrifice unto idols, we know that an idol is nothing in the world, and that there is none other God but one.*

Paul lets us know the food he is concerned with is only *those things offered to idols.* That is the key to understanding what vegans need to recognize about this chapter. It is any food offered to idols.

Enough already with the pagan meat issue!

Sorry about the repeats, but many activists open this book to an individual chapter, looking to answer a specific challenge on a single verse. A lot of this will be a rerun of what I said in a previous chapter, but I'll toss in a couple of new insights. Eh, it will only add 3 reading minutes and repeating is good for memorizing.

Many religious groups made animal sacrifices to their idols/gods. They kill an animal and offer its blood to the gods while the flesh (meat) might be eaten in the temple. Why is that a big deal? Because eating the food (meat or otherwise), would show allegiance to the idol or "join" with the false god. We've spoken about this in other chapters, and I'm as tired of it as you are.

The priests sold the leftover animal flesh (meat) to a wholesaler in the marketplace. The confusion begins here. If a new, weak Christian bought meat in the marketplace, they might not know it was part of a sacrificial offering made to an idol.

Christianity was still kinda new in Corinth. New Christian (weak in the faith) believers were still learning. The experienced and educated (strong) believers knew no other gods existed, so any sacrificed food was just plain ol' food. Christians are free to eat any food offered to false, imaginary idols or even un-kosher foods. However, new believers felt they would sin to eat food offered to idols.

> **6-** *But to us there is but one God,*

Paul says that these knowledgeable "stronger" Christians knew there was only one God.

> **7-** *Howbeit <u>there is not in every man that knowledge</u>: for some with conscience of the idol unto this hour eat it as a thing offered*

unto an idol; and their conscience being weak is defiled.

In the eyes of these "weak" Christians (the ones with little knowledge), eating food offered to idols would defile them. Calling them weak is not a negative. A child in third grade is nowhere near the intelligence or experience of a college professor, but you wouldn't call them stupid. Well, consider these weak Christians as third graders. They will grow, and they will learn, and they will become strong "college professor" Christians.

8- But meat commendeth (brings closer) *us not to God: for neither, if we eat, are we the better; neither, if we eat not, are we the worse.*

These stronger believers knew whatever they ate had no advantage in connection to God or any gods.

9- But take heed lest by any means this liberty of yours become a stumbling block to them that are weak.

Here lies the message. Imagine you're a strong believer eating a food item offered to an idol. A weak believer sits next to you, thinking that you (a strong and more educated) believe it's OK to eat this "idol food." You're causing them to consider doing something they assume is a sin. Get it?

To give a more current reference, consider this. You are married, and your spouse is an alcoholic. You're not an alcoholic, you don't have a problem with booze. You've got every right (liberty) to drink a beer. But you love your spouse and don't want to cause any temptations to drink. So, you decide not to drink any booze forever. It is a considerate, loving thing to do. Can you dig it?

12- But when ye sin so against the brethren, and wound their weak conscience, ye sin against Christ.

So even though these strong believers didn't force the weak believers to sin, it's still kinda sorta their concern. Not their fault, but as a loving, caring, Christian, they could have been more considerate of the new, weak believer they're hanging out with. As a strong Christian, be there to help the weak.

So now this brings us to why the apostle Paul said he won't eat animal flesh anymore.

13- Wherefore, if meat make my brother to offend, I will eat no flesh while the world standeth, lest I make my brother to offend.

I underlined the reason for Paul's rejection of meat. He did not want to offend someone by doing what they considered a pagan or unchristian activity. Even though meat (animal flesh) was the item, it could have been any unclean food item. Still, meat is usually the only food in question. Veggies are often just burnt up, with no remains to sell in the marketplace.

This context has everything to do with Paul being nice, <u>giving up his freedom for</u> someone weaker.

But Paul says:

I will eat no flesh while the world standeth. Does that mean Paul gave up meat forever? It could, but he may have been using hyperbole. Hyperbole is an exaggeration for the sake of emphasis. That's like picking up a suitcase and saying, "this suitcase weighs a ton." We know the suitcase did not actually weigh a ton, but that's hyperbole, and some will claim Paul was exaggerating when he said I'll never eat meat again. This is possible. But for sure, he did not give up meat for animal ethics.

A small win

Is there a vegan take-away from this verse? Yep.

In other scriptures, it appears Paul is big into eating meat, but this verse can prove otherwise. Paul's insistence on concern for new Christians shows how little value eating animals is to Paul. I reply: "eating meat is of so little importance to Paul, he will give it up forever just to be nice to other church people."

Vegans can present this verse to our carnist Christian friends when we go out to eat with them. We have the apostle Paul on our side when we ask them to give up meat for at least the meals they have with us. If they don't willingly, they are selfish. Being selfish is not a Christian virtue.

Causing others to stumble

This passage helps with the question of "What does a new vegan convert do with old non-vegan clothing"? Paul would recommend to wear them, but in a way without causing the vegan movement to stumble. For example, I had leather shoes when I went vegan. On Paul's advice, I wore them only when working in the privacy of my home. By self-restricting my "legal right" to wear them, I won't cause the vegan movement to stumble. It's no benefit to the animals to throw them away. Plus, I'm doing better for the environment by not buying another pair of shoes, even if they are vegan. So I can "legally" wear them in public, but for the sake of the vegan movement, I self-regulated my liberty and chose only to wear them privately.

CHAPTER 69:
1ˢᵀ CORINTHIANS 9:9 –
GOD HATES THE OX?

G od don't care about oxen, so let's eat cows

1st Corinthians chapter 9 verse 9
For it is written in the law of Moses, Thou shalt not muzzle the mouth of the ox that treadeth out the corn. <u>Doth God take care for oxen?</u>

The last line of verse 9 is the vegan problem. Paul implies God doesn't care about oxen. This is confusing because, in Deuteronomy chapter 25, God does:

4- Thou shalt not muzzle the ox when he treadeth out the corn.

God tells us to be kind to the ox working in the cornfield. How? The ox should be able to grab a mouthful of what they're helping produce. It's cruel to muzzle and stop him from eating, especially since he earned it.

So is the apostle Paul (Corinthians 9:9) contradicting God (Deuteronomy 25:4)? Not at all, because this verse is <u>about proper payment for work done</u>. And the principle applies to both humans and animals alike. Vegan win again!

5Ws

There was a mix of Gentiles and Jews in Corinth. They knew Paul as the apostle to the Gentiles, so they are questioning why Paul is talking to the

Jews. In verses 1-5, Paul addresses their concerns of his apostleship and authority to speak to everyone. When we get to verse 6, he talks of money, and it gets sticky:

6- Or I only and Barnabas, have not we power to forbear working?

Paul says he and his buddy Barnabas have the right (power) to ask for money because they are preachers (working) and can expect financial support from the people in the church. No problem there, very customary and appropriate. But he and Barnabas *did not take any money*. Instead, they choose to support themselves in unrelated businesses such as tent-makers.

Pass on the cash!

But why not take the money? After all, Paul started this church at Corinth. He preaches and deserves to be compensated. So why pass on the cash?

Paul didn't want anyone to say he was preaching for his own economic gain. Instead, he supported himself by making tents. I'm sure you can think of many television evangelists today who are preaching just for the money, but not Paul. To be above reproach, Paul considered it best to pass on the financial support and do it himself. Pretty clever, huh?

Even tho Paul himself rejects the cash, he makes the case it's OK to get paid for preaching. Understanding the exchange of support from the people to a preacher is necessary for verse 9 to make sense. Or should I say cents? Ha! That's a money pun I made there.

7- Who goeth a warfare any time at his own charges? Who planteth a vineyard, and eateth not of the fruit thereof? or who feedeth a flock, and eateth not of the milk of the flock?

Verse 7 says, if a guy goes to war, doesn't the government support him? If he plants a vineyard, doesn't he get to eat the fruit? If he cares for a flock, doesn't he get to enjoy the milk from that flock? Phooey, that's not a vegan verse, but at least it's just milk from the flock and not meat.

8- Say I these things as a man? or saith not the law the same also?

Paul says, "*I'm not making this stuff up. Payment for work is what the law teaches.*" Paul reaches back into the book of Deuteronomy, for the law teaching an animal (an ox) should be fed for its labor.

We spoke earlier about the importance of this law. Hundreds of laws were written around regarding care for animals. So Paul uses this law, because it is so well established in the mind of his listeners. Paul knew they wouldn't question the understanding.

9- *For <u>it is written</u> in the law of Moses Thou shalt not muzzle the mouth of the ox that treadeth out the corn. Doth God take care for oxen?*

    10- *Or <u>saith he it altogether for our sakes?</u> For our sakes, no doubt, this is written: that he that ploweth <u>should plow in hope</u>; and that he that threadeth in hope should be <u>partaker of his hope</u>.*

Verses didn't exist then, so read verses 9 & 10 as one continuous thought. *Doth God take care for oxen? Or saith he it altogether for our sakes?*

Here is how I translate it: *"You guys know back in Deuteronomy, God gave us a law saying it's cruel to make an ox work and not feed it. Do you think God wrote that for the ox or <u>for our sake</u>? Dudes, ox can't read; God wrote it for <u>our sake</u>, so we learn what is fair! Just like it's fair for the ox to eat, it's fair for the preacher to get paid."*

Did you get that? God does care about the ox, and He cares for the preacher. Paul wants this principle understood. If they get food from the ox, then feed the freakin' ox, or if they hear the gospel from a preacher, then feed the freakin' preacher! It's a believer's responsibility to take care of them both. Did that help?

Verse 9 is not establishing if God cares for oxen. That was already established in Deuteronomy 25:4. The entire chapter is about preachers rightfully getting paid for their work. Paul's use of the "ox law" from Deuteronomy is a way to draw attention to this fairness. If you look at it this entire chapter, it really makes no sense to take this one reference to prove God doesn't care for ox so people today can eat cows. Paul is using an established law about caring for animals to show we have to care for human preachers. This part is totally vegan.

We get a more detailed understanding when Paul ties it up in verse 12, when he says:

If others (preachers) *be partakers of this power* (power = requirement of payment) *over you, are not we rather? Nevertheless <u>we have not used this power</u>* (took no payment)*; but suffer all* things (worked other unrelated jobs), *<u>lest we should hinder the gospel</u> of Christ.*

Paul makes the case he and Barney (preachers) *can* demand (requirement of payment) money for preaching. Still, just so people can't accuse him of corruption (verse 12), he prefers to support himself as a tentmaker.

CHAPTER 70:
1ST CORINTHIANS 10 –
EAT WHATEVER

Didn't Paul say to eat whatever was given to us? Even meat?

1st Corinthians chapter 10 verse 25
Whatsoever is sold in the shambles (makello = a place where meat and other articles of food are sold)*, that eat, asking no question for conscience sake*

Verse 25 is used to maintain humans have universal and unlimited approval to eat animal flesh at any time, for all time. The problem is they're ignoring the context. Once again, the eating of foods offered to other gods/idols is the concern. So here we go again.

My 5Ws

This letter was written by the apostle Paul to the church in the city of Corinth. The Corinthian church was really screwed up. Their temples were involved in various pagan worship rituals. In these rituals, they pray to false idols, kill animals and offer the blood to their imaginary gods on temple altars. They often sold the leftover animal flesh from the sacrifices in the marketplace called "Shambles."

Paul already brought the gospel (good news of Jesus) to the Corinthians, and now they're serving the real God. These new (weak) Christians were having concerns regarding the source of foods they were eating. They did not want the leftover meats from sacrifice rituals to demons, idols, and false gods. If they bought meat from the Shambles, chances are, they would not have been told they previously offered it to a pagan idol. Why? The sales people knew these weaker believers wouldn't buy it.

Paul said the better educated (strong) believers knew the pagan deities were just empty statues. The foods had no connection to any god because no other god existed. The strong believers, knowing the other gods were imaginary, had the freedom to eat whatever, even if it was offered it to idols.

So, from a "Strong" Christian's point of view, eating food is of no consequence. The apostle addresses the situation in starting in verse 23:

All things are lawful for me, but all things are not expedient (beneficial), *all things are lawful for me, but all things edify* (build up), *not*

Paul also spoke of this in chapter 6. To help us understand how things can be good and bad at the same time, let's look at that verse before I go further with verse 23.

First Corinthians chapter 6 verse 12
All things are lawful unto me, but all things are not expedient: all things are lawful for me, but I will not be brought under the power of any

It's easy to see the similarity between these verses. There is an additional line I want you to pay attention to:
I will not be brought under the power of any
Lawful or good things can consume a person so much, it takes over their lives. In ways, it becomes their god. In our society today, eating food offered to idols is not a concern, so I'm going to relate it to gambling. Maybe you're rich and got a million in the bank. You can afford to lose 100 bucks. It won't hurt your family, and your children won't go without food, then ya, gambling a hundred bucks is "lawful" or good fun. But what if you are someone who gambled so much you're about to lose your home? Gambling is lawful to do, but not for you because you are under its power. Now you see it, don't you? Christians have the freedom to do many things, like gamble or drink. Still, we should be cautious not to become a slave to any of them. Or, as Paul said, *all things are lawful for me, but I will not be brought under the power of any*.

OK, let's get back to chapter 10.

24- Let no man seek his own, but every man another's wealth (wellbeing)

Paul wants us to take this lesson and apply it to those around us. Ask yourself, will this lawful action benefit those around us? So now we have two filters on what is permitted. Filter #1 from verse 12 - <u>Will it enslave me</u> and Filter #2 from verse 24 - <u>Will it hurt others</u>. That's good advice, and we can all get behind that. Now let's get to the animal part finally.

25 Whatsoever is sold in the shambles (makello = a place where meat and other articles of food are sold)*, that eat, asking no question for conscience sake*

The translation problem starts here. The word "Shambles" in the King James Version is "markello." Markello means "*a place where meat and other articles of food are sold*." Sadly, in many Bible translations, they have translated the word to "meat market," misleading readers into a false belief it only sold meat.

With our 21st-century minds, a place called a meat market will make us expect something like a butcher shop. That's called *Ethnocentrism*. Ethnocentrism is evaluating other cultures during their times based on our understanding of contemporary culture and our time. A place called a meat market sounds like a store with meat all over the place. Back in the first century, it wasn't so. The markets were mostly vegetables. Why do I say that? Because the meat was expensive, most people could not afford it (unless maybe it was this leftover pagan meat). Also, there were no refrigeration units to keep the meat fresh. It's not like there were individually wrapped styrofoam packages kept in refrigerators all day. Salespeople only brought small amounts of meat they knew would sell and make a profit before it spoiled. So the unfortunate part of this translation is we envision nothing but meat, meat, and more meat.

Paul is talking about *any foods in the "Shambles"* offered to idols. Yes, it's lawful, and we have freedom in Christ to eat meat offered to idols, but that doesn't mean we should.

How do I know we shouldn't?

Let's use those 2 filters Paul gave to determine what we should do.

Filter #1: Can we become enslaved by meat?

Yes, we can. Do I need to speak of gluttony? So many people today have high cholesterol and should not eat any cholesterol products whatsoever. Still, they continue to destroy their health because of their enslavement/addiction to animal flesh. This will affect their family life and their ability to serve God. They are so addicted to the meat they take medication daily rather than just eliminate the cause of their illnesses: eating meat. Think about that meat-eaters. If you are taking a medication to thin out your blood because of the food you eat, just stop eating that food! Where's the common sense in continuing the activity that harms your body? Face it, you're addicted and enslaved by meat.

Filter #2: Does eating meat affect others?

Yes, it does. Suppose Christians set an example of compassion and quit eating meat. We could use the resources to feed livestock and redirect it to starving humans. Consider this: we currently feed 60 billion farm animals every year, and we only have 7 billion people on the earth. If we just provided that plant food directly to the hungry people, we could end world hunger. Isn't feeding the poor something a Christian should choose? Duh!

So finishing up verse 25, when Paul says <u>eat anything from the marketplace,</u> it could mean vegetables, but yes, it could also be meat. And yes, we can eat it, but should we? No.

> *27- If any of them that <u>believe not</u> bid* (invite) *you to a feast, and ye be disposed* (want) *to go; whatsoever is it before you, eat, <u>asking no question for conscience sake</u>*

When Paul references *"them that believe not"* and *"for conscience's sake"*, we have confirmation that Paul's concern is foods offered to idols. We are not getting his approval to eat meat whenever.

Paul says if you're invited to dinner by somebody <u>who does not believe,</u> just eat what they give to you and don't ask if it was sacrificed to idols. Yes, fellow activist, this means meat too, but chill, because it does not apply to our scene today. We are not being confronted with food offered to false idols, and neither is today's meat-eating Christian. Activists now are dealing with issues of cruelty; Paul was dealing with issues of idol worship. Not the same thing. Today's carnist Christians honestly cannot use this verse to justify eating meat.

We get more vegan action in **verse 28**:

> *But if <u>someone says</u> to you, <u>"This has been offered in sacrifice,"</u> <u>then do not eat it</u>, both for the sake of the one who told you and for the sake of conscience.*

Paul says when you're invited to dinner and the host openly tells you the food was offered in a sacrifice, *then do not eat it*. Here's where I put my vegan spin on it. Ask your meat-eating Christian if he's invited to dinner, and the host says they made the food from the abuse, torture, and sexual molestation of an animal. Should they eat it? Nope, Paul would advise *"do not eat it"* since abuse, torture, sexual molestation of an animal is sin. Ahhh, good one, huh?

Wrap up

You can find the overall message in the 2 filters I gave. This passage is not about meat but about newly discovered Christian liberty and idolatry. It's about the responsibility of a Christian to make sure they are not doing any action that hurts others or themselves. In today's world, meat hurts the oceans, the environment, the planet, each other, and, of course, the innocent animals God created to be our companions, not our food.

CHAPTER 71: COLOSSIANS 2:16 – JUDGEMENT IN MEAT OR DRINK

Don't judge me for eating meat.

So often I am told *"You shouldn't judge Christians for eating meat, it's wrong"*. Don't they see they are judging me by saying I am doing something wrong?

Colossians chapter 2 verse 16
Let no man <u>therefore</u> judge you in meat (brosei = Eating, food), *or in drink, or in respect of an holy day, or of the new moon, or of the sabbath days:*

Colossians chapter 2 is about Christians being *completed* through the death and resurrection of Jesus Christ. Believers are no longer to be judged under the Mosaic laws regarding non-kosher foods eaten (*meat or in drink*), their attendance of religious festivals, or Sabbath observance (*respect of a holy day*).

And again, we have the poor translation of brosei to meat. This is the same stuff we just read about over and over.

5Ws

While locked-up in prison, Paul wrote this letter to the church in Colossae. There were guys in prominent positions known as Judaizers, causing trouble in the church. These Judaizers held on to the idea that Christians must also keep the man-made customs and laws they got from Moses and the Jewish Oral Torah. In today's Christian church, they are often called *legalists*.

Paul taught salvation is <u>only</u> through the "Grace of Jesus Christ." This "Grace" put an end to the man-made rituals and dietary customs. Jesus is the only thing needed. These Judaizers had 1 foot in *The Law of Moses* and 1 foot in *Grace thru Jesus*. Paul intends this letter to get both feet in Grace alone.

The commandments and doctrines of men

In verse 16, look at what upset the Judaizers:

1- The things they were drinking and the unclean (not kosher) things they were eating.

2- They were not taking part in religious festivals.

3- The improper ways of keeping the Sabbath.

These legalists/Judaizers started getting all up in people's faces saying, don't eat this, or only eat that. Then demanding worship of God on specific days or take part in a religious festival. Paul is telling Christians to ignore the Judaizers and their judgments; the legalists are wrong.

It isn't the same situation when a vegan tells a meat-eating Christian to stop eating animals. Vegans are saying to stop animal abuse. To use this verse against a vegan advocate is scripture twisting, yet so many pastors ignore the context and quote it to me in debates thinking they have a slam-dunk against vegan criticism. Don't let the carnists use this verse against your vegan advocacy. It is unlikely back in the year 60 AD, a vegan advocate was at the church of Colossae telling people not to eat animals. Verse 16 corrects legalism, not veganism.

What is "therefore" there for?

Want more proof this restriction on judgement wasn't about veganism? I underlined the word, <u>therefore</u>. When we see the word, therefore, ask, "what is that <u>therefore</u>, there for"? We have to hop back to verse 8 to see.

> *Beware lest <u>any man spoil</u> you through philosophy and vain deceit, after the <u>tradition of men</u>, after the rudiments of the world, and not after Christ.*

"Therefore" refers to any man who can impair someone's faith in Christ using <u>man-made traditions</u>. Beliefs such as salvation under the Law or spiritualism could hinder and lead people away from faith in Jesus Christ. No connection to judging someone for eating meat, but again, what eating meat represents.

> *10- And ye are complete in him (Jesus), which is the head of all*

principality and power:

Believers could, but didn't need to keep kosher in the food they ate. They didn't need to celebrate specific days or take part in religious rituals. Jesus Christ has made believers complete and did everything for them. That's what verse 16 is saying. It is not an anti-vegan verse in any sense.

Meat is food

Now, let's discuss the poor translation of the word "meat." I took the verse above from the King James Version of the Bible. Let me show you how it's written in other translations:

NIV: *do not let anyone judge you by what you eat or drink*
ESV: *let no one pass judgment on you in questions of food and drink*
NASB: *no one is to act as your judge in regard to food or drink*

The Greek word is Brósis, which translates: *eating, food.* But with the King James version being so popular, people see the word meat, and that's that. I am getting so tired of this KJV miss-translation crap. I'm sure you're equally annoyed hearing me kvetch about it. But, food here could mean meat or vegetables. The reason they were "*judging*" was that the food item (meat or veggie) was most likely un-kosher food or food offered to pagan idols.

We know the reply in verse 16 is to the Judaizers' legalism because they include the Sabbath, festival, special days, and even what is permissible to drink.

Ok, so what about judging their actions?

Christians are complete in Jesus, and they don't have to do a bunch of religious rituals, Groovy. What does that look like in a "complete" Christian?

1ˢᵗ John chapter 4 verse 8
He that loveth not knoweth not God; for God is love.

If you don't have love, you don't know God.

Galatians chapter 5 verse 22
The fruit of the Spirit is love, joy, peace, patience, kindness, goodness, faithfulness

If someone is a "Saved Christian," these attributes (love, peace, patience, kindness) should be noticeable in their life. But can these attributes be seen in a meat-eating Christian diet? Let's judge.

Joy: Not found in a Slaughterhouse
Love: Not found in a Slaughterhouse
Peace: Not found in a Slaughterhouse

Patience: Not found in a Slaughterhouse
Kindness: Not found in a Slaughterhouse
Goodness: Not found in a Slaughterhouse
Faithfulness: Not found in a Slaughterhouse
Come on, it's obvious if you're a Christian, you need to go vegan already.

CHAPTER 72:
1ST TIMOTHY 4 – A
DOCTRINE OF DEMONS

Veganism is a doctrine of demons.

Many carnist Christians will use 1st Timothy chapter 4, verses 1 thru 4 to say veganism is a *doctrine of demons*. They don't grasp this passage speaks of a future group who were once "Saved" but went back to ideologies of Gnosticism forbidding all pleasures of the flesh. Let's look.

5Ws

They assume Paul wrote this to his colleague named Timothy (duh!) in Ephesus. Paul wants to discuss the harmful "Gnostic" teachings creeping into the church. Note: Paul's concern was of <u>Gnostic teachings</u>, not vegan teachings. If this was a vegan/meat issue, there is no need for the added concern with forbidding marriage. You'll see.

Uhhh Steve, what's a Gnostic?

Well, I wouldn't call it a religion. It's more like a group of Church-going people that believed a variety of religious theories. Some good theologies and some bad. One of these gnostic doctrines shuns physical pleasures, so sex (marriage) or yummy foods would be considered sinful.

However, God commanded the opposite. God made tasty yummy food for humans (Genesis 1:30) and told us to be fruitful and multiply (Genesis 1:28). Can you see why the apostle Paul was ticked off with these Gnostics? Let's go through the verses.

1- Now the spirit speaketh expressly that in latter times <u>some shall depart from the faith</u>, giving heed to seducing spirits, and <u>doctrines of devils</u>

To *depart from the faith,* one would have to be *in the faith.* Paul is referring to a future time (latter times) where some Christians (in the faith) will give up (leave) their faith in Jesus and take on these Gnostic *doctrines of devils.* This is not veganism.

2- Speaking lies in hypocrisy; having their conscience seared with a hot iron;
     3- <u>forbidding to marry</u>, and commanding to <u>abstain from meats</u>, which God hath created to be received with thanksgiving of them which believe and know the truth

ARRRGGGHHH!

For the last time in this book, I will deal with the poor translation of the word meat. The Greek word used is *Broma,* and when translated into English, it can mean *food of any kind.* Sadly, animal flesh is implied in the King James version.
    For some proof it's a poor translation, read the same verse in the
NIV: Order them to abstain from certain foods
ESV: Require abstinence from foods
NASB: Advocate abstaining from foods
    These verses confirm it's about foodstuff of any kind. Geez, makes me want to punch King James in the nose sometimes.
    These gnostics were saying *any yummy food* was bad news. They claim Christians do not have the freedom to partake in any fleshly pleasures, even marriage. Paul's "doctrine of demons" warning was dealing with that heresy. This is not an anti-vegan thing; it's a false doctrine thing. Consider this, both Paul and Jesus recommended abstaining from eating foods and marriage, but not for reason of pleasure. For example, if it will make another person sin, or if they offered the food to idols. I discussed this in earlier chapters, but let's have another look at the verses.

Romans chapter 14 verse 21
It is <u>good not to eat meat</u> or drink wine or to do anything by which your bother stumbles

And—

Acts chapter 15 verse 29
That you <u>abstain from meats</u> offered to idols and from blood and

from things strangled.

Here are 2 places Paul says to abstain from eating meat. Now let's look at marriage.

1st Corinthians chapter 7 verse 8
I say therefore to the unmarried and widows, It is good for them if they abide (stay unmarried) *even as I*

The Apostle Paul is teaching to abstain from foods and marriage. Is he teaching a doctrine of devils? Nahhh.

Jesus and Marriage

Before we go on further with the food thing, jump back to what Jesus said in **Matthew chapter 19, verse 12.**

For there are some eunuchs, which were so born from their mother's womb: and there are some eunuchs, which were made eunuchs of men: and there be eunuchs, which have made themselves eunuchs for the kingdom of heaven's sake. He that is able to receive it, let him receive it.

"Eunuchs" are dudes that aren't able to have sex. Some are eunuchs from birth, some were castrated by force, and some guys castrated themselves. I get their reasoning, but ouch! Regardless of how they became eunuchs, they used their lack of sex drive to better serve God. I know when I'm horny, the last thing I want is a Bible study so I can see the benefits of being a eunuch in God's service. Jesus says the guys voluntarily making themselves eunuchs free up their time to serve God, which is a good thing. It's not for everyone, but if they want to, go for it. So Jesus himself is giving the OK to abstain from marriage. Is Jesus teaching a doctrine of demons? Nahhh.
Neither Paul nor Jesus is teaching doctrines of devils. Nope, the evil is in the reason one chooses to forego such things. Doing it as a requirement for salvation is a bad thing. However, choosing to free up time to be of more service is a loving thing. Totally acceptable. Catch the difference?

Getting drunk and getting laid

Consider to whom this was written and their understanding of what they were reading. These Ephesians would have read it like this: *"If you get a group of people telling you God doesn't want you to enjoy the pleasures of life, kick 'em out. You can enjoy un-kosher food, you can enjoy marriage. It's your choice, not an obligation".*
I want to address something before my critics accuse me of promoting

drunken orgies. This is not unrestricted approval to get drunk or run off and experiment in all kinds of debauchery. Trust me, I live in Las Vegas. I know how fun the debauchery can be, but the rest of the Bible suggests limits on fleshly pleasures. Will it hurt someone? Will it hurt you? Will it bring glory to God? I think you get the idea.

Now on to another poor translation in verse 4.

Every creature of God is good and nothing is to be refused if it is received thanksgiving

The Greek word for "Creature" is "Ktisma." Ktisma isn't always translated as "creature" but as "*created thing,*" that's a big difference. A carnist Christian will see the word creature and think only of a living animal thing. Read how other Bibles translate this verse:

NIV: For everything God created is good

ESV: For everything created by God is good,

NASB: For everything created by God is good,

HSCB: For everything created by God is good,

Ya see? It's not animals, but <u>everything created</u>. See how misleading the KJV is by using the word "creature"?

Now consider this verse through the eyes of Genesis chapter 1. Plants are the only *things* God created to eat. When I read *everything* created by God is good, I automatically think of plants. I don't read animals into this verse the way today's 21st century Christians will. A firm understanding of Genesis can be essential to interpreting New Testament scriptures.

What if?

What if the carnist Christian insists it means every creature? Vegans can work with that, too. For example, if *every creature* God created is good for food, humans would also be on the menu. Actually, the Bible doesn't come out and say no human eating. We know it's evil with all its connections to being a punishment or in times of distress. However, even though it's a curse, I can point out many verses that involve eating humans was a thing. And if all creatures are actually all creatures, it would include humans. Here are a few to rattle the meat eaters.

Leviticus chapter 26 verse 29
And ye shall eat the flesh of your sons, and the flesh of your daughters shall ye eat.

Deuteronomy chapter 28 verse 53
And thou shalt eat the fruit of thine own body, the flesh of thy sons and of thy daughters, which the LORD thy God hath given thee,

Jeremiah chapter 19 verse 9
And I will cause them to eat the flesh of their sons and the flesh of their daughters, and they shall eat every one the flesh of his friend in the siege and straitness,

Ezekiel chapter 5 verse 10
Therefore the fathers shall eat the sons in the midst of thee, and the sons shall eat their fathers;

So, if *every creature of God is good,* then we can't automatically ignore humans. See what I did there? Sneaky but effective.

Wrap up

So, we've established everything God created as food in Genesis chapters 1-3. Plants were the only thing God called good to eat. Abstaining from foods can be beneficial if by choice, but it's not mandatory to serve God. The warning in this chapter was, there will be Christians leaving their total trust in Christ for Gnostic spiritualism teachings. Beware them. Gnostics felt denying themselves pleasure was better than Jesus. So these good activities (eating, drinking, marriage), done to make oneself "holy" could also show rejection of Jesus' salvation through Grace. That is wrong and a doctrine of demons.

Christians willingly abstain from many activities, such as going to certain movies, using foul language, gambling, etc. Abstinence can be a virtuous, voluntary part of what believers do. Abstaining from foods created from violence (going vegan) can be virtuous. Vegans are not rejecting foods to achieve a better place before God. Vegans are rejecting foods made from violence because animal abuse is just plain wrong. Christians shouldn't be involved in animal abuse in any form.

CHAPTER 73:
JAMES 4:17 – DO GOOD
OR YOU'RE SINNING

Come on, you know better

In this chapter, James breaks sin into two categories. Sins of action and sins of inaction. When a person, with intent, actively engages in sin (murder, stealing, lying, etc.), those are called *"sins of commission"* because they are sins you commit.

In chapter 4 verse 17, James mentions *"sins of omission."* Those are things you exclude or omit. **Omission:** *a failure to do something, especially something that one has a moral or legal obligation to do.* Got it? Good. Let's see what James has to say.

James chapter 4 verse 17
Therefore to him, that knoweth to do good, <u>and doth it not</u>, to him it is sin.

For Christian vegans, this verse is a call to activism. For carnist Christians, this verse is a slap in the face kind of judgement. Why? Because animal abuse is bad, ask any Christian. Therefore, avoiding animal abuse is good. See where this is going? When a choice between evil and good activities (*knoweth to do good*) is an option, Christians have a moral obligation to do good. If given a chance to do good but don't (*doth it not*), they are sinning.

Ask the Christian

Shouldn't a Christian avoid food made from animal abuse?
    Shouldn't a Christian avoid food made from beastiality?
    Shouldn't a Christian avoid food that destroys the environment?
    Shouldn't a Christian avoid food that causes world hunger?
    As soon as an activist makes a Christian aware their food choices are coming from evil sources (animal abuse, beastiality, world hunger, pollution), that food becomes a sin to eat. See how that works? Memorize the facts about animal agriculture, the environment, world famine, and we've got another vegan win.
    I'll use this as a reminder to be nice.

To him, that knoweth to do good.

We need to cut them slack if they don't know. Only *if* the Christian is ignorant of their actions, consider them innocent. Remember Jesus when he said:

Luke chapter23 verse 34
Then said Jesus, Father, forgive them; for they know not what they do.

Even though they are 100% guilty, accept them where they are. They are unaware of the evil in their food choices, as many vegans once were.
    Once an activist makes them aware of the violence connected to eating animals, they can no longer claim ignorance. They must commit to veganism or continue on to sin. Challenge them with this verse. A Christian who actively takes part in a system of unimaginable pain and suffering is not living in God's image. They resemble the devil more than Jesus.

Obligation

Of their own free will, Christians accepted the responsibility to represent God's love, kindness and mercy in their lives with their actions. Even if it will cost the Christian something they enjoy, they must serve God over their personal pleasures.
    So ya, Christians can be guilty of sin by doing nothing. It's like this, say you are walking down the street and you see a grown man beating an old lady. What do you do? Walk past (omission) thinking "eh, not my grandma"? No! You do the good thing. You help the grandma or you are sinning. I'm not saying you're required to put yourself in danger, but anyone can whip out a cell phone and call the police. Christians are required to do good.

Similar approach

I have a couple more verses that offer a similar approach.

1ˢᵗ John chapter 3 verse 6
No one who abides in him <u>keeps on sinning</u>

1ˢᵗ John chapter 5 verse 18
We know that anyone born of God does <u>not continue to sin</u>.

God doesn't want his followers purchasing products made from physical mutilations, sexual molestations and torment forced upon animals on factory farms. Once the carnist Christian knows, ignorance is no longer a defense for them. If they <u>continue</u> purchasing, eating and supporting such an industry, they must not be of God. Because John says no one who *"abides in him"* or is *"born of God"* continues on sinning.

A Christian will never achieve a sinless life, that's a given. James and John are making a point. If a person, such as a thief, becomes a Christian, he would no longer continue on in thievery. He should turn to an honest career. Similarly, a meat eater should turn from animal abuse.

These can be great tools when you get some chuckle-head who replies: I don't care. It doesn't argue they can't eat meat; it argues Christians must give up eating meat.

CHAPTER 74: REVELATION 21:4 – WE ALL END UP VEGAN

A new heaven and a new earth

Here we are at the end of the book, both mine and almost the Bible. I'm sure you're sick of my babbling. Heck, I'm sick of me too, so I'll keep this short and sweet.

Revelation gives us a peek into the future new world that Jesus will bring.

Revelation chapter 21 verse 4:
And God shall wipe away all tears from their eyes; and there <u>shall be no more death</u>, neither sorrow, nor crying, neither shall there be any more pain: for <u>the former things are passed away</u>.

There are countless commentaries on the book of Revelation. Arguments on what they should understand as literal or figurative. It's a mess, but most believers acknowledge what I underlined is real. The future world (eternity) has no more death. The former needs of this life will end. Christians will agree death ends, but for some reason (can you say lust, addiction, gluttony), they won't let that apply to their food. Show them they can't have steak without death, they can't have pork chops without death, they can't have hot dogs without death. Then quote this verse to them. Watch their eyes glaze over with confusion.

The world started off vegan and according to this verse, it will end vegan. There is no getting around that. Fight as they may, Christians will have no choice but to go vegan for all eternity.

THE END

I'm outta here

Rock on my vegan family. If we don't meet on earth, I look forward to meeting you at a vegan potluck in Heaven. I'll bring donuts. Until then, my prayer for you is peace, love, and all things groovy.

www.ingramcontent.com/pod-product-compliance
Lightning Source LLC
Chambersburg PA
CBHW021132090426
42740CB00008B/761